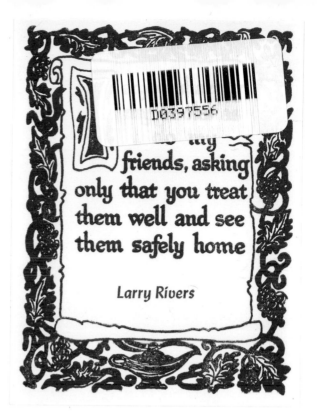

...my friends, asking
only that you treat
them well and see
them safely home

Larry Rivers

UTTER

INCOMPETENTS

ALSO BY THOMAS OLIPHANT

Praying for Gil Hodges

UTTER INCOMPETENTS

Ego and Ideology in the Age of Bush

THOMAS OLIPHANT

THOMAS DUNNE BOOKS

ST. MARTIN'S PRESS NEW YORK

THOMAS DUNNE BOOKS.
An imprint of St. Martin's Press.

www.thomasdunnebooks.com
www.stmartins.com

Book design by Philip Mazzone

Library of Congress Cataloging-in-Publication Data

Oliphant, Thomas.
   Utter incompetents : ego and ideology in the age of Bush / Thomas
Oliphant.—1st ed.
   ISBN-13: 978-0-312-36017-7
   ISBN-10: 0-312-36017-7
   1. United States—Politics and government—2001–   2. United States—Foreign
relations—2001–   3. Bush, George W. (George Walker), 1946—Political and
social views.   4. Bush, George W. (George Walker), 1946—Influence.   5. Political
culture—United States.   I. Title.   II. Title: Utter incompetence.
   E902.O47   2007
   973.931—dc22   2007031464

First Edition: November 2007

10 9 8 7 6 5 4 3 2 1

CONTENTS

ACKNOWLEDGMENTS

IN THE SPRING of 2005, my publisher, Tom Dunne, climbed aboard the shuttle to Washington with an idea in his expansive brain that would not become chic for at least another half-year—that the troubles then besetting President Bush in the first few months of his second term were much more than mere troubles. He thought the wheels were coming off this machine, and for reasons that went well beyond the ongoing, seemingly endless wars in Iraq and Afghanistan.

On his way for a chat with me before bringing out a memoir that summer of my New York childhood and my first love, the Brooklyn Dodgers, Mr. Dunne opened his laptop on the plane and let rip a most delightful screed, the main point of which was that there was no important topic one could list of which President Bush was not making a colossal mess—domestic as well as foreign. In another notion that would not become chic for at least a half-year, he used an adjective then not generally in use in descriptions of the Bush administration—incompetent.

His memo was both jarring and entertaining. But we still had another project to launch, and so I put the manifesto aside. Tom Dunne did not put the idea aside, pressing me to tell him what I thought and what people were saying as Bush's approval numbers continued their unusually steady slide. Asking around, I decided he was essentially correct, that there had not been anything remotely like it for years, and that the situation was continuing to deteriorate.

Then Hurricane Katrina changed the equation dramatically. In deciding to proceed with this project, we aimed at a hole in the work that had been done on the Bush administration's first five years. There was no dearth of examinations in minute detail of the unfolding catastrophe in post-invasion Iraq, and there was much in the way of traditional, insider-focused accounts of internal administration politics. What was missing was a search for explanations of how one administration could goof with such astonishing regularity, whether the issue was natural disasters, wars, taxes, energy, health care, or Social Security—a search for common themes and habits that could help a reader understand the gap between the economy Bush portrayed politically and the economy Americans actually lived in, not just between blind hopes and ugly reality in Baghdad.

It seemed to me this required deduction more than induction, as well as analysis of the voluminous public record (official sources from commission reports to texts of legislation and proposals, and statistical compilations of impacts on the public, where available) to hunt for patterns. Gradually a picture emerged strongly suggesting that this fish rotted from the head and that the administration handled taxes in much the same way it plotted strategy in the Sunni Triangle.

Through it all, my experience in politics and journalism had me convinced that no president could absorb all these self-inflicted wounds without at some point—going into the 2006 congressional elections or at least coming out of them—realizing something was fundamentally wrong and changing course. So the biggest surprise of all was how little, if at all, Bush has changed, not after the Democrats won both houses of Congress, not when the U.S. death toll in Iraq went above 3,500. The downward slide in the administration's sixth and seventh years was not noticeably different from the events of the first five.

It is presumptuous to choose sixteen topics for analysis. Others could easily pick different ones. I'm convinced, however, that the ones here provide sufficient breadth to show the pattern of emerging pitfalls ignored, of the hubris and arrogance that prevented responses to changing circumstances, of the excessive importance of short-term politics, ideology, and special interest cronyism in influencing decisions, and of the stubbornness that blocked obvious course-changing options. I prefer the left-of-center perspective in politics, but the Bush administration's record shows that behavior, not beliefs, was what counted.

Intellectually, I am indebted to the early dissenters on the right who illustrate this key point: to the neoconservative foreign policy expert Francis Fukuyama, who lectured on the dangers of over-reaching abroad in 2005 and published *America at the Crossroads* the following year; and to passionate conservative Bruce Bartlett, whose dissent from Bush domestic policy, especially on government spending, taxes, and trade, titled *Impostor,* was published in 2006. Many conservatives have since joined their chorus.

For Tom Dunne's inspiration and Job-like patience as I wrestled with all this, there is no adequate expression of gratitude. At St. Martin's, this was my second time around the track with a brilliant woman whose patience, insight, and nudging leadership were as ever invaluable—my editor, Kathleen Gilligan. And at home, my work was once again aided immeasurably by the loving, stern, get-to-the-point perusal of my wife, Susan Spencer, of CBS News.

But all the goofs are mine alone. I recommend this attitude to President Bush.

UTTER

INCOMPETENTS

JUSTICE

The scandal unfolding around the firing of eight U.S. attorneys compels the conclusion that the Bush administration has rewarded loyalty above all else. A destructive pattern of partisan political actions of the Justice Department started long before this incident, however, as those of us who worked in its civil rights division can attest. . . .

—Joseph D. Rich, chief of the voting rights section of the Justice Department's civil rights division, 1999–2005, *Los Angeles Times* Op-Ed, March 29, 2007

JUST DAYS INTO George W. Bush's second term as president, his assistant for politics, policy, and nearly everything else—Karl Rove—asked a direct question of his White House associates, recorded in a memo by the deputy White House counsel, David Leitch.

Rove's query involved the operating engineers of every president's administration of justice: the ninety-three United States attorneys. After four years in office, Rove wanted to know what was next, or as Leitch summarized it: "How we planned to proceed regarding US Attorneys, whether we were going to allow all to stay, request resignations from all and accept only some of them, or selectively replace them, etc."

By tradition and law, "we" could do anything. These jobs are a president's patronage. But also by tradition, the ninety-three prosecutors are supposed to be top-notch lawyers, good at their jobs, and the whiff of politics inevitably surrounding their employment is best kept faint.

But this was the Bush presidency in operation. Within two years, the administration had so completely messed up what is ordinarily a routine task that the already bruised and bloodied president had fresh wounds, his crony and second attorney general (Alberto Gonzales) lost his credibility and then his job after hanging for months by the frayed thread of their personal relationship, and a half-dozen senior officials of the shamed department were gone under clouds. The favored Republican verb for his latest series of White House screw-ups was "botched"; the Democrats preferred more sinister descriptions of an obviously politicized administration of justice. At least three of the departed U.S. attorneys had been under fire for a lack of zeal in making prosecutorial mountains out of evidentiary molehills involving a favorite GOP campaign topic, voter registration irregularities; one was gone to make room for a Rove crony, a move made with a customary lack of skill and subtlety, and at least two who stayed on had stage-managed "investigations" involving Democratic Senate candidates in 2006 that went nowhere.

It was classic Bush-in-action, Keystone Kops governance. The U.S. Attorneys Affair was an exclamation point after a long series of exclamation points involving war, terrorism, hurricanes, energy, health care, Social Security, and taxes (to name only a few). At the time Rove wrote his note, the president had just been handed his second golden opportunity to lead a lasting conservative reordering of the country's politics and policies. By the time the note surfaced in 2007, he had blown it sky-high. It would take the country years to clean up the many messes he had made abroad and at home; it would take conservatives years to have another chance like the ones Bush blew.

He had taken office as the first Republican president in forty-eight years to be blessed with a Republican House and a Republican Senate; he had then been handed an opportunity by the worst attack on American soil since Pearl Harbor to lead a united nation; and he had limped to reelection in 2004 with modest increases in his congressional majorities. He wrecked each and every one of those opportunities.

Rove's intervention was no aberration. It was written in secret about plans that would remain secret for nearly two years. There was no serious consultation outside the tight inner circle, the bubble that Bush had created to shield himself from scrutiny and accountability. There was no serious consideration of risks or alternatives down the road. And at the first (inevitable) sign of trouble there was a flurry of high-class political damage control, befitting the manipulative talents of some of the best in the business. But because there was no action to correct the underlying problems, all the political redirecting skill in the world was ultimately beside the point, and actually boomeranged. So it went for six-plus years, through one of the strangest presidencies in the country's history.

Obviously, this was not supposed to happen, wasn't planned to happen. But it did.

SCREWING UP

We've done a lot of hard work together over the last three and a half years. We've been challenged and we've risen to those challenges. We're climbing the mighty mountain. I see the valley below and it's a valley of peace.

—**President George W. Bush, first debate with John Kerry, September 20, 2004**

IN THE BEGINNING, there was an orgy of order, or so it seemed at the time.

The third conservative government since Ronald Reagan's ascension in 1981 prepared to take office deeply committed to a style of leadership befitting the first president to enter the White House with a master's degree in business administration under his belt.

In election campaigns, scores of presidential candidates down through the years, Democratic as well as Republican, had found utility in the hoary notion that running a government like a private business was not just good politics but the essence of successful leadership. George W. Bush, who had known disorder and chaos intimately in his life, was unusual in that he actually believed in it.

It fell to his diligent chief of staff—in the campaign of 2000 and then in the White House—to work out the details, taking advantage of what was universally believed to be a unique asset, and then communicating his design in a message of reassurance to a country that had just been through a bitterly contested election that did not end until the Supreme Court stopped it.

Andrew Card was the ideal chief for a Bush White House staff. He had been the deputy for Bush's father in a very different White House, working for John Sununu, an autocrat and self-promoter who eventually bombed out. He had worked in Bush politics for twenty years, from the bottom up. He had briefly run a department (Transportation) and then ably represented the automotive industry in Washington for nearly a decade. He lacked both the pretense and the background of a policymaker or spokesman and took pride in his relentless attention to detail.

In conversations before and after Bush became president, Card described a smooth, humming governmental system openly drawn from corporate models, in a message amplified throughout the administration and the Republican Party. The president, he said, would be the kind of chief executive officer who leads—his own organization as well as the country. He would decide the broad contours of foreign and domestic policy and then bring opinion, from the public to the congressional kind, along with him.

The operational mechanics of the administration would be delegated, scrupulously. Card enjoyed summing up his own responsibility as making sure that Bush got everything he needed and nothing he didn't; that he saw the right people at the right time on the right issues; and that the necessary communication of orders and decisions from the top was handed down the power ladder crisply and then carried out efficiently. At all levels, administration officials and staff members could recite the mantra of their smooth, relentless system—strategy, operations, and implementation.

To oversee the operational functions of his administration, Bush had already committed himself to empowering the most significant vice president in American history—Dick Cheney. His surprising choice as running mate the previous summer (surprising because Cheney had been running the selection process) had been among the handful of campaign decisions that put him in position to become president—a major, reassuring move for a rookie running against an experienced, knowledgeable public figure in national life, Vice President Al Gore. As Bush prepared to take office, Cheney's presence was widely seen to be as reassuring as Gore's. He had been a boy wonder chief of staff himself in Gerald Ford's brief presidency, a heavyweight congressman, a defense secretary, and then a CEO in the energy and government contracting business.

As Card outlined it, Cheney would control the development of major policies as well as relations with Congress. His uniquely powerful office would also make sure that the administration was not caught unprepared, that information was collected and analyzed thoroughly, and that the decisions made in the White House were faithfully implemented down the chain of command.

The repeated use of the corporate model, in practice and in propaganda, was illustrated by the presence of four former CEOs in Bush's cabinet, including: Defense Secretary Donald Rumsfeld (G. D. Searle and Co., the drug giant, as well as General Instrument Corp.), Commerce Secretary and close friend Donald Evans (Tom Brown, Inc., a large, independent energy company), and Treasury Secretary Paul O'Neill (Alcoa); the fourth was Cheney himself, fresh from a company called Halliburton.

Every presidency, especially since the modern era of media politics began in the twentieth century, has functioned as the stylistic antithesis of its predecessor. Bush famously recoiled at the imagery of disorder often conveyed by Bill Clinton, neglecting its substantive successes. No late-night pizza runs. No late-starting meetings. No informality in dress. No undisciplined leaking of backstage chatter. And no collegiality, either. This was always going to be a conservative government, but it was designed to work, to accomplish things for the country, even to change the tone and lower the temperature in national affairs that had become so divisively partisan and so hot for at least a decade.

It didn't. Not even close. It flopped—early and often. It messed up virtually everything it touched.

The Bush self-destruction was vividly on display more than fifty months into his presidency during one of the odder flights in the history of Air Force One.

Returning to Washington, at the end of a five-week vacation at his sprawling ranch near Waco, Texas, the president's plane took a detour. As the luxury airliner cruised northeast at 29,000 feet, Air Force Colonel Mark Tillman, the chief pilot, diverted to the south so the president could view firsthand (and be seen viewing) the unprecedented horrors Hurricane Katrina had visited on the Gulf Coast. As the huge plane approached New Orleans at 1,700 feet, a stone-faced Bush sat alone on the left side in a section normally occupied by his Secret Service detail.

Off the cuff, the president is often inarticulate and malaprop-prone, and on this occasion his press secretary, Scott McClellan, passed on a classic Bush-ism to traveling reporters: "It's devastating. It's got to be doubly devastating on the ground."

Months later, it was still not clear whether—and if so, exactly when—Bush appreciated the extent of the devastation. Below him was a ghastly human toll that included well over one thousand lives lost to raging waters that breached New Orleans' fragile levees, laid complete waste to outlying communities as far as the eye could see, and wrecked the Gulf Coast as far east as Mobile, Alabama. What was clear that day, even from the air, was that the Bush administration was frozen in the ice of its own ignorance and inability to process information and act. Looking down, Bush could only see one of the Coast Guard helicopters hovering over a flooded dwelling as the pilot tried heroically to rescue one of the tens of thousands of people trapped in the city. He could see few signs of activity over Mississippi as the occasional C-17 cargo plane landed in Pascagoula to deliver supplies. Mostly he saw nothing but water and ruin.

The vaunted corporate model of effective efficiency was nowhere in evidence. Before the storm hit, the White House and Bush himself had access to information about its extremely dangerous potential as well as information going back years on what a powerful hurricane could do to the New Orleans levee system. And while the hurricane was making landfall early Monday morning, there was information he should have received, but didn't, that the levees were being breached; and immediately after the storm passed there were reports of the catastrophe that was unfolding. But there was virtually no evidence of this information being processed by policymakers, much less received, analyzed, and acted upon by top officials. The president continued to vacation and make public appearances in the West for two more days; his vice president was vacationing in Wyoming; and his chief of staff was vacationing in Maine. Essentially, nothing of consequence happened while the country sat glued with horrified fascination to its television sets.

The astonishing bungling of the Katrina disaster showed Bush couldn't handle a disaster created by God; but when God didn't hand him a crisis, he was perfectly capable of creating one. He'd demonstrated this knack earlier that wretched month on two fronts—the war in Iraq and the government's most important domestic program, Social Security.

Throughout his vacation, Bush and his top advisers managed to make a cause célèbre out of a barely known Gold Star mother of one of the roughly four thousand Americans killed in the Iraq and Afghanistan wars that had unfolded in every way contrary to the administration's detailed plans and expectations. Cindy Sheehan is a person with an unspeakable burden of grief; but she is also an activist with marginal, leftist views. Her publicized efforts to win a personal meeting with the president (she had seen him in a small group of other grieving families after her son's death), and his petulant refusal created a bizarre scene in rural Texas that lasted for days. It could have been defused with, at most, thirty minutes of Bush's vacation time; what the president's fabled political team could not grasp was that Cindy Sheehan was important not as a solitary figure, but as a symbol of the ongoing, murderous mess in Iraq that seemed to have no worthwhile end in sight—and seemed especially so that summer. The mishandling of Sheehan also provided symbolic fodder for

Bush's increasingly focused image as a stubborn, out-of-touch president who radiated indifference to other people's views and feelings
as the war dragged on.

The second example of his uncanny knack for leaving a situation
worse than he'd found it was just as egregious—the mishandling of
Social Security.

Bush had begun his vacation in humiliating retreat from what had
seemed for months to be the singular domestic policy initiative of his
second term—a long-sought, huge change in one of the pillars of retirement in America. With the program facing the challenges of navi-
gating the costly retirement of an immense chunk of the country—the
generation born after World War II—while avoiding insolvency,
Bush had long sought to give workers the option of diverting a portion of their payroll taxes to private investment accounts in order to
accumulate wealth, as well as pension rights, in return for acceptance of reduced direct benefits.

More than twenty years before, a top aide to the late House
Speaker Tip O'Neill, Kirk O'Donnell, coined a famous phrase about
Social Security, calling the public pension system the "third rail of
American politics." O'Donnell, who has also since died, never meant
that politicians can't ever touch it, but that it takes broad consensus,
meaning important figures in both parties working together, to do
so successfully—whether to broaden the program's coverage and increase its benefits or to slow the growth in its expenditures. Though
Bush first started talking about his imperfectly framed notions as a
presidential candidate in 1999, he never succeeded in moving the issue beyond partisan, ideological politics. Circumstances (the burst-
ing of the high-tech bubble and a sinking stock market against a
background of major corporate scandals) blocked him during his
first term in office, as did his inability to extract a consensus proposal from a commission he himself established.

After his narrow reelection, Bush ran with the issue again—
straight into a wall. After six years of rhetoric, he and his advisers

remained unable and unwilling to develop a specific proposal, especially one that explained how the government could finance the diversion of payroll tax revenue without adding to Social Security's financial challenges. In an astonishing display of political and policy-making ineptitude throughout 2005, Bush appeared to increase the opposition to his vague stance on the issue the more he talked about it, and he talked about it dozens of times. By the time he retreated to Texas for vacation, his administration and its allies in the Republican Congress were at work on the thankless task of burying his initiative for the second time.

Following his defeat of Democrat John Kerry in 2004, the president inflated the scope of his victory beyond the facts, speaking constantly of the "political capital" he said he had earned, capital he intended to spend in alliance with the clear, if narrow, majorities his party had won in the Senate and House. But he and his allies then proceeded to waste whatever resources they had in the war-without-end in Iraq, and the president's inability to move the Social Security discussion his way.

For those addicted to opinion polls, Bush presided with a slender majority of the country inclined to his side as his second term began. In short order, however, he lost the inroads he had made among relatively conservative Democrats who had been in favor of his invasion of Iraq and supported his conduct of the battle against terrorism. Then he lost much of his support among those Americans who consider themselves as having moderate views, with no strong allegiance to either party. Then he lost significant support from the people who vote more regularly than any other demographic bloc—those who are above the age of sixty. Then, depending on the issue, he managed to lose support from the foundation of his once slender majority—10 to 20 percent of fellow Republicans and conservatives. Then, as 2005 ended, he managed to lose even more support from that foundation, from those Americans who had previously believed (by large margins) that the struggle with terrorism was going well, was being run by a likable president who at least talked straight with them, and was a strong, purposeful leader.

American history contains few examples of such a pervasive, systemic, persistent record of blunders by a national administration, much less an equally persistent record of a myopic refusal to face the facts. As the sixth year of Bush's presidency unfolded, serious historians were indulging in something much more than a parlor game, debating which presidencies equaled Bush's in its astonishing ineptitude in the face of major challenges across the range of domestic and foreign policy. The tentative nominees for this dubious, damning distinction included the passivity of Franklin Pierce and James Buchanan as the forces building toward civil war gathered momentum and the choking by Herbert Hoover in the face of the Great Depression's enormity.

Ever since Bush's contested Electoral College win over Gore, he and his political advisers had come to believe that he could get reelected as well as press a conservative agenda with only a slender majority of support in a divided country. The belief strengthened as the Republicans slightly increased their majorities in Congress because much of the country was still consumed with fears of terrorism and because there remained issues involving modern American culture (the hot one in 2004 was whether gay people should be allowed to get married) around which conservatives would mobilize. At various times, but especially after the off-year elections in 2002 and Bush's reelection two years later, his top political aide, Karl Rove, acquired guru status.

In American politics, however, the political pendulum is always moving, which makes adaptability an underappreciated skill in government. Slender majorities by definition can become minorities very quickly. What looks like principled leadership one year can morph into recalcitrant stubbornness the next. A relatively simple proposition—like invading a weak, broken country—can turn into a hideously complicated quagmire if the appropriate attention is not paid to the cost and the aftermath. The consequences of inattention, or worse, in the face of a plethora of serious domestic and foreign policy issues can be avoided in the short run, but eventually reality always trumps the mix of propaganda techniques known in modern America as spin.

The modern conservative movement has been an awesome election-winning machine for a generation, fueled by an intense ideology among its most important coalition partners—fervent believers in tax-cutting as the engine of minimalist government and economic growth, and equally fervent dissenters, almost all of them fundamentalist or evangelical Christians, from many of the elements of modern American culture. Even a partial list of their grievances hints at the power of this movement—taxes, regulation, crime, welfare, sexual permissiveness. As Reagan ran for president in 1980, hatred of communism was the movement's driving force in foreign policy, but under the second President Bush, conservatism found fresh fuel in the shock and then the anger felt in the wake of the horrific attacks on this country by international terrorists in 2001.

At every stage of its development, moreover, conservatism has benefited from the uncertain stances of the post–Lyndon Johnson Democratic Party; still groping for a fresh, unifying vision for a changing America in the aftermath of the Vietnam War, the civil rights movement, and what amounted to a second New Deal in the 1960s, it was a party that relied excessively on the constituency-driven politics of its ossifying majorities in the House of Representatives.

In many an election after the 1970s, the contest appeared to be between Republican clarity and Democratic laundry lists—and the list of successes is remarkable—the presidency in 1980, 1984, 1988, 2000, and 2004; the Senate in both 1980 and 1994; at last the House in the tumultuous second earthquake of 1994, and then the strengthening of these congressional majorities after 2002 and 2004; plus a majority of the nation's governors after 1994. There were setbacks along the way—the congressional campaigns of 1982, 1986, 1990, and 1998, not to mention Bill Clinton's two-term presidency between Bushes. But the underlying record of conservative success is undeniable.

The movement, however, has consistently stumbled on the day after its electoral triumphs. Compared to campaign politics, governance is never easy. But conservatism has had a constant problem fitting the square peg of its clear ideology into the round hole of actual programs. Nothing has symbolized the problem more dramatically than the adage: Nothing is easier in American politics than cutting taxes, and nothing is more difficult than adjusting government expenditures accordingly so that the country's finances don't hemorrhage.

Conservatism is often an inflexible, even radical, ideology that, beginning with Reagan, has had trouble adjusting to the realities and inevitable compromises of responsible governance. On more than one occasion, Republicans have split bitterly over difficult but unavoidable decisions involving domestic policy. The most memorable include the mix of spending restraints and tax increases that righted the Social Security system in 1983, the attempt at budget deficit restraint initiated by President George H. W. Bush in 1990, and despite a chance at one-party government from the right in 2001, the difficult issues of trade, the creation of a new benefits program covering some prescription drug expenses, and the control of surging illegal immigration. These post-election difficulties have been a recurring theme ever since Reagan's budget director, David Stockman, discovered in 1981 that he could not make his tax cut and spending numbers add up credibly or responsibly. The crucial difference is that Reagan and Bush's father were as famously adaptable as George W. Bush is famously rigid.

Through a combination of good fortune and first-rate political skills with continued Democratic disarray and the country's renewed concern with security, the electoral consequences of these difficulties have frequently been avoided. But every chicken appeared to come home to roost during George W. Bush's horrid second term.

The list is breathtaking. In the political media culture, it is common to claim that all of the president's severe difficulties stem from the frustration and anger over what has become at least the country's biggest foreign policy error since the decision to transform a civil war in Vietnam into an American war in 1965—the decision to invade and conquer Iraq in 2003 without a coherent plan to deal with the unavoidably murderous aftermath. There is no question that the intractable war lies near the core, but it doesn't come close to explaining the long list of major messes that have caused about two-thirds of the country to believe that the nation is heading in the wrong direction.

In addition to the loss of American lives and more than $400 billion so far in Iraq, the president's inattention and ineffectual stewardship has left a host of major issues on the table. Each is a major concern to a significant chunk of the country: the cost of energy and its availability; the cost of health care and its availability; a uniquely unbalanced economy; a huge shift of the tax burden away from capital and toward working families; the condition of family as well as government finances; the financial security of retiring workers; protecting Americans from terrorist threats under the law; the proliferation of nuclear weapons; the country's standing in the world and its military preparedness; relief from natural disaster; the environment; protection of public health; and the control of America's porous borders.

Bush has made a mockery of that long-ago effort to organize his administration along the hyper-efficient lines of a successful corporation. It brings to mind a long-ago moment at the Democratic National Convention in Atlanta in 1988, when the presidential nominee and governor of Massachusetts, Michael Dukakis, insisted on the insertion of a sentence in his acceptance speech that reflected his rich experience in government and his belief that governing effectively is as much a function of hard, wise work as it is of conviction.

With a passion he rarely exhibited, Dukakis's voice rose as he declared, "This election is not about ideology, it's about competence."

Throughout the political world, regardless of ideology, the cognoscenti clucked knowingly. On one level, Dukakis was simply incorrect; that election, like all elections, was not a Scholastic Apti-tude Test; ideas, character, and, yes, ideology matter to voters much more—and they mattered much more in 1988. But all these years later, the context of the colossal mess George W. Bush has made of his presidency suddenly produced a rediscovery of Dukakis's famous line within the public forum. Only a modicum of attention was paid to Bush's organization of his administration in 2001. Questions of "competence" in regard to his presidency were nonexistent. But by early in 2006, as the list of foul-ups seemed to grow weekly, the word "incompetence" was suddenly everywhere, and not merely on partisan lips.

In the Democratic world, a competition developed over incompe-tence rhetoric, especially after polling data showed that the word resonated with most of the public.

"The worst president of my lifetime," said baby boomer John Edwards, the former North Carolina senator who was Kerry's run-ning mate in 2004, adding that what stunned him was that "when I talk about his incompetence it runs across the board."

"I really think he shatters the myth of white supremacy once and for all," said Harlem's congressman, Charles Rangel.

The word appeared again in a passionate screed days after Ka-trina belted the Gulf Coast. Louisiana senator Mary Landrieu, de-crying "the staggering incompetence of the national government," noted Bush's claim that "I don't think anybody anticipated the breach of the levees during the storm." Actually, she said, "every-body anticipated the breach of the levees, Mr. President, including computer simulations in which this administration participated."

Even more noteworthy was the extent to which the president became the butt of competence jokes in the popular culture. Said the singer Linda Ronstadt, "If I did my job the way he does his, I'd be fired and so would you."

Added novelist Philip Roth, "He is a man unfit to run a hardware store, let alone a nation like this one."

"President Bush said catching a seven-and-a-half-pound fish in his lake was his best moment since becoming president," said late-night comedian Jay Leno. "You know the sad thing, a lot of historians would agree with that."

Garrison Keillor of NPR's *Prairie Home Companion* was talking about Minnesota's former governor, the loudmouth Jesse Ventura, but his shrewd observation cut equally to the president's quick: "After four years of him, it was a relief to go back to politics as usual, where soft-spoken people with ordinary chest sizes sit down and negotiate and get the job done."

Incompetence is a delightful pejorative, but it is also misleading and a stretch. It is a word that mixes images of inherent inability and disqualification with ineptitude, and in the Bush administration's bizarre case that goes way too far. The president can be a dim bulb at times, especially extemporaneously, and he has lived an often aimless life, but the fact remains that he was an intelligent, shrewd, and successful governor of Texas. And his most senior advisers were, without doubt, people of significant training, qualifications, and, above all, accomplishments.

But behind the increasingly closed doors of the Bush administration, with ideology and interest group politics (and on occasion corruption) as the driving forces, it was easy for inept, ineffectual governance to flourish—from the beginning, and not simply in 2005.

Quite possibly the finest appointment President Bush ever made elevated John DiIulio from academic to government life, to run one of Bush's singular initiatives—figuring out a way to funnel large sums of money to poverty-fighting programs operated by religious organizations that (unlike long-established religious charities) do not employ staff outside their particular religious affiliation. DiIulio is a recognized intellectual giant—a product of the tough South Philadelphia streets who ended up on the Princeton University faculty and spent much of his time toiling on the vexing problems associated with poverty among youth. Though he is a social conservative, DiIulio's appointment was widely hailed outside the conservative movement because of his famous propensity for good-natured inclusiveness. But he was gone before the end of Bush's first year, dismayed at what he saw close-up in the White House.

He did not spend the next few years publicly ratting out his former colleagues and boss, but in a little-noticed letter—to the writer Ron Suskind, the author of an important, early work about the Bush administration, based largely on the private, detailed disillusionment of Treasury Secretary O'Neill (gone after 2002), DiIulio described the Bush-Cheney-Card system:

> In eight months, I heard many staff discussions but not three meaningful, substantive policy discussions. There were no actual policy white papers on domestic issues. There were, truth be told, only a couple of people in the West Wing who worried at all about policy substance and analysis. . . .
>
> This gave rise to what you might call Mayberry Machiavellis—staff, senior and junior, who consistently talked and acted as if the height of political sophistication consisted in reducing every issue to its simplest, black-and-white terms for public consumption, then steering legislative initiatives or policy proposals as far right as possible. . . .

DiIulio's devastatingly shrewd observations were not intended to be public. A decorous man, he was genuinely shocked when they appeared, very briefly, on the Internet shortly after he wrote them. But they stand years later as a definitive portrait of the Bush administration in operation—the perverted triumph of ideological politics and interest group service at the expense of governance.

In an atmosphere like the one he so accurately described, superficially organized but in fact warped in its incurious insularity, the wheels come off the machine easily. The so-called outside influences that are routinely resented by insiders constitute "reality," and a diligent and wise president and his most important advisers take special care to respond. Politics can delay the impact of underlying reality, even past elections, but in the end reality will overcome the most creative fog machine.

Because of the enormity and the enduring shock of the attack on this country in 2001, the new era it ushered in, and the ongoing wars it spawned in Afghanistan and Iraq, there is an understandable tendency in Washington to focus on security issues to the exclusion of everything else. It is understandable but unfortunate, because the bumbling that has hurt the long-term confrontation with terrorism and produced the catastrophe in Iraq is itself symptomatic of a deeper problem that has affected every aspect of national life.

The truth is that government has stumbled and fallen down across the full range of domestic and international challenges facing the country in the first decade of the twenty-first century.

The list of ignored or messed-up situations is astonishing if perspective is broadened beyond terrorism, homeland security, invasions, and military occupations: Energy costs. Energy supplies. Health care costs. Insurance availability. The modern economy. The national tax burden. Public, family, and national finance. Retirement security. The law and personal rights. Nuclear proliferation. The country's international clout and military preparedness. Disaster relief. The environment. Public health and safety regulation. The control of America's porous borders.

There has never been an American government that didn't stumble badly at times. During the last two years of his time in the White House, Jimmy Carter often seemed a straw in the winds of energy crisis, ruinous inflation, the Soviet Union's invasion of Afghanistan, and the seizure of American hostages in revolutionary Iran. During his second term, Ronald Reagan was staggered by the revelation that senior officials had traded arms sales for other hostages with that same Iranian regime and used the proceeds illegally to aid guerrillas in Nicaragua. And Bill Clinton produced chaos instead of change during the first year of his presidency and paid for it dearly in the Republican congressional landslide and takeover of 1994.

What distinguishes the Bush administration is the breadth of its failings, the fact that they extend from the beginning to the present day. Even more stunning is the fact that they have not produced a recognition of, or a true response to, its abiding, underlying problems.

Just as war and terrorism have tended to obscure a much more extensive compendium of failures, so the dramatic combination of Iraq and Hurricane Katrina in 2005 tended to obscure the entire record of the administration—as if the principal problem was that President Bush simply had a bad fifth year in office, a rough patch seemingly made worse by the fact that so many of his most publicized woes occurred during a single month. In fact, the administration's problems have been apparent from the beginning. The same administration—and in many cases the same people—that chose not to assign the highest priority to defending against terrorism before the September 11 attacks also chose to remain passive in the face of international pressures on energy supplies and prices; the same administration that planned a ninety-day, in-and-out, oil-financed invasion of Iraq also chose to remain passive in the face of ruinous increases in the cost of health insurance; the same administration that chose to yield to private sector blandishments to limit certain key industries' precautions against terrorist attacks also chose to yield to other private sector blandishments and transform a broadly supported effort to include prescription drug coverage with Medicare's services to the elderly into a fresh round of subsidies to the pharmaceutical and insurance industries that nearly foundered in its initial months.

The temptation is to restrict an analysis of these breakdowns to their separate parts. It is a more than useful exercise, but it risks creating the false impression that the foul-ups, screw-ups, and breakdowns that produced a murderous, expensive, and open-ended occupation of Iraq are entirely distinct from those that contributed to soaring gasoline prices and health insurance costs.

They are not. The trick is to search for common threads. The danger is that this becomes the political equivalent of the fabled search for a unified theory in physics—the effort to unite all of nature's fundamental relationships and forces in one overarching theoretical construction, sometimes derisively referred to as the Theory of Everything. The term unified theory was coined by Albert Einstein, who famously regretted his inability to develop one.

Dangers and pitfalls aside, the fact remains that there are indeed several common threads to an analysis of the combination of grand electoral success and major governance goofs that has distinguished the modern conservative movement, culminating in the Bush administration. They could just as easily apply to governments by progressives.

The ingredients for trouble on a grand scale are several: tight ruling circles; a strong penchant for insularity and secretiveness; intense ideological motivation with a strong mixture of hubris; strong ties to demanding interest group supporters; and an obvious backseat for the habits of traditional policymaking that emphasize transparency and the give-and-take of consensus-building compromise. All have been present throughout the Bush presidency from health care to Iraq.

The costs to the country and to the grand designs of modern conservatism have been considerable. Terrorism and war peaks aside, President Bush has on his best days governed with the support of a narrow majority of Americans. Since his reelection, however, he has steadily lost ground. At 40 to 45 percent in the public opinion polls of his job approval ratings, he had lost the support of moderates and people with weak partisan affiliations; at barely 30 percent, he was facing erosion from his base of Republicans and conservatives.

The collision between reality and strategy is a reminder that, in the United States, politics is almost always dynamic and almost never static; the pendulum is never stationary and an election victory is a beginning, never an end. Except in very rare cases of landslides, election victory does not change a single policy effectively or enact a single piece of legislation. The Bush record in the aftermath of two narrow personal victories and two narrow congressional election successes is an epic example of how political success can be squandered by governmental failure.

There are many more elegant ways to summarize what happened, but sometimes the simplest explanation suffices—they screwed up.

2

PUMPING DOLLARS

*Our dependence on foreign oil is like a foreign tax on the American Dream—
and that tax is growing every year. My administration is doing all we can to
help ease the problem. We're encouraging oil-producing countries to maximize
their production, so more crude oil is on the market to meet the demands of
the world. And we're going to make sure that consumers here at home are
treated fairly. There's not going to be any price-gouging here in America.*

—President George W. Bush, June 15, 2005

WELL, NOT EXACTLY.

President Bush was expounding after having led the country
through several giant steps backward in a struggle that had been going on for more than thirty years, steps that helped neither the supply, the demand, or the price aspects of a huge problem that lies at
the core both of America's security dangers and of its economic
challenges. He was far from finished. Bush had more giant steps
backward to promote as he presided over an administration whose
energy policy record varied from the outset from inattention to dere-
liction, from special interest favoritism to impotence while cash
poured out of frustrated Americans' pockets.

Major national problems, and not just crises, inevitably become a
president's responsibility. As time passes, especially for anyone who
gets two terms, a president is either responsive and effective or he is
not. Right from the start, six months before the 9/11 attacks, Bush
took a series of actions and took a pass on several other responses

that produced an enormous transfer of wealth and income in the wrong direction and endangered the country's security. From the beginning, his one area of alleged expertise became a torn Achilles' heel.

Shortly before the end of his sixth year in office, the administration was hit with a pair of adverse federal court rulings. Each contained an unusual rebuke for Bush's failure to correct a price-gouging mess that was created early in his first year in office.

The rulings concerned a topic that Bush, as well as Vice President Cheney, was actually supposed to know something about when he took office—energy. The rulings proved, however, that nominal expertise is no impediment to the monumental mess that can occur when a president's ideology and political ties get in the way of the sound judgments and solid, compromising deals with Congress that effective chief executives routinely make—no matter their party or ideology.

The decisions, from the appeals court in San Francisco that has jurisdiction over the Western states, affirmed what seemed a simple proposition—that a state could seek to break a supply contract with a power company by showing that the contract was the result of illegal supply and price manipulation.

That was precisely what had been uncovered, and on an unprecedented, massive scale. During the first "crisis" the fledgling Bush administration faced, there was a series of severe problems in the freshly deregulated electricity market, producing brownouts in California and a massive explosion of rate increase throughout the region that in turn seriously disrupted an already weak economy. The high-profile situation provided the perfect backdrop for the development of a comprehensive national energy policy—one of Bush's more prominent promises during the 2000 campaign.

After 2000, though, instead of siding with the obviously injured customers and states, the government's principal regulatory arm had gone so far as to decline to even consider reviewing the underlying contracts for the evidence of manipulation and unfairness that would allow abrogation. And that refusal was the tip of a far larger iceberg of policies that favored producers over consumers, production over conservation, and fossil fuels over renewable sources—all accompanied by a self-defeating, passive posture in the face of a ruinous spike in prices not seen since the shocks of the 1970s. Worse, the iceberg also consisted of a stubborn refusal to adapt to changing (in this case, worsening) conditions to address a problem that was being discussed at kitchen tables all over the country. To still be dealing (in this case, not dealing) with the same serious problem six years after it exploded into the country's consciousness mocks the sense of administrative order Bush sought to convey from the beginning.

In ruling that Nevada, Washington State, and California could pursue claims and try to break high-priced supply contracts that a mountain of evidence showed had been the product of fraud more than economics, the court declared that the government improperly elevated the ideology of "markets" above the reality of manipulation and the demands of law. Precisely the same could be said about the administration's energy policy as a whole.

More than peanuts was involved in the long-running electricity melodrama. According to Senator Dianne Feinstein, California's energy bill jumped from $8 billion in 1999 to $27 billion the following year and then remained at these stratospheric heights for nearly two more years. The same agency that was blocking renegotiation of the power contracts, moreover, had already concluded that at least four major energy firms (including the notorious Enron) had been manipulating conditions in the Western markets, a finding backed up not only by voluminous documentation but also by actual tape recordings of hotshot traders gleefully pulling supply and price strings.

What happened to electricity in the West was itself a harbinger and a symbol of what would happen to the nation.

Energy came first, months before the 9/11 attacks, and long before wars and other snafus tied the Bush administration into knots of its own making. Indeed, the tone and much of the content of the administration had been established in its first weeks via a carefully considered, allegedly new approach to a problem that had vexed the country and politicians of all persuasions for a generation.

The supply of energy and the price of energy had been in the middle of the political dialogue and on top of the government's in-box ever since an embargo on crude oil sales to the United States was imposed by the Arab members of the international producers' cartel during the Yom Kippur War in late 1973. Presidents Nixon, Ford, Carter, Reagan, Bush Senior, and Clinton had wrestled with the resulting price spikes, shortages, gas station lines, a flood of hard-earned dollars overseas, and the environmental consequences of oil- and coal-burning ever since—and with mixed results. But the second President Bush was the first to screw the problem up on an epic scale.

He failed to see the crisis coming, and bet heavily on the wrong side of the mess to chase the fool's gold of more production to meet ravenous international demands. He wasted much of his time in office advocating subsidies and other government assistance to an industry flush with record profits, and ignored the most severe price spike ever that took hundreds of billions of dollars out of the pockets of ordinary American families and sent those dollars not only to the oil companies but also to some of the same governments that opposed the United States in the messy, dangerous, new world after 9/11.

When Bush took office, energy prices had been on a tolerable plateau for years, reflecting a rough balance in world and domestic supply and demand. Experts, however, saw trouble ahead, in part because major crude oil supplies were still hostage to crises in unstable parts of Africa and the Middle East, and in part because pressure on supply was certain to build as budding economic growth engines began to purr in such huge population centers as China and India. For years, moreover, U.S. policy had been asleep; motor vehicle mileage standards had not been adjusted for a decade, even as a new generation of fuel-gobbling light trucks and sport utility vehicles dominated the domestic automotive market. The most important regulator of consumption continued to be price, and the most important government decision by far was nearly a generation in the past—Jimmy Carter's critical move to gradually eliminate price controls on oil and natural gas and thus expose Americans to the realities of world prices. The idea was to use reality as an incentive for a dramatic increase in conservation practices that would significantly reduce demand; business by and large got the message; individual consumers by and large did not.

Unlike the 1970s, there was no sudden price spike in the first half of the twenty-first century's first decade. Instead, it was gradual, steady, deeply corrosive, and over time immense.

The world price of crude oil was barely $28 per barrel when the Bush administration came to power. It would eventually peak at roughly $80. The more important reality, though, was a steady series of ever-increasing plateaus beginning early in 2004. The fact that this rise was steady, almost inexorable, makes the failure to respond all the more remarkable.

Gasoline cost an average of $1.44 per gallon in late January of 2001. The worst spike sent the price briefly above $3 just four years later in the aftermath of Hurricane Katrina, and it happened again the following summer. Yet, the more important reality was a second steady series of rising plateaus over the same period that peaked at well above $2 early in 2007 and then spiked for a third time above $3 at record levels.

Through the administration's first five years, the overall amount of price inflation was around 11 percent. In more normal times, the fact that electricity prices rose more than a third faster and natural gas prices rose more than four times faster than inflation would have been treated as a serious national problem. But the cost of crude oil and gasoline shot up at least ten times as fast, and the pace was even higher for the cold weather consumers of home heating oil and propane. The price spikes were not a serious problem; they constituted a crisis.

According to the government's Energy Information Administration, the impact on ordinary American families bordered on the ruinous. In 2001, average family expenses for gasoline, electricity, and heat were about $3,300; five years later, the average household bill exceeded $5,100. The $2,000 difference, all by itself, more than wiped out average gains in wages and salaries over the same period. The rising cost of energy also more than eliminated whatever meager advantages ordinary American families gained from the tax cuts Bush pushed in 2001 and 2003.

The hit on businesses was equally severe as the economy struggled to return to the growth rates of the late 1990s. Higher fuel costs amounted to an $80 billion surcharge on their gasoline and diesel bills; the aviation industry alone paid $22 billion more for jet fuel; and natural gas costs to commercial and industrial consumers rose $45 billion.

The gigantic jump in oil prices not only produced huge increases in the flow of cash to the domestic oil industry, hundreds of billions of dollars; it also produced equally stunning increases in the flow of dollars abroad to oil-exporting nations, several of them not exactly allies of the United States, and a few of them avowed foes. When Bush was running for president in 2000, the then steady increases in oil imports that had satisfied most of the rise in domestic fuel consumption were a major feature of his rhetoric, especially in the face of relatively stable prices. He was fond of noting that the share of U.S. consumption filled by imports, then well above half, was the highest it had ever been and he vowed to do something significant about it.

When his vice president's task force unveiled a plan of action in the spring of his first year in office, Bush began selling it as a route to price stability at home and less dependence on imports. Four months before the 9/11 attacks, Bush said, "If we fail to act, our country will become more reliant on foreign crude oil, putting our national energy security into the hands of foreign nations, some of whom do not share our interests."

Bush spoke too soon. Six years into his presidency, imports had jumped to nearly two-thirds of domestic use, exceeding fourteen million barrels a day. What is more, the sharply higher world prices were fueling a kind of petro-prosperity in countries with competing international agendas (Russia, Venezuela, and Saudi Arabia) and in at least one country that was a declared foe, these monies were funding an increasingly worrisome nuclear fuel program and supporting terrorists in Lebanon and Iraq. That country was Iran.

Arithmetic suffices to calculate the enormous increases in America's fuel bill. At the beginning of 2004, when the worst of the price spikes began, crude oil was still going for barely $34 per barrel. Three years later, at roughly $60 per barrel, the country was shelling out at least $200 billion more per year for oil, with two-thirds of the money going abroad.

Amidst the wreckage of his efforts to promote more supplies in the long run while shortchanging conservation incentives in the short run, Bush began hinting in 2006 at a willingness to change course, but only by admitting the existence of problems—as if a partial recognition of reality could all by itself constitute a worthy response in the public's mind. But the reality of policy continued fundamentally unchanged. Headlines, for example, were generated by Bush's statement in his 2006 State of the Union address that the country had become "addicted to oil," and that the success of new technologies would "help us reach another great goal, to replace more than seventy-five percent of our oil imports from the Middle East by 2025."

Within days, however, his second energy secretary, Sam Bodman, took it all back, transforming his boss's great goal into "purely an example" of what might transpire over the next generation if U.S. oil demand were reduced. In fact, consumption and imports increased again that year, as if the president's allegedly dramatic words had never been spoken.

And it happened all over again the following year. For his seventh year in office, Bush's political operation was determined to show the president taking "action" to actually deal with the "addiction" he had acknowledged the previous year but never actually confronted. The result was a forgettable slogan, "twenty in ten," that was designed to create the illusion of a dramatic response. In precise terms, the slogan encapsulated a new government goal of reducing the consumption of gasoline 20 percent below the level it was officially projected to reach over the next ten years. Through the simple technique of repetition and abbreviation, the slogan made it sound as if Bush were courageously setting the nation on a course to actually reduce consumption instead of merely to reduce its growth many years in the future. Precisely the same political technique was used early in the Bush administration to dramatize his supposedly dramatic commitment to research ways to use renewable hydrogen to power motor vehicles—an interesting, potentially vital technological breakthrough that might or might not occur at least a decade hence. The president was given a topic to emphasize that was at least relevant to the subject of energy, but which did not require a huge federal investment and which could not produce results of consequence until long after he had left office.

The Bush White House is thoroughly polluted by politics, but its reliance on short-term sound-bite politics in the absence of actual responses to problems directly affecting millions of Americans was both dangerous and from Bush's own perspective ultimately self-defeating. To put a small amount of flesh on the bones of his "twenty in ten" slogan, Bush began his seventh year in office by committing the nation to a new requirement that the amount of gasoline containing renewable substances like farm products be increased fivefold—to roughly 35 billion gallons annually by the year 2017, or at least eight years after he would be gone from office.

Like all politicians with hopes of winning the Iowa caucuses, Bush had years earlier supported government subsidies for the manufacture of ethanol from corn, a rapidly growing segment of the energy business, but one that cannot supply more than half the increase in the alternative fuels Bush was committing the nation to. Knowing this, he also spent his seventh year in office publicizing his interest in stepping up the government's support of other renewable fuels that are currently in their industrial infancy—above all hardy grasses and wood chips. His rhetoric about their future was gushing, but his credibility was severely undercut by his own budget. On the surface, Bush's numbers seemed impressive—$50 million for general bio-energy research, more than $2 billion in new government loan guarantees for the financing of so-called cellulosic ethanol plants, and $15 million in annual grants for biomass development projects.

At the same time, however, Bush's 2008 budget was proposing nearly a 40 percent increase in federal support of research and development related to nuclear power, nearly $900 million annually, as well as a jump of nearly a third in direct support of fossil fuel projects reaching approximately the same dollar figure. This all dwarfed his more publicized embrace of renewable technologies that amounted to pennies by comparison.

Bush didn't mishandle energy policy entirely on his own. As with the messed-up conflicts in Iraq and Afghanistan and the smoldering nuclear issues with Iran and North Korea, energy was a slow-moving, gathering storm, not an out-of-the blue crisis. Fumbling it required not one, but several, governmental errors, repeated over years, and reaffirmed doggedly, stubbornly in the face of broad-based criticism. From the beginning, Bush had big-time assistance.

Energy—not terrorism or war—provided the country's first hard look at a new vice president with a uniquely powerful and central role in the Bush administration. From the beginning, Dick Cheney blew his big chance, not only leaving the country weaker and more exposed to dangerous forces but severely injuring the administration's political standing. When the Republican Party lost its control of the House and Senate in 2006, the most used and most effective television commercial on behalf of Democratic challengers all over the country was not related to the deteriorating situation in Iraq, it was the assertion that incumbents from Conrad Burns in Montana to Mike DeWine in Ohio to George Allen in Virginia and Jim Talent in Missouri were tools of the oil industry.

When Cheney was assigned the task of developing a new national energy policy by a freshly installed President Bush in 2001, he occupied dual roles. He was not only an elected official with the explicit role of chief operating officer for Bush's corporate-styled government; he was also the main source of reassurance for the country about a new president with unusually thin credentials—just as he had been about candidate Bush the year before. But he lost all credibility and trust by running an unnecessarily secretive task force and restricting most of his advice and information to people trying to make money in energy. Cheney blew a historic opportunity for himself, his president's administration, his party, and his conservative movement.

When he started, he was a highly regarded, deeply experienced official who had emerged in the Nixon years to run Gerald Ford's White House staff, strike up a lifelong friendship and alliance with a predecessor named Donald Rumsfeld, serve his native Wyoming as its congressman, and then the country as defense secretary during the collapse of the Soviet Union and the first Gulf War. When he returned to Washington after a stint in the private sector running an oil services and government contracting conglomerate with the then obscure name of Halliburton, he arrived with a reputation as an affable, avuncular, able politician and manager intact. But this did not last for long.

Cheney personified the administration's weird ability to be arrogant and inept simultaneously. Regardless of ideology, successful administrations from both parties are above all receptive enough to outside forces to stay on top of volatile situations and be adaptive in responding to changing circumstances. They have allies more than cronies, they form and lead coalitions, they put a premium on maintaining a president's independence and freedom to maneuver. From

Nixon through the first President Bush, Republican presidents were careful to develop and defend a broad public interest in conservative, market-based policies. Nixon made the decision that markets were not sufficient and that national energy policy must be vigorous; Ford first embraced government-imposed mileage standards for motor vehicles; the first President Bush negotiated a toughening of the Clean Air Act with a Democratic Congress.

But every one of those elementary rules for effective governance was broken by the Bush-Cheney handling of energy policy. The dangerous deterioration of the U.S. position in Iraq understandably eclipsed everything else as Bush's time in office passed. But his mishandling of kitchen-table issues like energy first eroded his position with the all-important center in American politics and illustrates the fact that the administration is a textbook How-Not-To-Do-It government—across the board, not merely in Baghdad.

Much of the attention paid to that first-year policy exercise, both then and now, has focused on its secrecy, the fact that Cheney and the White House adamantly refused to publicly identify the companies and individuals who met with his group during the first few months of the Bush presidency. With an office full of firm believers in reconstituting post-Watergate and post-Vietnam presidential powers, Cheney won the legal battle (in the Supreme Court, no less). The preoccupation with secrecy, however, was an early example of the triumph of ideology over common sense. Secrecy in domestic policymaking, especially involving access granted to private interest groups, always leaves a president vulnerable to inevitable disclosures. Sure enough, all it took was a minimalist probe by Congress's Government Accountability Office, as it's now called, to discover that indeed Cheney's operation to develop a new national energy policy favored energy companies and their allies, and paid at most perfunctory attention to consumer and environmental activists. The resulting, avoidable furor damaged the administration's prospects from the outset.

Even less attention was paid to the actual content of the Cheney report. High-profile policy operations like this one are often classic means of forging consensus. To succeed, they must not only withstand scrutiny but also define issues and solutions comprehensively. Cheney's energy policy document failed both basic tests, setting the stage for four years of inconclusive legislative politics despite Republican control of Congress. With the headlines focused on the unprecedented mess in California, Cheney attempted to jump from that highly regionalized crisis to a wild assertion about a national crisis that very few Americans could discern back then. Focusing almost entirely on inadequate U.S. production and outdated infrastructure (pipelines and refineries), his report claimed discovery of "the most serious energy supply shortage since the oil embargoes of the 1970s."

But what the Cheney group got wrong was what would become obvious by 2004 and was already being widely discussed by experts, namely that the main engine of the crisis was far more than merely unchecked U.S. demand; it was an explosion in consumption as the developing nations of the world (above all China and India) experienced rapid economic growth. This convergence of worldwide pressure on finite supplies drove an explosion in prices. Bush had an opportunity to change this course as America began to feel the pressure three years after Cheney's report was published and the administration went to work on Capitol Hill to get its policy initiatives enacted. In as clear an indication of his stubbornness as his refusal to plan for the aftermath of the invasion of Iraq, Bush never budged.

The administration's program from the beginning had focused on opening up as many new potential sources of crude oil and natural gas in the United States and off its shores as possible, and stimulating as much exploration and development as it could via new tax breaks and other subsidies. It promised more energy production— but how much more no one could really say and precisely when no one could really say either. But the jump in demand from the developing world and the continuing jumps in demand domestically were immediate as well as essentially unaffected by the administration's policies. The resulting imbalance produced both the tight supply situation and the explosion in prices.

The second major error by Cheney's group in addition to its secrecy, compounded by the Bush White House, was to invest far too much political capital in a hyper-controversial initiative—a political sideshow, really. Even the most optimistic of the experts argued that very little could make a major contribution to increasing domestic oil supplies. For years, the oil industry, aided by its allies in the Republican Party, had eyed a small portion of the environmentally fragile Alaskan coastal plain that had long been a wildlife refuge officially and thus off limits for drilling. Cheney meant to break the taboo, and traditional battle lines formed almost immediately. From what was a large package of proposals primarily to subsidize increased domestic production, drilling in the beautiful state's National Wildlife Refuge became almost the entire focus of the legislative politics—for three long, inconclusive years. This protean struggle unfolded despite strong evidence that even under the most wild-eyed projections, the wildlife refuge's potential output, if developed over a decade, would at the most be the equivalent of a motorist topping off his gas tank—in short a major political campaign disproportionate to the energy supply gains allegedly at stake.

The third major error by Bush and Cheney involved cronyism. In his brief elective office career, no company had supported Bush more with its executives' money and other political donations than Houston's notorious Enron. And no businessman had been more closely allied with the Bush family than Enron's chief executive officer, Kenneth Lay. Enron and Lay enjoyed easy access to top administration officials while the Cheney group was doing its work, and the result was a gratuitous endorsement of the company's business model, focusing on arcane financial products in the commodities markets called derivatives. These products, the Cheney report stated in glowing terms, "allow firms to substantially reduce their exposure to changes in energy prices. . . . The US government should continue to support the development of efficient derivatives markets."

This ringing endorsement came in May of 2001, just as analysts in the investment community were beginning to raise questions about the reliability of Enron's financial data. Within just three months, the first public indication that something was seriously wrong would surface, before the end of the year the company would go spectacularly and tragically bust, and within a year Enron's manipulative role in the California electricity debacle would be exposed. The Cheney operation was so eager to be supportive that it did not look into Enron's condition independently to validate its supportive inclinations. The administration's credibility was compromised gratuitously.

As domestic and international energy prices went through the roof beginning in 2004, and with no prospect of breaking the stalemate with Congress over comprehensive energy legislation because of the Alaska dispute, Bush and Cheney simply gave up. The tacit confession of impotence was embarrassing, but judged to be tolerable during a reelection year when other issues, above all the continuing terrorism scares, were presumed to be more politically important.

The following year, after Bush's narrow win over Democrat John Kerry and with the price crisis even more serious, the president and his embattled Republican congressional allies agreed to try for a scaled-down energy bill so that at least a minimal accomplishment could be touted in preparation for the congressional election season. The result was a comedy of additional political and policy errors.

Beholden as ever to its oil industry backers, the administration and Congress agreed on a fresh batch of tax and royalty relief measures largely focused on the expensive search for more oil in the Gulf of Mexico. In all, the package was worth about $2 billion in savings to the industry, but it was enacted just as gasoline prices were beginning to flirt with the preposterous level of $3 per gallon in the aftermath of Hurricanes Katrina and Rita. What is more, the

benefits were being passed out even as the industry was earning unheard of record profits because of the price spikes. It was from such
shenanigans that the Democratic Party's all-purpose television ad-
vertisement in the 2006 campaign emerged.

What is more, data appeared after the election indicating that the
legislative package of tax and royalty goodies was likely to have no
impact whatsoever on the problem it was allegedly designed to deal
with. According to a study done for the Interior Department by an
energy consulting firm, the so-called incentives were likely to produce at most a 1.1 percent increase in the country's oil reserves
above what would have been the case had the package never been
enacted.

In one of its first acts, the newly Democratic House of Representatives unceremoniously repealed the entire package early in 2007.
The vote produced a solid 264–163 majority, with some three dozen
Republicans joining their Democratic colleagues. Undeterred as ever
by these realities, Bush vowed to try to block the measure in the
more narrowly divided Senate.

At the time Cheney's task force was wrapping up its much anticipated work in the spring of 2001, Bush's initial posture as a knowledgeable new president willing to tackle a tough topic had largely
neutralized a post-Reagan tendency for the electorate to lean progressive on domestic policy issues. In the spring of 2001, an ABC
News survey showed Americans split on Bush's handling of energy
policy: 39 percent positive and 43 percent negative. In the inevitable
clash of policy options, 35 percent favored more domestic production, with 56 percent favoring an emphasis on conservation.

But by the sixth year of his presidency, Bush had seen the center
collapse, as it did eventually on his handling of everything else. In
the spring of 2006, asked if the president was doing enough about
gasoline prices, Americans answered no in a CNN/Gallup poll by a
71 to 24 percent margin. By the following January, Democrats were
preferred as the stewards of energy issues by 55 to 30 percent.

Bush had lost politically and decisively so, but the country had lost substantively. The current official projection of the Energy Department is that oil imports will increase inexorably to fully 70 percent of domestic consumption over the next two decades.

3

UNHEALTHY

On the critical issue of health care, our goal is to ensure that Americans can choose and afford private health care coverage that best fits their individual needs. To make insurance more affordable, Congress must act to address rapidly rising health care costs. . . . A government-run health care system is the wrong prescription. By keeping costs under control, expanding access, and helping more Americans afford coverage, we will preserve the system of private medicine that makes America's health care the best in the world.

—President George W. Bush, January 20, 2004

EXACTLY THE OPPOSITE occurred.

As it happened, a few years after that boilerplate State of the Union address, President Bush's beleaguered handlers picked Chattanooga in late winter for what in happier times would have been one stop on one of the photogenic tours modern presidents like to take to draw attention to the major elements of their freshly delivered annual messages.

Instead, his brief journey at the end of February in 2007 drew unwanted attention to Bush's astonishing mixture of false starts, ignorance of basic facts and trends, ideological myopia, and political ineptitude about one of the country's most serious problems—the crisis in health care—that was bad enough when he first took office and became increasingly horrendous.

An occasionally funny man, intentionally and otherwise, Bush was telling his typically handpicked audience about one of the basic things every consumer does in advance of a major purchase—ask around about the prices of his options.

"I do when it comes to a car, or I used to," he said, adding as he realized he was talking about life outside his famous bubble, one that is due to resume soon enough, "I will soon."

But where health care is concerned, Bush had a point that he makes periodically and is central to his conservative vision of a consumer-driven marketplace. It is also central to an understanding of how huge a failure his haphazard efforts in this vital area have been.

"I don't know about you," he said, "but I don't remember ever asking how much something was going to cost when it came to health care."

Of all the dangers a president faces, none is more to be avoided than looking ridiculous. His power is fragile, based in large part on his perceived stature and always in danger of erosion, so appearances count. Roughly nine of every ten dollars spent on health care in the United States is spent on the treatment of illness, raising the question of what Bush thought he was talking about. As if ordinary families with a kid down with chicken pox, or diagnosed with leukemia, or an adult with a kidney stone or experiencing arrhythmia treat health care as a giant suburban mall in which to look for sales.

The truth is that Bush's remark parted the curtain before a piece of conservative ideology that has been around at least since the late 1960s. In the face of the explosion in costs, both for care itself and for the insurance that inadequately covers much of it, some conservative thinkers have argued that the core of the problem is the "demand" for care fueled by group insurance—whether via government programs like Medicare for the elderly, or Medicaid for the poor, or coverage schemes available in the workplace. Under these umbrellas, so the theory goes, people procure services without regard to need or cost, thus propelling the costs skyward.

In the alternative, many academic conservatives have argued through the years, a system based on conservatism's iconic focal point (the individual) would solve modern America's dilemma about availability and affordability, empowering people to shop for what they need at prices they can afford. In Bush's case, this belief structure led to a series of ideas advanced in the infancy of his 2000 campaign and all the way through his presidency, to use tax deductions and tax credits, special forms of tax-favored savings accounts, and new limits on the tax-free status of contributions made by employers to their workers' insurance, to help ignite a revolution.

The problem, as with all transforming health care ideas no matter their ideological origin, is in figuring out how to navigate the transition. In health care, as in everything else, presidents are wise not to get flagrantly divorced from reality. What sounds brilliant in salons and think tanks can appear absurd in the real world. In health care it helps to keep two huge realities clearly in mind—the median household income in the United States is roughly $50,000, and around 85 percent of the population is (sort of) insured today either through work or the government. The danger, and this is precisely what happened during the Bush years, is that politicians can tinker with the uninsured while things are going haywire in the rest of the world, where nearly all Americans live and work. In this case, haywire meant not only an explosion in costs (that almost made the jump in energy prices pale by comparison), but also a decline in the availability of health insurance as hard-pressed firms began to drop coverage and new ones decided they couldn't afford to offer it to their workers. The number of Americans with no coverage at all swelled under Bush by more than seven million and approached fifty million people. The cost increases, whether in care itself or in insurance premiums directly, or in the deductibles and co-payments that degrade its value, were in the thousands of dollars.

At the time of his trip to Tennessee, Bush was pushing a freshened set of proposals to reform the insurance mess via the tax system. His main proposal would provide each household with a new standard deduction on its income tax return of $15,000 (half that for an individual) for the purchase of insurance coverage—whether bought as an individual or through an employer. At least in theory, the Bush idea was that it was both unfair and inefficient for people in workplaces that don't offer coverage to have to buy it on their own with no tax breaks, while those in places that do are heavily subsidized through the tax deductibility of part of the employer's contribution.

Or, as the president put it in Chattanooga, "Right now, there's a limited market for the individual. It makes it hard to find a product that either suits your needs or you can afford."

There is just one problem for that all-important individual with an ordinary job and an ordinary income: how can you afford the money up front to get coverage, in order to get the tax benefit later? The answer is that the vast majority of ordinary Americans can't, which makes Bush's plan of interest only to people at the extreme margins of the health care debate who have large incomes, and of virtually no interest to everybody else. That is why this idea and earlier versions of it (primarily involving tax credits instead of deductions) have been orphans on Capitol Hill—both when the Republicans were in control of Congress and when they were not.

To cover his inaction in the face of disastrous trends in costs and coverage, Bush's political advisers kept him in the proposal business constantly. At any given moment throughout his tenure, he had an idea on the table—to encourage some technological innovation in insurance record-keeping, to combat some marginal threat like the stale conservative bogeyman of "frivolous" malpractice suits. In Washington, the nonexistent congressional prospects were widely recognized for what they were, but for his travels around the country the White House proposal factory created the convenient illusion of action. As time passed, however, the danger of overreliance on short-term political strategies to cover for a deeper inability to respond became clear. The strategies can work on any given day, but over time people realize that nothing is in fact being done to relieve a situation they are directly experiencing. Bush has been in that bad habit on health care from the beginning.

The tax deduction scheme in fact elicited more derision than reaction. Representative Rahm Emanuel, the Chicago Democrat who is a major player in Speaker Nancy Pelosi's new leadership group and the person in charge of the Democrats' victorious campaign in 2006, sharply dismissed Bush's initiative for "its absence of appeal to ordinary Americans for whom up-front payments for personal insurance would be an extreme hardship, for its potential threat to the scores of millions of people with tax-favored coverage through work, and for its bottom-line, every-person-for-himself motif.

"He does nothing to control costs," Emanuel said, "and he does nothing to expand the number of insured. Other than that, it is incredibly helpful."

Progressives tended to prefer derision; Republicans in Congress mostly chose silent dismissal; but the problem was so severe that it evoked often vicious satire in the popular culture, the strongest evidence that Bush had screwed up on an issue whose resonance with ordinary households was as obvious as it was powerful. It's bad enough for a president to elicit more opposition than support; but when people start laughing, it's disastrous. Shortly after his 2006 State of the Union grab bag fell flat politically, Bush became the butt of some highly effective humor—none more so than the following offering from Stephen Colbert, one of Comedy Central's stars in its nightly parody of news on television.

Playing his familiar role of faux conservative talk show blowhard, Colbert absorbed the details of Bush's latest health care thinking and delivered the following analysis, which became an instant hit via the Internet megaphone:

"It's so simple. Most people who couldn't afford health insurance also are too poor to owe taxes. But if you give them a deduction from the taxes they don't owe, they can use the money they're not getting back from what they haven't given to buy the health care they can't afford."

Just as Bush was arriving in Tennessee, he got some more bad news. Reflecting the severity of the country's health care crisis, scores of networks of activism in localities all around the country have been spawned. Timed for his arrival, a local organization—the Community Research Council of Chattanooga—published a primer jammed with information about the finances and health care status of residents of the city and the surrounding Hamilton County. For starters, roughly one in five of the county's 310,000 residents was without any health coverage as of 2006, a figure higher than the national average but in line with the situation in most of the Southern and border states.

Of those, three-quarters of the uninsured get by on household incomes of less than $40,000, and fully one-fourth of them had family incomes below $20,000. This is a vivid illustration of the point that most working families simply don't have the cash to purchase decent health insurance packages, which usually run into five figures annually. And of the county residents who were insured, roughly 60 percent had coverage via their workplaces. Overall, in a poll of adults, fully two-thirds of the Chattanooga area's adults were firmly in line with the rest of the country in strongly agreeing that just as with minimum wage and overtime laws, employers should be required by law to offer their workers health insurance.

Bush, of course, has tried to move the country in exactly the opposite direction. His tax deduction proposal, however, is the kind of madness that nonetheless has ideological purpose. Undermining the work-based system that insures well over 150 million people is also designed to enhance the attractiveness of another favorite, ideology-based scheme in the conservative movement—so-called Health Savings Accounts, yet another tax-based idea that promotes the private insurance market. These investment vehicles were first widely available in 2004 (they were authorized as a last-minute sop to insurance and investment community lobbyists while the administration's version of a new prescription drug benefit for the elderly was being enacted). Contributions are tax-deductible up to a maximum of nearly $5,500 for a household, with withdrawals also tax-free as long as they are for medical expenses.

To qualify, a plan purchased by an individual or offered by an employer must include very high deductibles (more than $2,000 for a family in 2006). The combination of deductibles, co-payments, and other out-of-pocket expenses is permitted up to a maximum of $10,500 for a family. After three full years in operation, surveys by the Government Accountability Office showed that at most three million people had signed up for Health Savings Account plans that on paper had been given government approval; but many of these individuals had yet to actually open their accounts.

By definition, in other words, one of the centerpieces of the administration's health care rhetoric is literally designed to exclude Americans with ordinary or low incomes. A third of the households with no health insurance protection have less than $25,000 in annual income, and two-thirds of them bring in less than $50,000. For workers with earnings on that scale, federal income taxes are but a tiny portion of their financial reality; for those owing no income taxes there is no subsidy whatsoever for opening one of these savings accounts. And for those who pay the lowest income tax rate, the subsidy amounts to no more than 10 cents on the dollar.

Given the realities of life for middle- and lower-income families—particularly the soaring costs of other necessities like housing, gasoline, electricity, and heat—even the struggle to put aside $2,100 to cover a family's deductible in a savings account would appear unrealistic in the extreme. And for the full load of deductibles and other out-of-pocket requirements, the annual savings need would exceed $10,000, depending on how much of actual medical needs are covered under each plan.

The president, in other words, has been touting a scheme that is most attractive to the wealthiest and healthiest families. Indeed, one survey of participants in the benefits program for federal employees found that those picking high-deductible insurance plans were far more likely to earn more than $75,000 per year than those choosing comprehensive protection.

Even with relatively few Americans participating in them, the savings accounts have become a new source of dropped coverage as a growing number of employers cite the tax breaks as a reason to end insurance coverage for their workers and toss them on the rarely tender mercies of the private insurance market. According to one study of Health Savings Accounts, the addition of nearly four million to the ranks of the insured who can afford to put aside the money that triggers the tax breaks would be more than offset by the more than four million workers who would lose comprehensive coverage at work as a result.

And with no net increase in the number of insured Americans, billions of dollars would be drained from federal revenues that might otherwise be available for health care programs and other pressing needs. According to the administration's own budget office, the five-year drain from Health Savings Accounts would approach $20 billion.

On occasion, the Bush administration has let its underlying ideological fervor creep into official documents. According to Bush's annual economic policy report in 2006, for example, the combination of high-deductible insurance with the savings accounts is a way to "give consumers both the incentives and the information needed to become better shoppers for health care," in alleged contrast to comprehensive insurance that is said to "dull" such market mechanisms.

The danger of substituting ideology for common sense and hard data, when it's a topic of vital interest to everyone, is that it creates a clash between the words people hear from their leaders and the realities they confront when they discuss life at the kitchen table. The vast majority of Americans do not "shop" for health care. To the extent (increasing all the time) they confront the private insurance market on their own, they are encountering an industry whose profit model is based on denial—either of coverage for specific expenses or of coverage altogether. According to one study (of what looks much more like a racket than a business) for the Kaiser Family Foundation, applicants for private insurance are unable to get the standard advertised rates unless they are fortunate enough to have no health problems at all; more than a third of those whose health is considered less than ideal are rejected.

To operate this massive system that cherry-picks its customers, the industry spend tens of billions of dollars a year on administrative, marketing, and underwriting costs. A study by the consulting firm of McKinsey & Company estimated that this immense bureaucracy drains nearly $100 billion out of the health care system in bureaucratic costs—well above the $77 billion it estimated a system that offered universal insurance would cost.

For more than seven years—from presidential candidate and governor of Texas through all but the final lap of his presidency—Bush has vigorously promoted tax credits, tax deductions, Health Savings Accounts, and other schemes that by definition have extremely narrow appeal. The question is why—especially given the enormous increases in the cost of insurance and care that have severely injured the financial foundation of the vast majority of Americans.

The answer, apart from his enduring commitment to the fringe belief that insurance coverage is part of the problem—as opposed to the solution—of soaring costs and declining availability, is politics. In the face of a huge problem that affects everyone and is becoming more severe every year, any White House, no matter which party controls it, has essentially two political choices: go at the problem directly and at least appear to the public to be trying to tackle it or even make it less severe, or employ misdirection maneuvers to distract attention. The Bush White House has consistently chosen the latter in its domestic policymaking, usually getting a modicum of short-term advantage at the cost of much bigger trouble later—the very definition of a screw-up. Tax credits or deductions, or Health Savings Accounts, are interesting topics and have evoked passionate debate for years; any presidential proposal in a major area like health care is guaranteed to get attention even if it only has significance for a small slice of the population or little chance of congressional enactment (or both). Eventually, however, Bush's distracting noise was no match for pressing matters that affect huge chunks of the country—like the elderly, children, and working families. His attempts to tinker at the extreme margins of the problem for political and ideological reasons and his inaction in the face of ruinous cost pressures ended up not only setting the cause of conservatism back but also costing him the all-important center in the overall debate about the future of health care and insurance.

His other actions in the health care area only compounded the difficulty, politically and substantively.

In the next-to-last budget of his presidency, Bush did what presidents tend to do when budget pressures become intense—he made a thinly disguised attempt to make the government's books look a little less horrible by attempting to nickel-and-dime Medicare, at least on paper. He had also tried it at the beginning of 2006, an election year, an attempt that not only contributed to the atmosphere in which the Republicans lost control of Congress but also to their inability to reach agreement on a budget on their way out of power.

The new proposal was to take roughly $50 billion over the following five years out of the mammoth federal insurance program that covers about half the hospital and doctor expenses of the elderly and the disabled. That would have amounted to about one-fourth the amount by which the program is expected to expand in this period as an aging population pushes the government's tab toward a half-trillion dollars annually.

There were very few details, except that the budget documents said the cutbacks were to be concentrated among what are called "providers" in Medicare jargon—meaning the hospitals, nursing homes, and home care professionals who actually deliver services to beneficiaries. One reason for the absence of details in how, when, and where the cuts would be made was pure politics; no details were necessary because there was no expectation that the cuts would ever be legislated. If a Republican Congress hardly glanced at a proposal for a $35 billion Medicare cutback in 2006, the odds of a Democratic Congress taking a $50 billion proposal seriously the next year were laughable.

The real reason for the proposal was that the PR and politics-fixated White House was intent on proposing a budget in 2007 that on paper looked as if it would finally reach balance five years into the future. The reason the numbers worked was through preposterous assumptions such as unspecified cutbacks to Medicare providers and other propositions that had no chance of occurring.

This kind of sophomoric policymaking fooled no one. The initial reaction in Congress was totally negative (representing the center, Republican senator Arlen Specter of Pennsylvania called the smoke-and-mirrors effort "scandalous"). And for his trouble, the president also managed to earn opprobrium from any remaining segment of the national health care community that hadn't written him off already.

Deep down, as with Social Security itself, Bush has always been a closet privatizer, anxious to lure insurance companies and investment firms into Medicare as competitors for the healthiest and wealthiest beneficiaries. But after nearly seven years in office, his administration was only able to win approval of a six-year experiment in six metropolitan areas that will give Medicare patients the dubious "choice" of private insurance at a small discount that would be more than wiped out by the far higher administrative costs of the insurance companies.

Bush tried the same budget-maneuvering—and with the same effect—with the government's other huge health care program, Medicaid, which both provides health care services to the poor and has become the most important element of the safety net for chronically ill elderly people in nursing homes. Here, the proposal was for a cutback of more than $25 billion.

In general Medicaid operates as a joint state-federal program; since its inception in the 1960s, the split has generally been roughly fifty-fifty. However, the federal government has traditionally covered all but 10 percent of the states' considerable administrative costs of actually running Medicaid. What Bush proposed in 2007 was that the federal share of these costs should be slashed to 50 percent. His spokesmen could make the argument that with a more healthy economy at mid-decade, state governments were mostly running budget surpluses but the severity of the proposed cutback obliterated that point. A large chunk of assumed Medicaid money was included in the administration's preposterous projection of a balanced budget by 2012, but as with Medicare the assumption attracted no takers in Congress from either party, added yelps of protest from Republican and Democratic governors alike, and cemented the impression that Bush's ideological commitment was to shift Medicaid burdens from the federal government onto the states and onto already hard-pressed beneficiaries. He failed to earn even a chance of having what he proposed approved and further injured his political standing in the process.

Bush's reputation as a poor steward of Medicare and Medicaid, however, did not hold a candle to the self-inflicted wounds caused by his hostile intentions toward one of the few health care initiatives of the last generation not only to succeed but to win strong bipartisan support—and involving children no less.

It is called the State Children's Health Insurance Program, and in the late 1990s when it began, it was the reason that years of steady increases in the number of Americans with no health insurance were transformed into years of progress. In the wake of the failure of President Clinton's health insurance initiative in the first term of his presidency, it was the brainchild primarily of a very liberal senator, Edward Kennedy, and a very conservative one, Orrin Hatch of Utah. Its target was an important segment of the uninsured population that has a bit too much income to qualify for Medicaid assistance, but nowhere nearly enough to purchase adequate insurance privately, and it ended up hitting the bull's-eye.

At a cost of roughly $5 billion a year to the federal government, the program was originally designed to help children in families earning up to 200 percent of the official poverty level, about $40,000, though still well below the median household income. Eventually, states were encouraged by both the Clinton and Bush administrations to expand eligibility, and sixteen did so. After Bush's first term, the program was reaching families with more than six million children and would have been reaching even more if better efforts had been made to reach all eligible families.

But in 2007, a previously supportive Bush abruptly flip-flopped, proposing that the federal share be restricted to helping families with no more than double the poverty level in income—in effect, pulling the rug out from under all the states he had encouraged to expand their efforts. Instead, spending, Bush proposed, should be held to slightly less than the current level indefinitely.

The result was another bipartisan uproar—from Republican Arnold Schwarzenegger's California to Democrat Eliot Spitzer's New York—warning that states would run out of money within months to maintain existing caseloads. Negotiations for a short-term fix quickly began, but unlike his position regarding Medicare and Medicaid, Bush had more leverage to squeeze the children's program because its ten-year statutory authorization was due to expire in 2007.

For a generation, one fact about the country's long-running health insurance mess has been clear no matter which party was in control—without persistent efforts to reform the system and enlarge coverage the inexorable trend is toward a larger uninsured population and toward higher out-of-pocket costs to those still covered.

Between Bush's election in 2000 and the seventh year of his presidency, the number of uninsured Americans jumped by more than seven million people to roughly 47 million Americans, with another sixteen million struggling with minimalist policies that left them exposed to major expenses.

As for the more than 150 million Americans with some kind of coverage at work, the costs skyrocketed in the face of governmental inaction. The amount workers paid in premiums nearly doubled, up 84 percent over the first six years of the new century—quadruple the increase in wages and in overall inflation. On top of the explosion in energy costs, this was another consumer necessity where the increases in prices all by themselves wiped out the value of the administration's income tax cuts.

For businesses, the average employer contribution to family

coverage jumped by 80 percent to nearly $3,000 a year. The increase for employees on the average was actually a little bit more than that.

According to the Kaiser Family Foundation, one of the major sources of information about the worsening crisis, the cost of the average health insurance policy for a family soared by nearly 60 percent over this ruinous period—reaching just below $10,000, a jump of more than $3,000 above what the same policy cost in 2000.

Not surprisingly, there was a political cost for this appalling record of neglect, mismanagement, and self-inflicted wounds. When Bush took office, opinion polls showed that the public continued to follow the Democratic Party's lead on health care issues, as it had for the generation since Medicare and Medicaid were created. But Bush had at least managed to persuade most people that he was making an effort and that his administration was likely to help more than hurt.

After three months in office, a Gallup poll for CNN and USA Today found 51 percent of the respondents believing that the new administration would at least improve the situation.

Six years later, Bush's reputation was in shambles. By 66 to 30 percent, a Zogby International survey found the public preferring Democrats on the issue, and by 73 to 25 percent, respondents said they were dissatisfied with the availability of affordable health care. At those levels of nonsupport, Bush's record was opposed by self-described moderates and independent voters as vehemently as by Democrats, and he had lost the support of roughly a fourth of the Republicans.

It was no accident. It took years of hard work for Bush to transform a genuine Bush opportunity into a severe Bush liability at an enormous cost to the country.

4

HOT AIR

A recently released Department of Energy Report, "Analysis of Strategies for Reducing Multiple Emissions from Power Plants," concluded that including caps on carbon dioxide emissions as part of a multiple emissions strategy would lead to an even more dramatic shift from coal to natural gas for electric power generation and significantly higher electricity prices compared to scenarios in which only sulfur dioxide and nitrogen oxides were reduced. This is important new information that warrants a reevaluation, especially at a time of rising energy prices and a serious energy shortage. Coal generates more than half of America's electricity supply. At a time when California has already experienced energy shortages, and other Western states are worried about price and availability of energy this summer, we must be very careful not to take actions that could harm consumers. This is especially true given the incomplete state of scientific knowledge of the causes of, and solutions to, global climate change and the lack of commercially available technologies for removing and storing carbon dioxide.

—President George W. Bush, letter to Senator Chuck Hagel (R-Neb.), March 13, 2001

JUST DAYS BEFORE President Bush's next-to-last State of the Union address early in 2007 and six years after that retreat from an explicit 2000 campaign promise to regulate carbon dioxide emissions, Washington's rumor mill sprang an unusually specific leak.

After years of denials and dodges—not unlike his father's more than a decade before—the president was said to be ready to acknowledge the existence of serious global warming caused by cars, power plants, and other forms of human activity and to propose some first steps to credibly confront it.

With a documentary film produced by his 2000 opponent, Al Gore, headed toward an Oscar, with the scientific community as close to unanimity as it ever gets on the gravity of the crisis, with public opinion overwhelmingly tilting toward an activist agenda, the leak rang true.

That's because it appeared to use the jargon of environmental policymaking, an odd step by a notoriously anti-environment government. No less a figure than the head of the White House's Council on Environmental Quality—the mechanism through which Bush governed in this area—had let it be known that at least in principle he (James Connaughton) favored putting regulatory limits, or "caps" in policy wonk patois, on the emissions that contribute to global warming.

In an administration legitimately notorious for its arrogant stubbornness in the face of conflict—from the war in Iraq to the explosion in health insurance costs—this signal was taken at face value.

It shouldn't have been. The claim was too one-sided, missing the critical ingredient of hard information from officials closer to the Oval Office, or from the Prince of Fossil Fuels himself, Dick Cheney. As it turned out, the administration once again ended up dashing the hopes it had raised, compounding the six-year self-inflicted damage in this increasingly high-profile area.

Regulation of carbon dioxide emissions was but the tip of a very large iceberg of inattention to a core, Constitution-supplied presidential mission—taking care that the nation's laws are "faithfully" executed to protect the public's health and safety. Bush used his power more to serve the specific needs of interest groups than to serve conservative principles, warping policy on everything from pain medicine to birth control pills. Much of it worked for a while, but every one of his actions planted the seeds of far more serious trouble later on—for himself as well as for the conservative cause.

On global warming, Bush confused mentioning a national problem with tackling it seriously as he operated from deep inside his isolated bubble. It was said by his spokesmen to be significant that he had actually mentioned the problem in 2007—preferring the softer-sounding term "climate change." But in fact he had brought forth another mouse—his proposal to try to reduce gasoline consumption by 20 percent below what it was projected to be in the year 2017. The initiative—to be accomplished via a large increase in the use of alternative fuels like ethanol mandated by government regulation—was neither important to effective environmental regulation nor to America's dangerously unchecked fossil fuel consumption habits. From all sides of the debate about global warming it was recognized that meaningful action meant caps.

Nothing weakens a president more than inaction in the face of such a broad consensus. It is a virtual invitation to everyone else on the policy playing field to take over. In the case of global warming, the policy initiative that should have been the president's was ceded to a very long list of major players. It included, beyond the international scientific community, all the other developed nations, state and local governments with Republican as well as Democratic governors and mayors, growing segments of the business community including some major energy companies, and a newly Democratic House and Senate after 2006.

Facing this huge coalition of Bush's own making, it was surprising that his White House even attempted to take some credit for having only mentioned climate change in the prime-time address. Within the same news cycle, people who follow the issue were pointing out that Bush had been mentioning the problem for nearly two years—most pointedly during a European trip in 2005 when one of his texts contained all the right words: "I recognize that the surface of the earth is warmer and that an increase in greenhouse gases caused by humans is contributing to the problem."

The words, however, were more boomerang than pronouncement, calling attention to the broader inaction and signaling all the other participants in the debate in this country and abroad to pick up the reins he was dropping.

While President Bush is deservedly infamous for his truculent stubbornness on issues like Iraq, health care, and taxes, it is also true that when pressed (either by unavoidable reality or special interest pressure groups) he is capable of turning on a dime. He has done it in nuclear arms talks with North Korea, on anti–free trade tariffs to help the steel industry, on the formation of the Homeland Security Department, and on the formation of the 9/11 Commission—to name only a few. When handled correctly, policy lurches can be portrayed as commendable responses to reality by an effective president; but in Bush's case, they were uniformly simple cave-ins and only gave another jolt to his already depleted credibility.

But as flip-flops go in public life, his cartwheel on the subject of carbon dioxide pollution and its regulation is one for the record as well as the history books.

From barely a month before his disputed victory over Al Gore in 2000 to less than sixty days after he took office, Bush managed to go from being a surprise and welcome addition to the massive consensus behind an action agenda on global warming to establishing himself as the most important opponent of that agenda in the entire world. He also opened an early window on a regulatory record that would produce some of the most significant self-inflicted wounds of his presidency, without coming close to succeeding in their typically venal purpose.

During his reelection campaign four years later, Bush's camp managed to take skillful advantage of a silly verbal goof by his opponent, John Kerry, and use millions of dollars in devastating television commercials to affix the flip-flopper label forever to Kerry's forehead. What Kerry did was describe how he had voted for an amendment to legislation sending billions of dollars off to the Iraq War that would have funded it with a small increase in taxes paid by high-income Americans and then voted against the bill after the amendment attempt failed. His sin was in saying he had in effect voted for the bill before voting against it.

Those were merely very wrong words describing an eminently defensible action. Bush's flip-flop, however, affected the course of national policy. More than that, it sheds light on one of the defining elements of his administration: his ability to mix ineptitude with the worst kind of crony capitalism in one of the most basic of government's endeavors—the regulation of business activity in the interests of public health and safety. Bush's actions and proposals ranged far beyond the environment, warping policies that affected new drugs and the safety of coal mines as well as air pollution.

What Bush has never fully realized is that the liberal-conservative argument on regulatory issues is over means, not ends. Conservatives do not merely argue for voluntary as opposed to mandatory measures, they do not merely urge consideration of costs versus benefits, they do not merely favor supporting new technologies as opposed to mandated reductions in output from existing ones. Conservatives argue that the public interest can be served in these ways because they pose less of a danger to the economy.

Through the years, the real danger has occurred when conservatives let themselves get hijacked by the private agendas of business lobbyists. When it happened early in Ronald Reagan's administration, when borderline corruption surfaced at both the Environmental Protection Agency and the Interior Department, he responded by changing course abruptly in 1983. With his EPA administrator, Anne Gorsuch Burford, the issues included corrupt administration of the Superfund program for highly toxic waste sites (one of her top officials actually ended up in jail); and with his interior secretary, James Watt, they involved public land giveaways as well as the use of administrative procedures to gut statutory requirements (also a Burford-favored strategy). In the face of public outcries, which reached moderate Republicans in Congress, Reagan acted decisively, both firing the two officials and reversing policy. His new EPA administrator had been the agency's first back in the 1970s, the highly regarded William Ruckelshaus.

But on Bush's watch, with neither accountability nor adaptability high on the list of approved virtues, things only tended to get worse.

The then Texas governor's first carbon dioxide position was stated very clearly down the stretch of his battle with Al Gore in late September of 2000, as in an appearance in Saginaw, Michigan.

"We will require all power plants to meet clean-air standards," Bush said, "in order to reduce emissions of carbon dioxide within a reasonable period of time."

Bush not only made that firm promise, he also put it in the broader context of a promised tough assault on the three other components of serious air pollution—sulfur dioxide, oxides of nitrogen, and mercury.

After taking office, and after selecting Dick Cheney to produce an energy policy, Bush decided to ditch his promise quickly (the political equivalent of lancing a boil) rather than absorb the change into the overall energy initiative later. To stage-manage the flip-flop, the White House's skilled tacticians arranged for Bush to get a public letter from four Republican senators worried about the economic implications of carbon dioxide regulation—Chuck Hagel of Nebraska, Jesse Helms of North Carolina, Larry Craig of Idaho, and Pat Roberts of Kansas.

What is usually forgotten is that the president went well beyond a decision to leave carbon dioxide alone. He did it in the context of several other important maneuvers during that first March of his presidency: he not only repeated his implacable opposition to the international accord negotiated in Kyoto, Japan, four years earlier but also withdrew from participation in the international process itself. Moreover, he in essence reversed on his position regarding the other three major components of air pollution by proposing changes to the landmark Clean Air Act that would reduce the extent of emissions reductions and delay their enactment much longer compared to existing law.

And the following year, he went even further, attempting via executive action to maintain the most egregious loophole in the entire thirty-plus-year history of air pollution regulation—a provision that left certain coal-fired power plants alone (those which had been operating before the original statute was enacted). For a generation, these companies had avoided the regulations of the Clean Air Act by investing heavily in their older facilities (coal-fired ones) to keep them operational. As time passed, however, these investments were creating the functional equivalent of new facilities, but ones that still evaded controls on their emissions. President Clinton had fashioned a means of bringing them into compliance with the Clean Air Act; President Bush was determined to turn the clock back.

And he attempted one more subterfuge that in a backhanded way recognized the validity and the power of the evidence that fossil fuel consumption was creating a clear, present, and increasing danger to the planet—the announcement of a particular policy goal that appeared to be responsive but which in fact wasn't.

The Bush administration liked to call it "intensity"—a concept that deftly fudged issues involving amounts of pollutants in order to provide a broader "context," in this case the overall economy. In 2002, after his first year of living dangerously by attempting to roll back the policy commitments of the Clinton administration, Bush began celebrating intensity (defined as a ratio between emission amounts and units of economic output), and vowing to reduce it. The number chosen for a reduction in intensity to be unveiled by the president was a serious-sounding 18 percent, and its deadline was long after Bush's departure from office—2012. The theory enunciated was that as the intensity of greenhouse gas emissions dropped toward equality with the annual increase in gross domestic product, emissions themselves would at long last stabilize and then start to decline.

With continual repetition, the ever-active political communicators in the White House were able gradually to make it appear that it was emissions themselves or even energy consumption overall that was going to drop.

In fact, however, the administration's own Energy Department had numbers in its possession that showed how puny this initiative really was. Without any actions at all by Bush, simply because of ongoing efforts to promote efficiency throughout the economy, energy intensity was already projected to decline by 14 percent through 2012. In pushing for an 18 percent drop, Bush was seeking to accelerate the process by the minuscule amount of barely 1.7 percent annually.

The president's manipulation of the government's regulatory responsibilities regarding greenhouse gases was a classic, and predictable, case of short-term advantage purchased at the price of longer-term trouble. Presidents who don't institutionalize the vital practice of thinking through consequences usually end up facing them.

Renouncing the 1997 Kyoto treaty requiring reductions in greenhouse gases by the developed countries was at first easy—politically and even substantively. Even before Bush took office, a symbolic Senate vote on the treaty, which Clinton never bothered formally to submit, produced a unanimous no. However, in not only renouncing it but also withdrawing from the international process, Bush dealt the United States completely out of a game it could not afford to watch from the sidelines.

The risk was that Kyoto would be viewed differently in this country and abroad as the years went on, which is exactly what happened. Eventually, with ratification by Russia, it actually went into effect. Efforts to bring China and India into the process accelerated, and Kyoto began to spawn regional efforts to build on it, notably within the European Union. The result, for the United States, was an Iraq-recalling combination of defeat and isolation.

To build consensus despite the administration and a do-nothing

Congress, individual states began adopting policies that dovetailed with the Kyoto treaty's requirement that emissions over a decade gradually be reduced to 1990 levels—initially in green New England, and ultimately in California. And almost on the eve of Bush's ineffectual State of the Union address in 2007, a coalition of ten large corporations (including BP, Duke Energy, Caterpillar, and GE) joined with the core of the environmental movement to support a congressional agenda that would require greenhouse gas emissions cutbacks on a specific timetable but with flexible methods.

His domestic environmental initiatives were stalled in even the Republican Congresses of his first six years and did not even make it to the table after the 2006 elections. His international standing was in tatters. Bush had managed to get routed by centrist politics in the climate change debate, setting the stage for the policies conservatives have said they most feared. At the end, he was left as the guy who had taken $2.8 million in campaign cash from energy and mining interests in 2000 (ten times what Gore got) and whose party had collected $47 million (more than triple what all Democrats got) and delivered delay but little else.

When it comes to government regulation, it seems Bush always acts reflexively, although historically regulation has been neither a partisan nor an ideological matter. Spawned during the industrial revolution, regulation was a necessary response to the obvious excesses of the marketplace around the turn of the twentieth century. Republicans and Democrats supported it, a point Bush seems to have forgotten. He forgot it on climate change. He forgot it on carbon dioxide emissions, and he certainly forgot it when it came to the FDA.

The Food and Drug Administration epitomizes the regulatory function, overseeing the safety and effectiveness of substances people ingest. Down through the years, it's been axiomatic in politics that it is extremely stupid to fool around with the FDA. The advantages of good stewardship and diligence so clearly outweigh any short-term political gains.

President Bush's failure to grasp this simple truth was obvious even before he was sworn in. Presidents get to name their own FDA commissioners, but the tradition has been that they choose people with strong medical and scientific credentials and with well-established reputations. The first whiff of politics was apparent when the highly regarded person already in the job, Jane Henney, was abruptly dismissed during the transition period. The fact that it happened before Bush had a new, overall boss as secretary of health and human services and the fact that Henney was let go before Tommy Thompson had the job as secretary was only the first of numerous hints that the White House would be pulling many of the strings controlling the popular Republican moderate and governor of Wisconsin.

What followed was a comedy of governmental errors. For more than half of Bush's presidency, one of the most important positions in government was vacant. The FDA labored under two acting commissioners of diminished stature, a pal of Bush's from Texas (Mark McClellan) and one fellow who left two months after he was confirmed, for financial improprieties (Lester Crawford).

An atmosphere like this was designed for trouble and in the fall of 2004 it arrived in the form of a sudden announcement by the giant drug company, Merck & Co., that it was yanking off the market a popular drug used by millions of arthritis victims called Vioxx. When first approved in 1999, the drug promised to relieve chronic pain without side effects like stomach trouble and thus quickly achieved near-miracle drug status and multibillion-dollar sales.

There was just one problem. The main ingredient in Vioxx had been identified as a major factor in causing heart attacks and strokes. By then, the drug had been implicated in nearly thirty thousand incidents. The family of what are known as Cox-2 inhibitors was apparently magnificent at preventing inflammation and stomach damage but could also block a substance important to maintaining a healthy circulatory system.

The predictable result was a torrent of lawsuits and opprobrium directed at Merck for its actions and inactions in the face of accumulating evidence of trouble, but it didn't take long for knowledgeable fingers to be pointed in the FDA's direction as well. It turned out that at the time of its approval, when Jane Henney was still in office, there had been indications from the Vioxx trials of possible heart impacts but no detailed studies of the potential problem had been required.

In the years leading up to the recall, however, there had been several studies raising a red flag that produced no response at all from the weakly led agency—at just the moment when corrective action was most needed. There had been an early FDA rebuke of Merck's marketing policies, but after viewing the disturbing paper trail, the highly regarded British journal *Lancet* concluded that Vioxx should have been recalled years before.

The following year, the FDA did it again, this time less out of negligence than slavish adherence to the administration's social policy agenda—precisely the kind of consideration that is not supposed to intrude on professional regulation of food and drugs. Abortion politics, as opposed to the safety and effectiveness of the country's medicine and food, had primarily been the reason Jane Henney was quickly dismissed. She was in charge when the FDA approved the so-called abortion pill, RU-486, for sale in the United States. Social conservatives had the same attitude toward that pill as many liberals had toward missile defense systems—it would have been opposed whether the pill worked or not.

In 2005, however, politics polluted the FDA's work even more dramatically. Already there had been delays—not explicable by reasons having to do with safety or effectiveness—in permitting the sale without a doctor's prescription for what has also been called the "morning-after pill." It can be taken for up to a few days after unprotected sex in order to prevent a possibly fertilized egg from implanting itself in the female womb.

There had been no scientific or medical objection to the medicine, but social conservatives were once again aroused, and once again their concerns were put on a White House transmission line directly into the FDA. By the time Bush nominated Dr. Lester Crawford to replace Texas ally Mark McClellan as head of the FDA early in 2005, the morning-after pill controversy had already been simmering, unresolved, for two years, ever since its manufacturer, Barr Laboratories, applied for over-the-counter status.

At the end of 2003, one of the FDA advisory committees handling the application voted 23–4 to approve it with no restrictions, a position later supported by the agency's scientific staff. Politics then intervened.

With McClellan still the commissioner, the professionals who had worked on the matter were summarily overruled in the spring of 2004; the grounds cited were concerns about the pill's use by younger women. The possibility was raised that the result of its use could be rampant promiscuity. In an unheard-of departure from the norm, no studies, no evidence were cited in support of this assertion. Instead of rejecting the application outright, however, administration officials encouraged Barr to submit a new one that still required a prescription for teenagers. In the interests of incremental progress, Barr did precisely that in July, but the rest of the year inexplicably passed without a decision.

Bush's nomination of Crawford set the stage for a revealing confrontation. What was at issue was whether the president could manage a serious political fight and advance his social issue agenda. He could do neither.

The Crawford selection was immediately blocked through a common if arcane maneuver by the minority Senate Democrats. Two of them, Patty Murray of Washington and Hillary Clinton, immediately put what are called "holds" on Crawford's nomination, effectively blocking its approval. To break the impasse the administration had to promise that if he were confirmed, the FDA would act on the pill issue by that September.

Instead of acting, however, the White House attempted—and failed—to manage a double cross. A freshly confirmed Dr. Crawford announced that in fact the FDA would delay its decision indefinitely. The result was a monumental backfire, starting with the resignation of Dr. Susan Wood, the career official in charge of women's health issues, who became an instant public figure by charging that politics had overruled the agency's professional regulators and that politics had put the decision on a shelf.

And then, as bad luck would have it, the administration lost Crawford to a sudden resignation shortly thereafter. After four years in senior positions, improprieties were discovered in his personal finances, which meant the White House was again without a commissioner, but facing the impossibility of getting one confirmed without what amounted to surrender.

Instead of another political crony, Bush quickly nominated a longtime Bush family friend—Dr. Andrew von Eschenbach, then running the National Cancer Institute—and just as quickly agreed to a demand from more than enough senators to stop his confirmation that a decision on the morning-after pill would have to precede a vote. Meanwhile, nine states had decided on their own to approve the medicine.

In August of 2006, the FDA approved the pill, though as a sop to right-to-life activists that did little to dull their frustration, it was decided without the backup studies and evidence that normally accompany such rulings, it would only be available to women seventeen years of age and older without a prescription and would have to be sold from behind the counters of pharmacies. After more than five years of bumbling, Bush had tried and failed to politicize one of the government's most important agencies, had been caught and blocked, and ended up advancing the agenda of religious conservatives not an inch.

With the venerable FDA, Bush had to be cautious about injecting politics into the high-profile agency's activities. He failed miserably. But it is equally instructive to glance at a government regulatory operation that gets less attention in the press, one where conservatives have felt less constrained ever since the days of Ronald Reagan.

That would be the Interior Department, with responsibility for 500 million acres of public lands (that energy companies covet) and important regulatory duties including the safety of coal mines. The infamous fire sales of huge tracks of open space and oil leases in the Reagan years was now repeated twenty years later. What amounted to both lax and relaxed regulation of coal mines in the Reagan years returned even more flagrantly after 2000. Presidents who indulge in cronyism and special interest favoritism are wise to beware of events that can suddenly shine a bright light on this misbehavior; that's why the typical, effective chief executive avoids such wretched excess. President Bush, however, knew no limits as he placed Gale Norton, a conservative fox from the West with a long record of industry support and political activism, in charge of the chicken coop.

As things turned out, however, Bush and Norton were caught completely unprepared for the scrutiny resulting from two of those kinds of "bright light" surprises: the 2005 fall from grace toward prison of an astonishingly brazen influence-peddler with White House connections named Jack Abramoff; and the explosion in a coal mine in tiny Sago, West Virginia, that killed one worker outright and left eleven of twelve survivors trapped to slowly suffocate.

The Abramoff scandal, which was a factor in the Republican defeat in 2006, focused attention on Norton's top deputy—a poster boy for the promotion of private interests by public officials who rotate between service in conservative governments and lucrative lobbying practices focused on their policy expertise. His name is Steven Griles—a key participant in the sweetheart land deals done under Reagan's notorious first interior secretary, James Watt. He spent the post-Reagan years getting rich as an energy lobbyist and then returned to take charge of land and lease sales under Norton, blessed with a $250,000 annual package from his firm to supplement his government salary.

Though he resigned after Bush's first term, he remained in the spotlight because of the Abramoff affair, snared by his work on behalf of the Native American clients with major casino gambling interests. Eventually, federal prosecutors told him that he had become a target of their ongoing criminal inquiries, and in 2007 Griles pleaded guilty to obstruction of justice.

The explosion in the Sago mine, the tragic, drawn-out aftermath of which was covered nonstop by the cable news networks, focused still more attention on the department's questionable activities. Within days the nation—and not just interested parties in political battlegrounds like West Virginia—would learn that federal regulations governing coal mines had been significantly relaxed during Bush's first term—by still another industry-connected official. David Lauriski, like Griles, had departed after 2004, but his work after arriving in Washington from a major Utah-based mining company was understandably held up to scrutiny and then ridicule. It turned out the agency he headed, the Mine Safety and Health Administration, had watered down or eliminated numerous department safety regulations relevant to the disaster. The average fine for the scores of violations this one mine was cited for the year before the explosion was less than $250. That same year, moreover, Lauriski supported budget cuts that cost his already hard-pressed regulatory agency another 150 inspector positions.

Presidents who are slipshod or worse in handling the government's regulatory affairs run risks beyond mere exposure for causing significant damage to the public interest, health, and safety. They also risk doing lasting damage to the very philosophy they claim to represent. To many conservatives and Republicans, Bush gradually came to seem as large a threat to their beliefs as the most liberal of Democrats—no more so than through his mishandling of global warming.

The core of conservative thinking on the issue was that the most significant threat to the economy was mandatory reductions in greenhouse gas emissions. As time passed and the scientific evidence became undeniable substantively and politically, the position of several conservatives close to and inside the administration was that there had to be some kind of cap on future emissions, backed up by some form of price incentive (most likely in the form of a carbon emissions tax) to keep the situation from worsening until new technologies could provide a lasting solution.

But by dodging the issue again in 2007, they worried that Bush had in fact guaranteed that the next president would be a supporter of Kyoto-driven requirements that emission levels be cut substantially. By regulating poorly, he had made much more likely the very policy steps he had most loudly opposed. That was true of a lot more fields than climate change.

5

THE MAYBERRY MACHIAVELLIS

The Knights [of Columbus] are soldiers in the armies of compassion. You're foot soldiers. You've heard the call. You're helping this nation build a culture of life in which the sick are comforted, the aged are honored, the immigrant is welcomed, and the weak and vulnerable are never overlooked. You have a friend in this administration. You have somebody who wants to work with you to change America for the better.

—President George W. Bush, speech to the Knights of Columbus convention in Dallas, August 3, 2004

THE FIRST PERSON chosen in 2001 to lead President Bush's flagship initiative to redeem a high-profile promise during the previous year's campaign took a hike after barely six months on the job—muttering about the triumph of image politics over substantive governance.

Another top official in the same operation waited a while longer but eventually quit more flamboyantly—writing a book about the continuous dominance of politics over results in the Bush White House.

And still later, as the end of Bush's presidency loomed closer than its heyday, the fellow who coined the term that had more usage than any other propaganda phrase in the long journey from Austin to Washington, tried to remain loyal but felt obliged to summarize Bush's record where it counted as "moderately weak."

Ruining Bush's status as a self-proclaimed "compassionate conservative" was hard work, the result of numerous missteps and misjudgments over several years, each feeding on the next. Through it all, however, there were consistent, defining themes that permeated so many other elements of his administration—attention to interest group politics, to imagery, to rigid ideology, and to rhetoric that masked a curious inattention to detail and to the grubby, hard work that translates ideas into accomplishments.

As flops go, this one was both micro and macro—a signal achievement. Bush first botched his own attempt to give church organizations a significant role in the operation of government programs that assist the poor. And he also botched huge opportunities to transform much larger domestic programs—most notably in public education and immigration. His most noteworthy achievement, in fulfilling a pledge to begin an effort to provide insurance coverage for prescription drugs that older Americans require, began and continues to be mired in controversy because of his own mistakes.

Dr. Marvin Olasky legitimately takes the credit for coining the compassionate conservative moniker, one fruit of a long, personal journey as interesting as Bush's—the product of a Jewish family in Boston, moving to atheist and leftist, to born-again Christian, and an oddly relevant post as professor of journalism at the University of Texas. Karl Rove initially brought Olasky and Bush together before the first presidential campaign had taken shape; the political and philosophical gurus supplied Bush with books and sages to whet his genuine appetite for a way of thinking that mixed Christian concepts of abiding concern for others, especially the least fortunate, with conservative tenets embracing smaller, decentralized government that emphasized character-building as much as direct assistance.

"But those accomplishments fell far short of the original hope for a tough-minded approach that would help the poor while shrinking welfare spending and that would create for years to come a level playing field for all groups involved in helping the poor, whether religious or not," Olasky wrote in an essay early in 2007, one of fifteen assessing the Bush presidency that *Texas Monthly* commissioned. "While we got compassionate conservatism on the board, it became distorted. It came to be looked upon as either a political gambit by Republicans trying to buy minority votes or a rhetorical device hoping to fool soccer moms. And so Bush, in this area, has been moderately weak."

This elegant and accurate description of how politics ruled over actual change was what lay at the root of John DiIulio's quick resignation after barely a half-year as the first director of what was called the White House Office of Faith-Based and Community Initiatives. Though he has never disowned either the president or his work, his widely circulated Internet letter damning and describing the dominance of sound-bite politics over serious policymaking in the pre-9/11 Bush White House still stands.

More serious damage was done by another senior official in that office, David Kuo, who lasted much longer (until Bush's reelection campaign began to take shape in 2003). He left, also in despair, to write a book on the extent to which conservative Christians who took their New Testament seriously had been used by politicians, especially conservative ones.

During his book tour for *Tempting Faith*, Kuo said the reaction of Bush aides (meaning top Bush political and communications aides) to the surfacing of DiIulio's views was more intense than any of the work they ever performed on behalf of the religion-centered agenda the president had supported.

"After that occurred," he said, "the White House paid more attention to the compassion agenda in the forty-eight or seventy-two hours after that than they ever paid in the two-and-a-half years that followed."

It is often forgotten that this agenda was specific, from long before the 2000 election to well after Bush had taken office and organized his administration. There was always much more to it than merely the florid, intentionally religion-influenced words that Bush constantly used to describe his concern for "the least, the last, and the lost."

Bush's commitment was to carve out some $8 billion annually for religious groups active in social causes where before there had been virtually nothing.

In terms of dollars, the most important element by far was to give every American up to a $500 credit against his income tax bill for money donated to organizations helping the poor. This would have been worth some $6 billion in terms of government revenues, but it obviously would have stimulated much more than that in charitable activity. For a while, the tax credit survived most of the larger congressional debate over tax cuts in the first months of the administration; however, in June of 2001, it was suddenly and unceremoniously stripped from the legislation, never to surface again. In a literal clash between the sacred and profane, Bush's signature initiative was tossed overboard to keep the budget impact of all the tax cuts as low as possible. It was promptly forgotten except by the evangelical Christians who had championed it for years.

Bush had also pledged to funnel $1.7 billion annually directly to poverty-related organizations operated by religious organizations and to change federal law so money could go to denominations that only hired their own believers to run programs. He never got the change in law through Congress while it was Republican-led, and the money was still well short of $1 billion cumulatively as the twilight period of his presidency began.

During his tight reelection race in 2004, it sufficed that Bush had the loud, active support of fundamentalist religious groups concerned with battling abortion rights or keeping gay people from getting married—and who had no significant record displaying concern for the poor. But presidents who flagrantly walk away from self-defining principles and agendas have trouble holding on to support when they run into larger political trouble, as Bush eventually did.

It certainly didn't help that poverty shot up throughout Bush's first term, only stabilizing in his fifth year before the poor came under renewed pressure late in 2006 as the housing market bubble burst, and the cost of necessities continued to soar while the overall economy began to slow. With more than 37 million Americans officially poor (12.7 percent of the census-counted population), compared to more than 31 million (or barely 11 percent in 2000), compassion's backdrop deteriorated markedly.

At the height of Bush's popularity, just before the invasion of Iraq, Americans were believers in him, with 64 percent telling *Washington Post* interviewers in a poll published in February of 2003 that they believed the president was a compassionate leader. Barely one year later, that advantage—an important means of increasing Bush's support among political moderates—had been squandered, and the country was evenly split on basically the same question.

Most revealing, however, was the way Bush handled three other initiatives, all involving far more money and people than the narrowly defined, faith-based programs. Two of them were partial successes (public school education and a new prescription drug benefit for the elderly) and one was a political and substantive failure well into 2007 (immigration policy). In a larger sense, each was a golden opportunity for effective presidential leadership and on that more significant level Bush missed his chance.

For one brief, shining moment a year into his first term, the president appeared to have pulled off a stunt worthy of Bill Clinton on welfare or crime—achieving a significant legislative victory on traditionally progressive turf, the country's troubled public schools.

After a year of the hard work to which he was usually and notoriously inattentive, Bush and Congress had managed to enact the first huge change in the system of federal aid to schools John Kennedy had put on the national agenda in 1960 and Lyndon Johnson had enacted five years later. In exchange for a significant boost in federal assistance, a new regime of accountability had been constructed, based on the annual testing of pupils in schools that would be strictly monitored for progress. Substantively, it was a stunning achievement, coming twenty years after the first of countless studies documented the sorry state of American public education in an increasingly competitive international environment.

Politically, it was equally as stunning. Bush found running room amidst a confusing array of centrist Republicans and Democrats that also managed to attract the most important progressives in Congress; with that level of support, the defection of a few dozen very conservative legislators hardly seemed noteworthy. In the wake of Bush's legislative victory and a national bill-signing tour, a *Newsweek* survey found that 55 percent of the public preferred his policy on schools to the Democrats'. Building on his popular record in Texas, Bush even felt strong enough to title his initiative with the phrase used for nearly forty years by the most important of the advocacy groups in this field, the Children's Defense Fund. "No Child Left Behind" it was.

But within eighteen months, the president had lost that auspicious edge, and within five years, another survey found a decidedly displeased country. Indeed, at 58 to 39 percent in a survey taken early in 2007, Americans appeared only slightly less grumpy about the government's handling of their schools than they were about everything else associated with the Bush presidency.

What happened was that Bush ignored a basic fact of governmental life: the establishment of a new initiative is not the same as its effective implementation. Where major change is involved, presidents need to keep on selling and prepare to show results quickly or the coalition assembled for enactment will splinter.

Ironically, Bush was most inattentive to the right and to the center of the political spectrum. The new program created a bewildering variety of administrative requirements to monitor state and local performance, and considerable costs to localities to accompany them—the kinds of "unfunded mandates" that conservatives abhor.

With the polls headed south, it was no surprise that the lawsuits soon followed—from districts in conservative states (Utah and Bush's own Texas) to relatively progressive ones (Vermont and Maine, bastions of local control). The first statewide suit came from Connecticut, which like the others argued through Attorney General Richard Blumenthal that the Department of Education in Washington was either capricious in its rules or was establishing mandates without providing the resources to meet them.

From the outset Bush never made overtures to his wayward fellow Republicans. He simply beat them during the legislative fight and then assumed they would cease their opposition once the program started running. It was a dangerous, flawed assumption about people who believed they were keeping with conservative tradition.

The first time Ronald Reagan ran for president, in 1976, he had proposed ending about a third of the federal government's activities that were subject to annual appropriations, leaving them to states and localities to continue if they chose to. Education was at the top of his hit list.

The second time, in 1980, his most reliable applause line, in the wake of Jimmy Carter's elevation of education to cabinet status, was his vow to eliminate the department along with its fifteen-year-old core programs.

But Reagan was a flexible ideologue. Congressional reality combined with sudden, passionate interest in the country's troubled system persuaded him to shelve his ideas. So instead, he settled for budget cuts. When he took office a generation ago, federal aid made up just under 10 percent of the far larger state and local monies going to public schools. When Bill Clinton took office a dozen years later, the federal share had dipped below 6 percent. Even with a large jump in federal dollars under No Child Left Behind, the number today remains below 8 percent.

For many conservatives that is still much too high, and the opposition's ire has only intensified as the strings attached to the federal money have become stronger. But throughout his presidency, Bush never confronted this opposition. In the end, it turned on him with a vengeance.

Early in 2007, with the program's five-year authorization due to expire, the opposition's ranks swelled well beyond the forty or so congressmen who had opposed Bush in 2001. They now included the second-ranking Republican in the House, Minority Whip Roy

Blunt of Missouri, and the new chairman of the Republican National Committee, Senator Mel Martinez of Florida. Their effort was not to see the program die, but moving deftly they proposed relaxing its testing and sanctions components, and giving increasingly hard-pressed states more flexibility in meeting goals.

As a practical matter, this meant Bush would be forced to rely even more than he had in 2001 on Democrats to get the program reauthorized with its accountability standards intact. Here, however, the president faced still another mess of his own making—over money. From the moment of enactment and regularly thereafter, the two most important Democrats nominally supporting the program—Representative George Miller of California and Senator Edward Kennedy—pointed out with increasing harshness that the money actually budgeted for No Child Left Behind was falling further and further behind Bush's original pledge. Cutbacks in 2005 and 2006 had infuriated Miller and Kennedy, and with an eye toward the 2007 legislative fight the money was eventually restored. However, each year's budget since 2002 had been at least $10 billion below the authorized level. Democratic support hinged on more money—as well as funds for such other underfunded activities as Head Start and aid to higher education. Bush, however, was running into one of the consequences of his lust for deep tax cuts: having chosen sharp cuts in the top income tax rate and still wedded to elimination of the estate tax, there was no money under his priorities for the very activities that supposedly made him compassionate.

Normally, a president who is getting serious, sharp criticism from left and right is able to argue that he is effectively steering a moderate course. In Bush's case, though, he had helped launch a new effort that was now stumbling in its infancy and thus prompting thoroughly legitimate complaints from both left and right. The mess wasn't his critics' fault; it was Bush's fault.

This odd ability to be less in the middle than between a rock and a hard place was even more apparent in the president's handling of another new initiative—meant to redeem his campaign pledge from 2000 to establish a prescription drug benefit for Americans eligible for Medicare.

During the brief period that Democrats ran the Senate from the spring of 2001 through 2002, actually enacting a Medicare drug benefit was impossible on anything close to Bush's terms; he simply did not have the votes. Above all, this was because the typical progressive had this weird (from the right's perspective) notion that one of the choices available to elderly Americans should be a prescription drug benefit that was simply grafted onto the basic Medicare package (hospital insurance plus optional coverage for doctors' care). The simplest idea was that for $20 or so per month a person would be covered. To Bush, conservatism in this area meant rigid adherence to his larger health care vision of intelligent, empowered consumers shopping independently for the best deal. More practically, it meant providing a set of benefit choices that didn't include Medicare itself, but invited insurance companies and health maintenance organizations into what would be a gigantic new market, complete with government subsidies to tilt the playing field in their direction.

Nonetheless, the crisis in drug coverage and cost was so severe at the turn of the century that while stalemate prevailed in the one-vote-majority Democratic Senate, the Republican House still had to be seen as "doing something." Accordingly, Speaker Dennis Hastert of Illinois saw to it that the House passed what amounted to Potemkin legislation—bills that the insurance and HMO businesses' lobbyists heavily influenced. These included coverage schemes not involving Medicare itself, but ones that the disciplined majority could pass so that members from competitive districts could have "accomplishments" to campaign on.

But after the Senate switched back to narrow Republican control in 2003, the president had an opportunity to get a bill mostly on his terms. The result was a legislative strategy that worked, though just barely. The substantive mistakes made in 2003 helped cost the Republicans control in 2006.

The idea was that the House would approve something essentially to the administration's liking while bipartisan negotiations in the Senate would produce something that could command a majority there. As all who have survived high school civics know, the final product would be the product of negotiations between the two chambers. The doctrinaire Republicans realized that if Democrats were excluded from the serious horse-trading that ensued, the result could be tilted much more toward the House version with the final product still surviving an up-or-down Senate vote unencumbered by amendments or delaying tactics.

It was simple, smart legislative politics, embraced by Bush, and a way to enact conservative, pro-business legislation. But for those worried about the actual issue, the crisis in prescription drug costs and availability for retired people, it was also a way to create a controversial and confusing mess—perhaps causing Bush more trouble than a "victory" would. That is exactly what happened.

In the fall of 2003, the president had a choice. In terms of Senate politics, he could tilt toward a measure that had already passed that summer in an overwhelmingly bipartisan vote, 76–21, with the no votes largely comprising doctrinaire conservatives opposed to the creation of any new entitlement program. But in choosing to make the House measure more to his liking and able to get past a conference committee and then later the Senate, he ended up losing twenty-one of those yes votes (all Democrats). His end result, moreover, is a program that is controversial and mixed in its results. It also created fresh political fodder for Democrats, who charged that Republicans were against importing cheaper drugs from Canada, opposed price negotiations between the government and drug companies, and had left huge holes in the new coverage allegedly to hold down costs.

For a large portion of the elderly population that previously had no coverage at all, the program is obviously a major step forward;

for those who have very low incomes and few assets, it is just as obviously a godsend. However, Bush's cave-in to both ideology and business interests created an inadequate mess that is politically easy to assault.

The best example involves about six million people who are not only eligible for Medicare but also qualify for Medicaid because they are relatively poor. To save money, the Senate Democrats took a huge, compromising step. For the first time, they would exclude people eligible for Medicare but keep them (when applicable) in Medicaid where costs are shared between states and the federal government. In the final product, the very poor were allowed (in income terms up to 150 percent of the very low official poverty line) subsidies to help pay their premiums. But there was also a coverage gap, called a doughnut hole, in which people had to pay out of their pockets for drug costs, between $2,000 and $3,500, and this involves a great many people. Not surprisingly, it was in this area involving so-called dual eligibles that many of the highly publicized problems with the new program occurred.

But there were many other problems. The final version for the first time introduced means-testing to a social insurance program, affecting premiums for the voluntary part of Medicare that covers physicians' services. There were also special subsidies to promote partial privatization of Medicare (to the delight of the insurance people)—including new subsidized vouchers to purchase private insurance plans, and a special $12 billion program (called, accurately, a slush fund) to subsidize them directly. And for good, venal measure, it even tossed in nearly another $7 billion in tax breaks for the Health Savings Accounts conservatives love, which of course have nothing to do with prescription drug coverage for the elderly.

In addition to a much closer, hotly contested vote in the Senate, the final version also had to survive an unprecedented nail-biter in the House. To keep conservatives in line, Bush tried to maintain the fiction that the first ten years of the program, which wasn't due for inauguration until 2006, would cost no more than $400 billion, even though Medicare officials already knew it would be at least $100 billion more than that. Even so, Hastert had to keep the House vote open for more than three hours in the middle of a long night (an unprecedented step) so that the last few votes could be strong-armed into submission.

In the end, the special interest favoritism was so flagrant that Bush's top Medicare official (Thomas Scully) cashed in to join the health business he had helped stimulate, the top House Republican working on the bill (Billy Tauzin of Louisiana) cashed in to become the drug business's top lobbyist, and even his health and human services secretary (Tommy Thompson) cashed in after Bush's first term to run a consulting business before starting a long-shot campaign for president.

The pains clearly outweighed the gains, for the country as well as for the president. Bush had an opportunity to go for something akin to the marginally less contentious No Child Left Behind. Instead, he got a short-term, modest boost at the cost of huge problems later. The best evidence is the vigor with which the newly empowered congressional Democrats assaulted the program's major weaknesses within weeks of winning control in 2006—starting with an effort that was attracting moderate Republican support to permit price negotiations between the Medicare authorities and the drug companies.

The administration was left, as usual, with the need to mobilize its skilled public relations machinery to trumpet favorable developments in estimates about costs far into the future. In the summer of 2006, Thompson's replacement, Mike Leavitt, crowed over a fresh projection that a fully operational program was now expected to cost $964 billion between 2007 and 2016, instead of the previously projected $1.1 trillion. Bush had his program and it was indeed conservative, or at least business-oriented; just not very compassionate.

The same cannot even be said about Bush's handling of the country's increasingly severe dilemma over an old issue—one that touches raw nerves on all sides—immigration.

On January 7, 2004, beginning his reelection year in an uncertain foreign, domestic, and political atmosphere, President Bush's handlers arranged something of a surprise—a dignitary-saturated gathering in the East Room of the White House assembled to hear him expound on immigration and offer the first significant changes in American law in nearly twenty years.

As befitted his record back in Texas, Bush was welcoming, warm, nearly florid in his rhetorical description of the true condition of the ten to twenty million people who toil in undocumented, fearful obscurity in the United States:

> Their search for a better life is one of the most basic desires of human beings. Many undocumented workers have walked mile after mile, through the heat of the day and the cold of the night, risked their lives in dangerous border crossings, or entrusted their lives to the brutal rings of heartless, human smugglers. Workers who seek only to earn a living end up in the shadows of American life—fearful, often abused and exploited.
>
> When they are victimized by crime, they are afraid to call the police, or seek recourse in the legal system. They are cut off from their families far away, fearing if they leave our country to visit relatives back home they might never be able to return to their jobs.

This was classic Bush compassionate conservatism, reflecting a record in Texas that had never involved playing the Anglo card. He had never once played the demagogue on hot-button issues like bilingual education, or basic government services like health care and access to the public schools for all residents of a community. He was, like Ronald Reagan before him, basically a human Welcome Wagon Republican.

But on this big test of his leadership and ability, Bush blew it sky-high. The first clue was the audience. It contained the Mexican ambassador, but there were no Democrats and only a few Republicans associated with Bush's more inclusive position—already in danger of becoming a minority within the minority party. There was no Speaker Hastert, much less the real Republican broker in the House, Texas's Tom DeLay; there was no Jim Sensenbrenner of Wisconsin, who chaired the House Judiciary Committee and would preside over any actual legislation.

There also wasn't any legislation. Presidents who make a large fuss and then walk away always take a risk—that other forces, other politicians will fill the vacuum. That is what happened because Bush abdicated. There have been undercurrents of nativism in America as long as America has existed; they ebb and flow, often following economic trends. In 1986, sensing another opportunity, Reagan and leading congressional figures in both parties had rewritten the law to allow some three million undocumented people to remain in the United States and in those days no one flinched from calling the policy what it was—amnesty. In return, they also legislated a tougher regime of sanctions on knowing employers of illegals, but it turned out to be honored mostly in the breach. By the turn of the century, the number of illegal immigrants was soaring, the economy was sluggish, 9/11 had offered at least an excuse if not a solid reason, and the political agitation was therefore growing.

Bush reflected the early, impending political change that day in the East Room. His proposal's core was a system to entice everyone into the open. He called it "a new temporary worker program" that day (the more loaded word "guest" would come later). Employed people who stepped forward would get legal status in return for a fee. But it would be time-limited, and after the expiration of their permits, workers would be required to return home, where they could apply to be legal immigrants in the normal way.

Experts quickly spotted the flaw—the incentives were too puny to work. It would be rational for an illegal to prefer to remain in the shadows, where millions had existed for years, rather than risk so much for so little. Bush's proposal, however, at least was capable of getting a serious conversation started. It also kept his share of the

Latino vote that year reasonably high for a Republican, an essential element in his political advisers' hopes for a lasting GOP majority.

But by leaving the field, the president was vulnerable to events and to the activism of others, and he paid dearly for his passivity in the 2005–2006 congressional session—as he did on so many major issues, from Iraq, to gasoline prices, to natural disaster response. Responding to a much higher level of political noise, House Republicans completely ignored Bush's priorities in crafting their own astonishingly punitive legislation—built around large increases in Mexican border patrols, the construction of an expensive fence, and much harsher sanctions to gradually force illegals to leave.

The chance for consensus-building, once again, existed in the Senate, and several politicians—most notably John McCain and Edward Kennedy—took advantage of it with occasional administration assistance. To get something passed in a tougher political climate, however, required legislation that in the end looked as if Rube Goldberg had authored it. The measure lamely constructed three tiers of the undocumented, requiring different steps of different groups depending on how long they had been in the country. That, however, was not the point; the point was to pass a bill and then enlist the president in a serious negotiation with the hard-line House.

But in the middle of an election year, Dennis Hastert stiffed Bush and got away with it. With no negotiations held at all, the House Republicans, on their way to losing their twelve-year-old majority, played the Anglo card. For their trouble, in the end, the Latino vote in the congressional elections split 70 to 30 percent for the Democrats according to exit polls, with the Republicans even losing border state seats to moderate Democrats—most notably in Tucson and Phoenix where the issue was most intensely debated because that was where it was most intimately experienced.

This was one issue, however, that would not go away. Bush had begun what looked like an era of friendly feeling with Mexico shortly after taking office, only to let it slip away in the aftermath of the

9/11 attacks. He had made what he liked to call a "comprehensive" proposal early in 2004 and then not lifted so much as a finger to help move it through Congress; it appeared mostly to be an effort of showcasing goodwill to a Latino voting community. Then he was blindsided by his conservative friends in the House of Representatives in 2005.

It was, in short, extremely late in a presidency to have a credible chance to deal successfully with such a complex, divisive issue. As it turned out, Bush was helped by leaders from both parties in Congress who were more concerned with facing the problem than waiting on the president. For much of 2007, they negotiated back and forth at least in the Senate on the outline of a bill that might emerge with less of the maddening, probably unworkable complexity of the previous year's product. To his credit, Bush dispatched members of his cabinet to join the process. This time, the provisions supposedly enhancing security—hundreds of additional miles of tall fencing and an apparently simpler means of identifying workers and thus holding their employers accountable—were to be followed before those involving people in the United States illegally and trying to get in would take effect. The so-called path to citizenship for the millions here without legal documentation was not so obstacle-strewn as to be impossible to navigate. And there was a "guest worker" commitment to allow at least a few hundred thousand people to work here for two years at a time with some protection against the worst kinds of exploitation.

Nothing, however, was going on for much of the year in the House, and immigration remained a vexing issue that divided every constituency. It was very late, and Bush had already squandered six years. In his heart, he was the kind of Anglo who in Texas had never been a hard-liner on issues like bilingual education and immigration; and he tried not to be one in the White House. However, the combination of his own passivity and frequently his ineptitude had wasted six long years.

In the end, the noise of the opponents proved more politically important than the advocacy of the proponents, Bush included. Early in the summer of 2007, Bush lost a test vote that in effect blocked final Senate consideration of the bill. Only seven of forty-nine Republicans stood with him, causing the new majority leader, Democrat Harry Reid of Nevada, to pull the stalemated legislation off the floor. In the weeks that followed, Bush was only able to find five more Republicans to vote with him. The bill died ignominiously.

Bush had campaigned as more than merely a rhetorically compassionate conservative. He had even on occasion tried to govern as one. But his attempts largely foundered because of his poor work habits, his preference for imagery over accomplishment, and his ties to business and other special interests. As in so many areas, a truly large opportunity was largely wasted, with conservatives almost as angry and disillusioned as progressives.

6

THE ECONOMY, STUPID

In the last three years, adversity has also revealed the fundamental strengths of the American economy. We have come through recession, and terrorist attack, and corporate scandals, and the uncertainties of war. And because you acted to stimulate our economy with tax relief, this economy is strong, and growing stronger.

—President George W. Bush, January 20, 2004

DOWN THE STRETCH of a losing campaign more than thirty months after that self-congratulatory summary before Congress, President Bush took a brief rhetorical break from his most important message—that electing Democrats to Congress would undermine his war effort in Iraq and the larger struggle against Islamic terrorism. With less than a month to go until the first electoral defeat of his presidency, Bush reached for an issue whose failure to help him politically continually frustrated him—the economy.

In a Washington commentary that fall on some budget numbers that were moderately less dreary than the usual fare, Bush indulged in self-praise that neatly summarized his defiantly myopic worldview—a posture at demonstrable odds with the experience of most Americans living in a new world that the president had trouble acknowledging, much less understanding.

Largely because of the immense tax cuts enacted during his first term, Bush celebrated what he called the "37th straight month of growth," blithely neglecting the fact that economic output is reported quarterly and that at this point in his tenure, thirty-seven months stretched back to the summer of 2003 when he had already been in office through roughly thirty months of very different results.

"The theory was that if we can encourage entrepreneurship and investment and consumption by reducing taxes," Bush went on, "it will cause the economy to recover from a recession, and a terrorist attack, corporate scandals, war, hurricanes—and it has. The pro-growth policies have worked."

A half-year later, after Bush had led his party to what even he called a genuine "thumping," CBS News asked Americans in an opinion survey what they thought of the president's handling of the U.S. economy. By 57 to 36 percent they disapproved, in a reflection of sentiments that had not significantly changed in more than four years. Reflecting the depth of the negative sentiment, the disapproving majority included 60 percent of self-described independent voters, and nearly 30 percent of the Republicans. Ideology, short-term politics, and rigidity had in this case managed to bungle the most important job a modern president has besides protecting the country's security—to the nation's detriment as well as, ultimately, to Bush's own standing and legacy.

In a mischievous question probing that latter phenomenon, the CBS pollsters also asked if today's Republican Party was following the "principles" of Ronald Reagan. On this one, sentiment did not differ noticeably among all political segments of the public; by 65 to 23 percent, the Republicans in the poll said no.

They were not entirely correct. The late icon may have been a slow convert to the fervent tax-cutting ideology of the late-twentieth-century Republican Party but his fervor was genuine; if anything, the younger Bush was even more fervent, in marked contrast to his president-father. But there the similarity ended. In governance, where Reagan was flexible and tacked continually, Bush was rigid and uncompromising; where Reagan could take a step backward with a smile on his face after two steps forward, Bush almost never retreated tactically. And above all, where Reagan came by his common touch naturally, Bush was more a preppie with a Texas accent whose feel for ordinary Americans' concerns outside of religion was imperfect on his best days. Reagan's instinct was to loathe government regulations; Bush's was to listen to his business cronies.

As befitted a president whose government followed his habit of allowing politics an exalted place at the expense of traditional policy-making in domestic affairs, Bush developed a narrative about the American economy. It went like this:

He took office as a recession was beginning to grip the economy. Just as the vise was tightening, the United States was attacked by terrorists in its financial capital and then went to unavoidable war in two countries. And while conflict continued abroad, scandals undermined business confidence and the country's Southern states were hit by two of the most severe hurricanes ever. Fortunately, tax cuts had been enacted in 2001 and 2003 that helped the economy recover from these potentially devastating and sinister forces. Prosperity returned.

In the famous words of a popular radio commentator from the 1940s, Fulton Lewis Jr., "Interesting, if true."

But it wasn't. Bush had concocted an economic narrative that fit the requirements of short-term spin more than the facts. The great danger when an administration is as politicized as George Bush directed his to be is that spin and reality will collide. Where the economy is concerned, the danger is especially grave, because reality always has a greater impact on sentiment. The reason, simply, is that Americans already know how they're doing before the economic statistics have been processed through the government's computers, and well before any politician can start spinning their meaning. In complete contrast with Bush, Reagan was never publicly satisfied with the economy; he could be encouraged and he was indefatigable in defending his policies, but he never let his trademark optimism blind him to reality.

Bush did, and the result was that reality belted him in the face. The blow was much more than just political and personal; his rigid ideology and slavish attention to business interests left the economy near the end of his presidency naked to the uncertain winds of higher poverty rates, sky-high energy prices, burst investment bubbles—especially in the crucial housing sector—and slowing growth. The stern disapproval of roughly 60 percent of people was not the result of diabolical Democratic politics; it was the result of habitual inattention to the character of a very mixed economy in a much smaller world, the kind of ostrich-like inattention that would have been anathema to Republican presidents as different as Richard Nixon and Ronald Reagan.

During Bush's time in office, the economy has borne no resemblance to the mortally imperiled, then rescued and then prosperous model described in his politically driven narrative. The real story, recognized across party and ideological lines, is much more interesting and challenging than that. It goes likes this:

When Bush took office, the economy was nearing the end of a boom cycle characterized by explosive employment growth, income gains that gradually became widespread and put a visible dent in poverty, and the first federal budget surpluses in a generation. Those surpluses dramatically pushed back the date of fiscal reckoning for Social Security and Medicare. The bubble eventually burst early in 2001 with a steep decline in business investment leading to only a single quarter of declining output. Even after 9/11, the economy continued to grow, fed by public and private explosions in debt and by gains in real estate values that assumed bubble-like proportions. The real issue was never severe recession but instead the pace of recovery, the slowest in the modern record book, especially in employment and household income. The economy grew modestly, business investment recovered, but a great many Americans (probably most) were having difficulty making ends meet on the alleged strength of their relatively flat earnings in the face of a major spike in the costs of necessities. Continued job losses in older industries fed a growing anxiety about future prospects as the expansion (such as it was) matured and the bubble in housing began deflating.

That narrative may not give adequate weight to the fact that by traditional standards the economy is indeed expanding, has been producing new jobs for the most part since the late summer of 2003, and remains largely free of serious inflation. However, it does help explain why more than half the country is dissatisfied, uncertain about the future, and justifiably displeased with the Bush administration.

The president, however, is a vivid illustration of what can happen when politics overrules common sense in a White House, and the gray that is always present in the modern mixed economy is ignored. In his last frontal defense of his poor record, and therefore his poor polling status, with the 2006 elections looming, Bush ignored the underlying realities, thereby worsening their impact.

"The economy has expanded for seventeen straight quarters," he said in April during a choreographed tour of the economic horizon as well as the country, "and last year the American economy grew at a healthy rate of 3.5 percent. That's the fastest rate of any major industrialized economy. These gains are the result of the energy and the effort of American workers, small business owners and entrepreneurs. They're also the result of pro-growth economic policies. The tax cuts I signed left $880 billion with our nation's workers, small business owners and families. They've used that money to fuel our economic resurgence."

Or, as he put it ten days later as the tour was winding down with no noticeable change in public opinion, "We've got a good economy right now and, you know, it's growing at rapid paces and there's a lot of new jobs being added and productivity is high and people are owning homes. That's all positive."

Actually, it was, but the president's blind spots were too visible to the electoral audience he was attempting to reach.

By then, it was becoming clear that progressive opinion was more comprehensive and thus more accurate and politically effective. Shortly after the 2006 elections, one of the major beneficiaries of the shift in power—Congressman Barney Frank of Massachusetts, a veteran progressive who was about to become chairman of the Financial Services Committee—put his sharper understanding on display in an essay for *The American Prospect.*

"The most important lesson to be learned by Democrats from recent events in both the real and political worlds is that economic growth alone is not enough," he wrote. "Expansion of gross domestic product (the total output of goods and services) is a good thing, but four percent annual growth does not guarantee that Americans will see significant improvement in their own economic positions; and eroding real wages in the midst of a growing economy translates into an important political fact as well."

Frank cited one set of numbers he considered "particularly stark." Between 2001 and the first quarter of 2006, corporate profits as a percentage of total national income nearly doubled, from 8 to 14 percent, but in the same time frame the share represented by wages actually dipped 3 points to 63 percent.

That is just the tip of a sizable statistical iceberg which Bush totally ignored at his peril, and ultimately at the cost of his personal standing and political position.

The increasingly severe squeeze on ordinary families from relatively flat earnings on the one hand and relatively steep increases in the cost of necessities on the other was dramatically publicized by a mother-daughter research team in a bestselling book, *The Two-Income Trap,* which was published just as the 2004 election cycle was beginning. Harvard Law School professor Elizabeth Warren and Amelia Warren Tyagi updated much of their study of the squeeze in a paper they produced late in 2006.

"Never before have middle-class families worked so hard just to break even," they wrote. "The typical two-parent family now has both mom and dad in the workforce, even if the children are small. Increasing numbers of one-parent families are juggling both work and home life with no back-up help. Even households without children are struggling to pay the bills and try to put something aside."

The Warren-Tyagi research and conclusions are an illustration of why a concentration on macroeconomic data—focusing on output,

retail sales, employment levels, and other broad gauges of activity—
can miss a central point even as it makes others. Without steady
above-inflation improvement in a household's income, without significant savings, and with major increases in debt levels to pay for
necessities, improvement in the overall economy can lose its meaning
at the level of the individual and his household. They draw a stark
contrast between life in the mid-1970s and life early in the twenty-
first century, charting the virtual disappearance of the post–World
War II model of family life.

According to information primarily from the Census Bureau, a
statistically typical family a generation ago could prosper on one
paycheck, affording a home usually purchased with roughly 20 percent of the price in the form of a down payment and coming mostly
from the portion of earnings (typically more than 10 percent) that
was saved. There was enough left over for at least a two-week vacation annually.

Just twenty-five years later, not only were both parents working,
but the home they might have managed to buy was eating up a much
larger portion of their income, they weren't saving anymore, and yet
they had also taken on unprecedented levels of debt. With significant, downward pressure on wages and salaries and with job security a fading memory from a vanished era, the struggle (present and
future) was very real.

It was this economy that Bush—fixated on tax cuts and a succession of deals with business interests, positive of his chosen course,
and unwilling to alter his perspective to make room for a broader
view—neglected. The result was a revival of the worst of the Republican Party's and conservatism's reputation for inattentive economic
governance.

For much of the Reagan era, the right seemed to have shaken off
the image of Depression-era indifference that persisted all the way
through the deep recessions of the 1950s, the 1970s, and even the
early 1980s. This was due to several factors: the explosion of inflation and high interest rates toward the end of a passsive-seeming

Jimmy Carter presidency; Reagan's revival of optimism and pro-growth philosophy; and his successful portrayal of progressivism and Democrats as apostles of gloom, green-eyeshade fiscal policy, jealousy-driven class warfare, high taxes, big spending, and heavy regulation. None of that for Reagan, who never appeared satisfied, not even with the recovery from the especially deep recession of 1981–1982, even as it provided the foundation of his landslide re-election.

Almost single-handedly, Bush resurrected the image as well as the reality of the conservative past—not because conservatism is necessarily wrongheaded, but because Bush mismanaged its implementation.

While he was cheerleading, the real economy was performing quite differently. In a briefing paper updated in 2006 for the progressive Economic Policy Institute, research director Lee Price emphasized that it is the nature of a recovery, as opposed to the downturn that preceded it, that matters most, calling his effort the Boom That Wasn't.

"Since the Great Depression," Price wrote, "the resilient U.S. economy has always had gains over such four-and-a-half-year periods [referring to the period dating from the official end of the brief and shallow recession, the mildest on record, in November of 2001]. The appropriate question to ask is: How well has the economy performed compared to similar past periods?"

Price did precisely that, concluding: "By virtually every measure, the economy has performed worse in this business cycle than was typical of past ones, including that of the early 1990s, which saw major tax increases."

His analysis covered the major elements of macroeconomic data:

• *Total Output.* The economy's gross domestic product rose by just under 14 percent over this post-2001 period, an average annual pace of 2.8 percent. The average of the previous four recovery cycles was 3.4 percent. Measuring GDP's flip side, called gross domestic income from all activity, the 2.3 percent annual pace of the Bush era recovery was more than a percentage point below the 3.6 percent rate of previous cycles. The differences might appear small, except for the fact that this is a discussion of trillions of dollars in aggregate economic activity.

- *Employment.* The government data collected by Price showed but a 1.6 percent increase in nonfarm jobs as of March of 2006 over the level reached at the apogee of the previous expansion in March of 2001. This is way short of the average of 9.1 percent over the previous four cycles, during which the gain had never been less than 6.5 percent. In the private sector alone, the gain was only 1 percent, compared to more than 9 percent in the past, and gains in the post-9/11 surge in military spending more than cover this increase. With the labor force rising by more than 1 percent annually, Price noted that within the working-age population of 226.7 million people, there would be four million more people working if the recovery had reached the level of the previous cycle.

- *Wage, Salary, and Other Personal Income.* After adjustment for inflation, the average annual increase in what matters the most to the most people—their paychecks—was 1.2 percent, not only lower than any of the other modern recovery periods, but less than half their average. Even with other forms of income added, such as from investments and rent, the recovery's pace of 1.8 percent growth annually was far below the average of 3.2 percent during the other periods.

- *Spending.* Whether measured as sales to all purchasers or just to individual consumers, the story was the same. So-called final sales to all buyers from businesses to government to people were up at a 3 percent annual rate in the post-2001 period, compared to 3.7 percent in past recoveries. As for personal consumption, two-thirds of the economy's entire output and the reason growth was at least positive after the brief recession and terrorist attacks, the housing spending rate was up at a 3.1 percent rate, a half-point below the average in past cycles. In both cases, however, the level of increase was below the level of increase in income, meaning that increases in spending that were less than in past recoveries were being financed by increases in debt—huge increases, as it turned out.

- *Business Investment.* Spending on buildings, equipment, and software had plummeted at the beginning of the decade, the true cause of the overall mild recession. After the trough, it was up 7.1 percent by the end of 2005, less than half the 14.3 percent recovery pace during the slowest of the prior recoveries, and barely one-fourth the rate in the most rapid.

- *Housing.* This was the exception among the major components of national output analyzed by Price. During the housing boom that became an investment bubble after early 2001, residential investment jumped more than 38 percent, 8 full percentage points above the average during the four prior cycles, though not quite as rapid a recovery as that recorded after the 1981–1982 recession. Interestingly, Price noted, this occurred despite the fact that the lowering of income tax rates reduced the value of the tax code's substantial housing-related subsidies—a reminder to tax-fixated Bush administration loyalists that tax cuts are not the solution to every perceived problem.

This actual economic underperformance in what was technically a period of "recovery" is clear enough from the statistics measuring overall economic activity. It becomes much more so when the impact on individuals is measured. The research paper by Elizabeth Warren and Amelia Warren Tyagi began by figuring the increase in average hourly earnings for nonsupervisory employees working full-time since Bush took office. They used what are called nominal dollars for their illustrations, unadjusted for inflation. They could not use so-called real dollars, because with inflation counted, these average hourly earnings were actually down over the period. In these nominal terms, wages and salaries for employees working full-time rose cumulatively by 8.5 percent from 2001 on, or an average of 1.7 percent per year. Annualized, that was an income gain of slightly less than $3,300, or roughly $275 a month.

Warren and Tyagi tried to see what had happened to that $275 when measured against changes in just a few of life's necessities. It wasn't a pretty picture.

No expense is more significant than housing. In the five years after Bush took office, the cost of owning and keeping up a residence rose 23 percent. The average cost of a package of basic housing expenses was therefore up by $300 a month above what they cost in 2000. All by itself, in other words, higher costs for the same housing wiped out that $275 wage gain.

But there was more. Just to get around in their cars, average households had to absorb roughly a doubling in the price of gasoline, from $1.45 per gallon in January of 2001 to a high of $2.95 on average in August of 2006 (after a pre-election dip that fall, the price was headed back toward $3 by the spring of 2007). There was substantial variation in the impact, but for the average household, the sharp increase in gasoline costs exceeded $150 monthly.

For families with children, day care for the young ones and college for the adolescents is another serious burden. According to the Warren-Tyagi study, families with full-time working mothers spent an average of about $5,400 annually on day care; five years later that cost had jumped to more than $7,100, meaning that for each child under the age of six, there went another $140-plus a month.

College was worse. To pay for just one young person in a four-year public university, the basic costs shot up 44 percent for the five years after 2000. The study reported that college costs are now eating up nearly 30 percent of a fully employed male's earnings. His household bill is now more than $300 higher each month for college than it would have been for a similar family in 2000.

And that was just during college. After graduation, families were belted by enormous increases in the costs of servicing the large loans often necessary to finance higher education. Bush reversed Bill Clinton's policies favoring direct loans from the government in favor of much more expensive (to the student and his family) loans from banks and new financing entities, many of whose officials peopled the ranks of a lax Education Department. Because of the cost issue and because of bribes paid to university officials to favor individual lending firms, the situation eventually attracted the attention of both the new Democratic Congress and prosecutors.

After years of inaction, Bush attempted to promote changes in 2007, but lost the initiative to Congress, which was hard at work in 2007 reducing the government subsidy to the private lending firms by much more than the president had proposed, requiring a significant cut in their interest rates and increasing grants to the most needy students.

Health insurance was even worse than college—another $378 a month, often for less coverage and higher co-payments and deductibles. Adding it all up, the Warren-Tyagi paper estimates that just from housing, health insurance, and gasoline cost increases, the typical American family is nearly $550 a month further behind than it was in 2000—before inflation.

The primary coping mechanism in the real world has been a halt in saving and a fresh pile of debt. The research paper, citing Federal Reserve statistics, reported an increase in the average revolving debt burden per household from about $5,800 in 2000 to more than $7,500 five years later, raising the burden (not counting housing-related debt with "creative" terms that will increase the cost substantially in coming years) from 10.2 percent to more than 12 percent of income. In data compiled separately by the Congressional Budget Office and the Federal Reserve, the estimates of the ratio of household and mortgage debt to disposable income was the highest in 2005 since the frightening double-digit interest rate period of the late 1970s and early 1980s.

"The numbers are unambiguous," Warren and Tyagi concluded.

"The middle-class American family is caught in an economic vise—squeezed by flat earnings on one side and increased expenses on the other."

This is the economy Bush ignored. While the politics of terrorism provided his most important political cushion—before, during, and, until the Iraq War lost the public's support after his reelection—the president relied far more on politics and spin than on policy where the economy was concerned. The most significant Bush move was a political decision to declare that all economic statistics worthy of public citation should cover an artificial period whose commencement was decreed to be the late summer of 2003, more than thirty months into his tenure.

Thus, during the 2006 campaign, Bush could proudly declare that "In the past two and a half years we've added more than 5.2 million new jobs." The danger in that kind of presidential jibberish, however, is that it is too easily exposed and therefore ends up backfiring. After subtracting the three million jobs lost during his first two and a half years in office, the net gain was not just far below the 22.7 million jobs added during Bill Clinton's administration and the more than eighteen million added during Reagan's, it was the slowest pace since Herbert Hoover was president during the Depression.

More important, Bush consistently opposed specific measures to begin helping workers make up lost ground, or insisted on conditions for such measures that doomed their chances in Congress. The most significant example was the federal minimum wage, flat as a pancake since 1996 at a poverty-level $5.15 per hour. For the first five years of his presidency, Bush played a game with his dutifully compliant Republican Congress. Nominally he supported an increase but by caving in to business lobbies' pressure, Bush allowed tax breaks and other subsidies to be added to minimum wage legislation (ostensibly to compensate smaller enterprises for the added cost) that eventually produced legislative monsters progressives would refuse to support. Result: nothing happened, at least not until the Democrats won control of Congress (in part by using Bush's tactics as a helpful campaign issue against him). They almost immediately began moving a measure that mixed a $2 increase with a much less generous package of business subsidies. Bush's stance, like so many others, had won him short-term political and business support but his trademark absence of flexibility had cost him dearly, and cost American workers much more in the interim.

The main coping method for families—more debt—became the main coping method for the country. Unprecedented accumulations of public debt by the government, amounting to trillions of dollars in obligations at the expense of future living standards, required unprecedented levels of borrowing abroad, including some new customers for the Bush Treasury's unprecedented sales of debt obligations, most notably China.

When Bush first took office, he had visions of a new skepticism, bordering on official antagonism, toward this complex country that managed to mix breathtaking economic change with brutal repression and a rapidly expanding military for uncertain purposes. In time, however, he discovered that to keep the Chinese buying and holding American debt obligations (and thus helping avoid a disastrous spike in interest rates from destructive domestic policies) he was forced to tolerate flagrant violations of the new world economic order of which China had only recently become a member—from manipulation of currency rates to shore up an export-driven economy, to continued piracy of everything from American movies to American computer software.

In the process, Bush risked wrecking the shaky political consensus in the United States that has consistently existed behind a steady opening of markets in a shrinking world. This positive trend has been unfolding for nearly a half-century, ever since John Kennedy won business and labor support, as well as bipartisan backing, for the first of four rounds (named after him) of worldwide trade negotiations to reduce tariff and nontariff barriers to trade.

As Kennedy recognized, opening markets, including America's, involves the risks of change and disruption. The trick has always been to mix a steady opening course with the great care it takes to enforce agreed-upon rules and to craft new ones to meet new challenges, all the while taking care that domestic casualties are helped back on their feet.

Bush began his presidency with a victory, just barely winning five years of authority to negotiate deals that Congress could accept or reject but not amend. He won it by consensus, the only way such agreements can be concluded. A new round of worldwide talks quickly began, named after their place of origin in Qatar's Doha municipality. But nearly seven years later the effort was close to a bitter collapse—reflecting deep divisions between developed and developing countries and, more important, a weakening of the U.S. leadership role that had been so crucial.

Bush's negotiators concluded a series of bilateral and regional market-expanding treaties, but the breakthrough in the world talks eluded him. Soaring U.S. trade deficits and job losses to cheaper overseas locations so eroded Bush's domestic position that the prospects of renewing his negotiating authority seemed bleak on their best days. These were self-inflicted wounds.

They were salved mildly after the 2006 elections when the administration's economic policy officials negotiated an agreement on basic principles with segments of the new congressional majority. For six years, Bush had stubbornly resisted a concept Bill Clinton had embraced on its own merits and in the interests of getting his most important agreements approved. The concept involved a widely heard complaint that trade agreements negotiated simply to open markets or lower tariffs ignored at least two additional sources of competitive advantage—weaker environmental laws and weaker labor market protections in nations running large trade surpluses. After six years of saying no, Bush agreed that future deals would have to include environmental and labor provisions, but his agenda was still facing the steepest of uphill climbs because of his own intransigence.

Early in the spring of 2007, there was a symbolic event that underlined the position of the country under his confused stewardship. In international trading in mid-April, the British pound one day rose to a value of $2. That hadn't occurred since Bush's father was president under very different circumstances. The benchmark moment was far less testimony to British strength than it was to American weakness.

The U.S. economy was growing, no doubt about it. Consumers were still spending, and going into debt to do so. There had been a fresh boom—in housing—to replace the 1990s explosion in technology investment. That is called prosperity. But households, or at least nearly half of them, were nonetheless performing poorly in this exciting but uncertain world. Bush heralded the growth but ignored the family pressures. Big mistake.

7

TAXING PATIENCE

Let me talk about how to keep this economy growing. You know, one of the main jobs of government is to create the conditions for economic growth. A main job of government is not to try to create wealth. The fundamental question we've got to ask here in Washington is, what do we need to do to encourage investment and risk-takers, and to encourage entrepreneurship? And I believe the heart of good economic policy is keeping people's taxes low.

—President George W. Bush, speech to the National Cattlemen's Beef Association, March 28, 2007

POLITICIANS LIKE GEORGE BUSH were not exactly what a largely forgotten nineteenth-century French soldier and nobleman had in mind when he penned one of the better aphorisms ever about leadership.

When the Duc de Lévis (born François Gaston) added to his list of maxims the observation that "to govern is to choose," he was attacking indecision—the self-paralysis of leaders that renders them unable or unwilling to act, especially in the face of less than ideal alternatives.

His gift to history, however (the term *noblesse oblige* was another), also covers a less common affliction—the desire to avoid choosing by going after everything, whether through greed or fervor or both. That is George Bush to a T, especially on the subject of income taxes.

Long before 9/11, in just the third month of his administration,

Bush faced one of those defining moments, and proceeded to make a defining mistake. He screwed up in the eyes of his opponents, who wanted to aim tax cuts at ordinary households and the poor and who were ripe for serious co-option by a smart conservative; and he screwed up from the standpoint of true-believing conservatives who longed for a permanent, sustainable slashing of income tax rates and an end to the taxation of estates. Above all, he screwed up by trying to use subterfuge to have it all, and ended up succeeding in the short run, but only by sacrificing the very permanent changes in the tax code he cared about the most.

Having campaigned on specific proposals for serious reductions in tax rates and the elimination of estate taxes, Bush faced a common presidential dilemma. The way the system works, the vehicle for his proposals had to include the annual congressional budget resolution, which sets the broad parameters for the government's spending and revenue targets for the year ahead and, via projections, for the five- and ten-year period following it. At the time, post–Bill Clinton, optimistic talk of enormous budget surpluses from both fiscal restraint in the 1990s and a booming economy filled the political air, most commonly a ten-year projection of $5.6 trillion. But the largest chunk by far of that hoped-for sum was projected to come in later in the decade between 2002 and 2011. Rather than design a package to fit the actual surplus as it was materializing, Bush instead designed one to in effect spend the projected surplus whether or not it materialized (it didn't, of course). He did this in part by phasing the tax cuts in over an unusually long period, up to five years.

Bush's party had a slender but working majority in the House of Representatives, but the Republicans and Democrats were split fifty–fifty in the harder-to-manage Senate. President Bush's tax cut proposal was worth something like $1.6 trillion over a ten-year period, most of it from a slash in the rates paid by the highest-income earners. However, in a series of test votes on deftly structured amendments—so much more in the budget for broadly supported purposes like education and health care, financed by so much less for tax cuts—a consistent majority of Democrats and moderate Republicans had whittled the figure down by almost a third. Normally, the Senate and House split their differences at such moments, but the new administration faced the need to find fifty-one senators for a higher tax cut figure and it simply couldn't find them.

This was President Bush's moment. A president focused on effective governance as well as clearheaded thinking about politics over the longer term (say, Ronald Reagan after the first year of his presidency) would have settled for the best deal he could get. Not every single rate reduction, especially at the top of the income scale where the most money was at stake, would have been possible; perhaps, instead of the complete repeal of federal estate taxes whose cost in revenue would balloon to hundreds of billions of dollars in the second decade of the new century, a significant cut from existing levels would have to be accepted. There was always the option of proposing more tax cuts later.

Instead of choosing, Bush went for it all, enabled by his new vice president, who at the time was focused far more on domestic policy issues like taxes and energy than on the foreign policy issues that would make him infamous later. Dick Cheney, it turned out, used his skill and experience in politics and government to do pretty much what he did to sell the invasion of Iraq. He combined a toxic mixture of obfuscation, misdirection, brute force, threats, false promises, and misleading statements—all to Bush's great advantage in the short run and all to his extreme disadvantage as time passed.

Instead of trimming the proposal to fit the budget hole, Bush decided to fiddle with the estimated size of the hole. It was both ingenious and breathtakingly reckless. To get everything he truly cared about, the president designed his tax cut package to expire at the end of the decade. In budget terms, that "saved" money on the back end of the cycle, at least on paper. The political assumption was that by then the case for making the changes permanent would be overwhelming and a future Congress would sheepishly comply rather than risk the voters' ire for "raising taxes." As a dream it is certainly interesting, but effective presidents have rarely been so reckless that they hitched their success and legacy (not to mention the good of the country) to a series of questionable assumptions piled on top of each other.

Fast-forward six years. The adventures in Iraq and a host of other screw-ups have not only cost the Republicans control of Congress, they have also nearly ruined Bush's political position. He is in no shape to demand much of anything from a Democratic Congress, and as a result, at least half of the tax cuts shoehorned into law in 2001 are in serious jeopardy of expiring. The prospects of eliminating the estate tax are essentially nil. Not only that, but the tax cuts have opened a huge hole in a hemorrhaging federal budget, the national debt has exploded in the direction of $10 trillion, and the distribution of wealth and income in the United States has skewed sharply toward the extremely wealthy to an extent not seen since the Gilded Age at the end of the nineteenth century.

None of this was inevitable. It was the result of a series of blunders that were made by a president greedy for everything, blinded by ideology, fixated on short-term political concerns, and oblivious of the foreseeable consequences of his actions. He all but ruined a long-standing goal of modern conservatism and breathed life into very different tax principles embraced by progressives, even as he did damage to the country's fiscal condition that will take years to repair. As with nearly all the administration's manifold messes, from gasoline prices to the cost of health insurance to the war in Iraq, the issue was never what Bush's opponents did to him; it was what Bush did to himself.

The first major clue is the bewildering variety of explanations and justifications for large-scale tax cuts that has come from the president, beginning with his first campaign in 1999. It is a given that any modern president can say just about anything on any given day that will get him safely through that day's news cycle. However, it is also a given that, as time passes, presidents who fall into the political trap of offering multiple, even conflicting, justifications for the same act are playing with fire and eventually lose their ability to persuade.

From the outset, including his very first full-scale campaign trip to Iowa in the spring of 1999, Bush made it clear that cuts in the income tax rate structure and elimination of the estate tax were his goals. By the end of the year he had a published proposal that did not differ significantly from what he pushed shortly after taking office in 2001. His economic policy guru, Lawrence Lindsey, said back then that the tax cut package was designed as "insurance" against any risk that the then booming American economy might falter. Bush himself also argued, on ideological grounds throughout the campaign, that the large, looming budget surplus that began to show up on the books as the Clinton administration drew to a close would be better spent by taxpayers than by the government itself. Once in office, Bush began using whatever current events were in the news to argue for his package while Congress was considering it. Tax cuts, he said, would alleviate a short spike in gasoline prices early that first year; they would be an effective counter to the very brief and very mild recession that a sharp drop in business investment produced that spring; they would accelerate the unprecedented slow pace of post-recession economic growth. And eventually, after the fact, tax cuts had been the medicine that saved the economy from the perils of recession, the 9/11 attacks, and the ravages of disastrous hurricanes; they had been the key to the economy such as it was down the stretch of the Bush presidency—an economy most Americans felt had undermined their households' present condition and threatened their future.

In all these examples of a policy searching for a justification, there is more than a whiff of politics—partly because tax cuts per se have always been popular, and partly because in a political economy, the next election always looms when a president and Congress are considering changes in tax law. But Bush took this to an unprecedented, absurd degree.

The next major clue is found in the bewildering specifics of the tax package as finally approved at the end of his first May in office. Virtually everything of consequence was to be phased in over up to five years (negating its economic stimulus value) and everything in the package was written to expire at the end of 2010.

At the bottom of the income scale, a new tax rate of 10 percent was created for the first portion of a taxpayer's income. Because the rate was created for that year, 2001, this meant rebate checks from the Treasury would go out that fall, ranging in theory from $300 for a single person to double that for a married couple (to the extent there was genuine economic stimulus in the package, this was it). In addition, the income range for what had previously been the lowest rate (15 percent) was broadened considerably. And in two other elements of considerable potential consequence to ordinary Americans, the so-called child tax credit (deducted from the income tax bill for each minor in a household) was gradually doubled, and the standard deduction for people who don't itemize the allowable deductions on their tax forms was raised as well.

In addition to increases in the tax-deductible limits for retirement accounts and investment vehicles at work, this portion of the package (roughly half) represented the political consensus as of Bush's first year in office. His opponent the year before, Vice President Al Gore, had proposed an essentially similar approach—in order to keep a portion of the looming surplus available to spend on presumed national priorities like health care and education, and to keep paying down the national debt so there would be budgetary room for the enormous costs of the baby boom generation's retirement that would begin toward the end of the decade. With both so similar, there would have been hardly any controversy over such a package; it would have passed Congress overwhelmingly.

What set Bush apart was what he wanted to do for people with the highest incomes and the largest pools of assets. When he took office, there were four additional tax rates in effect as a person's income rose toward and above six figures—28, 31, 36, and 39.6 percent on the last portion of a high income (above roughly $350,000). The eventual package gradually slashed the first three by 3 points each and the president considered himself a moderate compromiser for accepting a cut to 35 percent in the top rate, 2 points higher than he had proposed. This top rate is where the serious money was. Lowering it was the most important cause of the skewing of incomes that followed the tax cut's enactment.

But there was more. Ever since the Republicans won control of the House of Representatives in 1994, conservatives had been agitating to get rid of the nearly century-old estate tax. Then-Speaker Newt Gingrich's great contribution to the language was the invention of the term "death tax" as a key element of the campaign, despite the fact that there was in fact no tax on death but instead on the value of assets that had been accumulating without taxation throughout a dead person's lifetime. Even in the 1990s it only applied to a tiny percentage of the population with taxable assets above $675,000.

Bush's proposal was to immediately cut the estate tax rate 10 points to 45 percent and increase the amount of assets exempted to $3.5 million by 2009. But like all the other provisions in the package, the cuts would expire after the following year. If the tax were in fact repealed after that, a standard projection for the coming age of the billionaire was that the government's revenue would drop by some $775 billion over the first estate-tax-free decade. In addition, another common projection, figuring in the added interest costs on a swollen national debt, put the total cost to the Treasury for ten years at more than $1 trillion. More than once during his first term, Bush was able to persuade a compliant House of Representatives to support full repeal, but the Senate just as consistently narrowly blocked him. After his political position started deteriorating during his second term, Bush eventually gave up.

A funny thing happened after the income tax cut package became law in those first heady months—nothing. Job losses in the economy continued into 2003, and overall growth rates were anemic at best.

A stab at further tax-cutting passed after the 9/11 attacks—allowing faster tax write-offs for business's capital expenditures—failed to have significant impact. Instead of gratitude from his wealthy friends and admirers, the president was mostly getting grief because the post-bubble stock market remained in the doldrums. Out of options, Bush hosted a conference on the economy in the summer of 2002 in Waco, Texas, near his vacation home. During a mind-numbing series of show-and-tell presentations without a common theme, one bit of determined advocacy caught Bush's attention. The multizillionaire stock broker titan Charles Schwab argued that investment was being held back by a familiar bête noire of conservatives—the fact that corporate profits were being taxed as they were recorded, and then taxed again when they were paid to individuals as dividends—called the "double taxation" argument.

Schwab urged Bush to propose that dividends paid to individuals be tax-free, a not surprising idea from a stock market player; what was surprising was that Bush swallowed it whole, making it a cornerstone of the tax proposals he made the following winter.

Once again, Bush and his congressional supporters attempted to play fiscal games under the federal budget rules. The president actually began by proposing just one year of tax-free dividends, assuming that extensions and eventually permanence would follow. In Congress, this idea was cast aside by Chairman Bill Thomas (R-Calif.) of the House Ways and Means Committee in favor of a measure that would cut the top rate on dividends to 15 percent from roughly 38 percent and slash the rate on profits from the sale of assets (so-called capital gains) by 5 points, also to 15 percent. Because of the legislative procedure the administration needed to use to avoid a Senate filibuster and because of the budget rules, this made possible tax cuts that could last only through 2008. Whenever investment-related taxes are cut there is always a short-term increase in activity to take advantage of the new rates, but the revenue cost to the government is still considerable—roughly $50–60 billion annually for the two changes. As with the larger package enacted in

2001, the actual economic impact of this windfall, based as it was on gimmickry, and offering at most short-term incentives, was at most minimal. To try to add some more stimulus, the legislation also made immediate the 2001 tax cuts that were still scheduled to be phased in during 2004 and 2006. By then the ordinary elements of a business cycle recovery were already producing positive economic growth (just not very much of it) and the tax changes paled in comparison to the constant, sharp reductions in interest rates engineered by the Federal Reserve.

However, the investment tax cuts did have a major impact on what the 2001 reductions, combined with the impact of stagnant household incomes, had already begun to produce—a significant redistribution of income to the wealthy. According to the Tax Policy Center in Washington—a joint venture of the Urban Institute and Brookings Institution—53 percent of the billions in capital gains and dividend tax cuts flowed to the 0.2 percent of the population making more than $1 million annually, and more than three-quarters went to the 3.3 percent of Americans with annual income above $200,000.

Bush's lust for his higher-income and investment tax cuts is also illustrated by his comparative disdain for more ordinary Americans who might have benefited from the same fancy fiscal footwork the administration performed for more comfortable fellow citizens. For example, in one gesture of casual unconcern, Bush and his congressional supporters slashed the value of the original rebate to taxpayers in 2001 by at least half, simply by restricting eligibility for it to those who already faced an income tax liability. This not only had the effect of reducing the size of the rebates by more than half the $100 billion budgeted at the beginning of the process. In practical terms, it also meant that more than fifty million people who paid taxes would not get the full rebates as advertised; and nearly 35 million of those would get nothing at all.

But nothing makes the unfairness point more powerfully than Bush's unwillingness to face a serious problem that had been highlighted by tax experts long before he became president and which he claimed to be concerned about. Bush's bungling of tax issues is classically illustrated by his deceptive and inept handling of what is called the Alternative Minimum Tax (or AMT). It is a sneaky levy, originally designed to make sure that the very wealthy paid at least something—no matter the size of their deductions or allowable exemptions and credits; but in recent years it has been pinching people much further down the income scale.

The Alternative Minimum Tax became part of the tax code in 1969 after national outrage erupted following a government report that many people with seven-figure incomes were paying no income tax at all because of loopholes in the system. The tax as originally designed required people making above a certain amount to do their taxes two ways. One of them involved the calculation of tax liability without the use of most popular deductions and credits; it has just two brackets, 26 percent and 28 percent. Taxpayers are then required to do their taxes the normal way and to pay whichever bottom-line amount is higher.

There was just one problem—the income ceilings above which Alternative Minimum Tax rules applied were never indexed to reflect inflation. Through the years there was a steady, if slow, increase in the number of people covered under it until by the late 1990s it threatened to explode into the living rooms of nearly one out of every five families, some earning as little as $50,000 and the vast majority earning amounts that are comfortable but hardly evidence of loophole-crazed tax cheats.

In President Bush's White House world, the issue did not loom large, however. For one thing, his ideological priorities were reducing the top income tax rates and then slashing taxes on investment income. For another, there was that pesky set of budget rules he had to work constantly to circumvent, and the great political advantage of the AMT was that it not only was a stealth tax with nowhere near the political impact of published tax rates but also one with considerable revenue-providing virtues. And for another, Bush's political advisers noticed that the AMT in practice applied most broadly in states and localities where the property, sales, and income tax burdens were relatively high—in other words along the East and West Coasts, which were already trending Democratic and thus not considered worthy of the president's closest attention.

Fully reforming the tax—meaning setting a high exemption level and indexing it against future inflation—would cost the government perhaps $1 trillion over a decade. Rather than face that music, which would have required changes in the rest of his tax packages, Bush took the huge risk of settling for just enough reform each year to avoid a huge jump in the number of households subject to the levy.

He gambled, and he lost—substantively and politically. The great danger for presidents who put off big decisions about serious problems (apart from the resulting damage to the country) is that their opponents have an opportunity to step into the void and seize the initiative, with major policy and political consequences.

Thus the country was faced with an additional, and avoidable, strain on the household budgets of millions of families who could hardly be called super-rich from a law that was never designed to hit them. But by the spring of his seventh year in office, the president was confronted by a powerful movement in a Democratic Congress that threatened to turn his tax policy on its head.

The new leadership in the House of Representatives began circulating a proposal, with support from the new Ways and Means Committee chairman, New York's Charles Rangel, that would exempt from the AMT all households with less than $250,000 in annual income—all but 2 percent of the country, and provide relief even to those making up to $500,000.

To finance a change of this magnitude, the Democrats were proposing that there be a much stiffer AMT for households with more than $500,000 annual income plus other changes in the tax code designed to increase taxation of the very highest incomes by about 10 percent.

Miles remain between this trial balloon and success or defeat, but it illustrates Bush's loss of control over an issue that used to be owned by conservatives. It wasn't supposed to be this way. As he prepared for the convention in New York that would nominate him for a second term, Bush's campaign managers came up with the idea of promising a complete reform of the tax code in a second term—a way of acknowledging that there were problems after all in the tax cuts that needed to be addressed (namely the issues of unfairness and a widening of the gap between the very rich and the struggling majority that even Bush has come to recognize) without committing in advance to specifics.

Sure enough, the president appointed a commission early in 2005 (the Democrat helping run it was one of the tax cuts' enablers in 2001, former senator John Breaux of Louisiana) that eventually gave him several big-ticket options—flatter rates, for example, as well as a move to tax consumption more than income. But Bush simply walked away from the issue and the commission—not only leaving a neglected mess under current law but also ceding the initiative to others, fatal presidential flaws both. In Bush's view after his reelection, changing Social Security was more important than tax reform and as 2005 unfolded the mess in Iraq, Hurricane Katrina, and his own shrinking political fortunes moved tax reform toward the back burner and then off the stove. Those were not irrational judgments but the fact remained that he lost the initiative on taxes—a big-ticket item on American kitchen tables—through his own inactions.

The most telling contrast was with Ronald Reagan—a fascinating study in flexibility during his eight years in the White House. Having succeeded, probably beyond his wildest dreams, in getting major personal and business tax cuts enacted during his first year in office, Reagan did not hesitate to give up roughly a third of them the following year—a price he gladly paid to close a large budget gap during the worst recession since the Depression and to persuade the Federal Reserve to shift its policy from inflation-fighting tight money to stimulation. And when Democrats threatened to take back the tax issue by supporting the essence of tax reform—fewer and sharply lower rates in return for far fewer deductions and other loopholes—Reagan gleefully jumped aboard the bandwagon and helped produce the landmark legislation of 1986.

Bush, on the other hand, now faces the prospect of leaving office with the tax code's reputation under his stewardship in tatters, and with no strategy for saving his cherished cuts for high-income earners and investors from those 2010 expiration dates.

Surveying the wreckage in *Texas Monthly*'s roundup of big thinkers, conservative activist Bruce Bartlett (a senior official in both Reagan's White House and the Treasury Department under Bush's father) summarized a growing discontent on the right, a growing conviction that Bush Junior had both missed a historic opportunity and deeply damaged the conservative cause in the process. He put this Bush right after Herbert Hoover and Richard Nixon as the country's worst president in terms of lasting accomplishment:

> As for Bush's tax policies, I think they have been overestimated in terms of their positive impact. I do believe in reducing marginal tax rates, but none of the tax rate reductions that he has rammed through Congress are permanent. More than likely, they'll be repealed or fail to be extended in coming years.
>
> I'm not sure what the point is of bothering with all kinds of tax changes if they are not going to be made permanently to affect people's behavior. I think that the tax cuts added perhaps a few tenths of a percent to economic growth, but undoubtedly there are other kinds of policies that would have done just as well. The growth that the administration is so proud of is essentially what we would have gotten if they had done nothing.

Progressives, of course, are much, much harsher, and thanks entirely to the president they now hold the reins.

8

A SURPLUS OF DEFICITS

Our nation has seen two years of serious and steady challenges. The recession and the decline in the stock market slowed earnings and cut into tax revenues and created a budget deficit. And in this time of war, I can assure you this government is spending what is necessary to win the war. But the Congress must also understand this: The American people deserve and expect spending discipline in Washington, D.C. With spending discipline and with pro-growth policies, we will expand the economy and help bring down this deficit.

—**President George W. Bush, January 7, 2003**

BARELY TWO YEARS into George Bush's presidency, and just two months after those Bush words, and just a few days into the invasion of Iraq, a somewhat rumpled, quite conservative Democratic congressman from South Carolina had some news for his colleagues, but it was lost at the time to the fog of war.

Bush had inherited arguably the government's strongest financial position since before the Mexican War in the 1840s, but John Spratt told his House colleagues in March of 2003 that it had all crumbled.

Where two years before, the government's official (and credible) projection was that the next decade could bring roughly $5.6 trillion in accumulated surpluses given a reasonably healthy economy, and just two months before that figure still stood at nearly $2.5 trillion in the post-technology-bubble economy, Spratt said the budget then on the floor would eliminate it all in a flood of red ink.

"Now," said the Democrats' go-to guy on budget issues, "just two years later, that $5.6 trillion surplus is gone."

What is more, Spratt warned his colleagues that they were about to compound their sins of two years ago and by doubling their tax cut bets of 2001 dig the government's hole even deeper even as they slashed away at important domestic priorities—an act of breathtaking irresponsibility considering the inevitability of the biggest public finance challenge in American history: financing the retirement safety net for the aging baby boom generation without crippling the two generations behind it.

Spratt made it clear that day in 2003, backed by unassailable arithmetic, that this time Bush and his allegedly conservative congressional enablers had an even clearer choice than they did in surplus-clouded 2001.

"If you forgo the tax cuts, you can also forgo the spending cuts, and you can put the budget in balance by 2008," he said.

Bush and his enablers made their choice, not unlike the fateful choice made on tax cuts—to go for everything. That meant not only tax cuts galore, but tax cuts unencumbered by any serious (or politically demanding) choices to restrain expenditures and ease the impact on the budget.

For the first time in American history, wars (in Iraq and Afghanistan and against international terrorism) were not only accompanied by two rounds of deep tax cuts on the home front, they were unaccompanied by any other request (symbolic or otherwise) for sacrifice on the part of the people in support of these multiple war efforts—no Victory Gardens, no War Bonds, and most certainly no rationing.

It is also true, however, that no American war has ever been paid for out of budget surpluses. Deficits are a fact of government life in times of war, worldwide and smaller. The red ink in the Bush era, though, was unique in that it stemmed only in part from spikes in military expenditures, though these were the main causes initially, along with a fall-off in government revenues after the brief business downturn in 2001. Eventually, the combination of tax cuts, the historically anemic pace of the business recovery, and a remarkably lax attitude for an alleged conservative about domestic spending (Bush did not veto a single spending bill until the seventh year of his administration, and even then the issue was Iraq war policy, not spending per se), came to be the dominant causes.

The situation might have been even worse without the benefits of the international economy's so-called globalization. Traditionally, high (in his case, record) budget deficits translate fairly quickly into much higher interest rates because of the financing burden. In Bush's time, however, the enormous trade and financial deficits the country ran with the rest of the world left the planet awash in dollars. Many of those dollars, especially in trade surplus countries in Asia generally, and in China especially, came back to the United States in the form of super-generous purchases of Treasury notes. This gusher of dollars helped restrain the traditional impact of budget deficits on interest rates and thus shielded Americans from the most noxious traditional impacts of the government red ink.

And it was a gusher. President Bill Clinton's final days in office coincided with the largest overall budget surplus in the country's history—$236 billion, a level that was projected to continue for a decade, hence the famous $5.6 trillion figure. Within a year, however, the budget had swung wildly into the red by $158 billion, with the high point ($423 billion) coming five years later. Indeed, to the extent the weak economy was being stimulated by the government, it was this flood of dollars (along with the interest rate cuts at the Federal Reserve) that provided it, far more than the slowly phased-in Bush tax cuts—more of a traditional liberal's remedy than a conservative's one.

Along the way, though, the national debt exploded again. It had roughly tripled during the 1980s in response to the Reagan era's brew of deep tax cuts and sharp increases in military spending. After steady declines throughout the post–World War II years, reaching a low of about one-third of the economy's total output in 1981, the national debt had spiked toward two-thirds the size of a year's output by the end of the decade.

Following a period of fiscal reform in the 1990s, when the share of output represented by the debt fell back toward 50 percent, the total exploded again under the second President Bush, once again approaching two-thirds the size of one year's economic output in 2007. The national debt's total jumped after 2000 from $5.6 trillion to nearly $9 trillion during his next-to-last year in office.

Beginning in the Reagan years, there had also been a marked change in the composition of the country's creditors. Increasingly, foreigners and foreign government found Treasury securities attractive. Japan was the first large holder to emerge, but the first decade of the twenty-first century saw the addition of China as an increasingly huge purchaser for its growing pool of dollars. By 2007, foreigners and foreign governments held more than $2.2 trillion of the U.S. national debt, nearly half the total amount of the debt in non–United States government hands.

The jump in government debt in the Bush years also produced an explosion in the unavoidable interest costs associated with the financing of it. This automatic but budget-draining expenditure roughly doubled during the president's first term, reaching nearly $400 billion in 2006, on its way toward $600 billion early in the next decade when it will become the government's largest single expenditure.

The record levels of deficits in the 1980s, early 1990s, and after 2001 have spawned a new political language in the country as Republicans and Democrats argue over the merits and demerits of their fiscal beliefs and policies. They have also spawned a gradual political realignment, with Democrats largely replacing Republicans in opinion surveys as the party seen as more likely to practice restraint and control spending. No morsel of political rhetoric, with the possible exception of the assertion that politicians on the left are typically "weak" on national defense issues, has had more staying power or more impact than the claim that their primary impulses are to "tax and spend." The words are still used but their impact has largely dissipated.

But for more than two decades, ever since it became clear that Ronald Reagan was going to be reelected easily in 1984, there has been a strong vein of opinion in the conservative movement that budget deficits are of little economic or political importance and that they can be a useful, if not a backdoor, way of restraining the growth of government. They are not unsupported arguments, but without care and context they can become feeble excuses for budgetary inaction, and a cause of trouble eventually, as President Bush has learned the hard way.

Reagan's reelection occurred in the middle of a sharp economic upturn from an extremely deep recession, and the second President Bush's reelection occurred during a decidedly mixed economic cycle with the country still hyper-preoccupied with the post-9/11 fears of terrorist attacks. By contrast, President Bush's father was soundly beaten by Bill Clinton with the economy barely recovering from a brief downturn in 1990–1991 and in the presence of a third party candidate, Ross Perot, who managed to make the budget deficit a major issue as a symptom of the country's gridlocked inability to face its most pressing problems.

In other words, the lesson of recent history is that deficits tend not to matter—except when they do. Moreover, mishandling of the budget can produce or feed other problems that have direct political salience—affecting a president's ability to win enactment of major proposals or fund important priorities, as well as public views of his character and credibility.

For example, in order to help win enactment of his original fiscal program—based on deep tax cuts—Bush borrowed an old Reagan trick of assuming that the projected budget surpluses would still exist because economic growth would become and remain vibrant throughout the decade. This resurrection of Rosy Scenario—the sultry political wench who beguiled the public with false promises in the early 1980s—was then replaced by a Bush White House political tactic of starting each year with deeply pessimistic deficit projections that could be replaced by the allegedly glorious news later in the year that the red ink had been nowhere near as bad.

None of that worked, much less masked the growing concern about the country's precarious financial position. In January of 2007, a *Washington Post*/ABC News opinion survey found Bush's position on the issue slightly worse than his wretched standing overall; by 62 to 28 percent, Americans said they trusted the newly empowered Democrats in Congress more than Bush to handle the federal budget.

Along the way to serious trouble, Bush also deviated from his standard political practice: rarely getting to the left of his conservative base of support in order to aid and comfort the slender majorities Republicans enjoyed in the House and Senate. The result was that Bush and his Republican supporters took old-fashioned pork barrel spending to unheard of levels as the deficit ballooned. The principal mechanism for this is language in congressional spending bills that directs, or "earmarks," money to particular projects.

In 2006, the year Bush lost his congressional majority, the watchdog organization called Citizens Against Government Waste identified slightly fewer than ten thousand particularly odious projects in the eleven pending appropriations measures, authorizing nearly $30 billion in expenditures. That was roughly double what had occurred in its comparable study during the final year of the Clinton administration, when the Republicans also controlled Congress. With this kind of record, the president's occasional plea for the authority, declared unconstitutional by the Supreme Court in the 1990s, to individually veto such items in individual bills fell on disbelieving ears.

A president's handling of the federal budget involves far more than the grimy politics of dividing up revenue spoils or loftier decisions regarding national priorities. More than a character question, it also involves his leadership, stewardship, and therefore his legacy. As time passes and history takes over, one of the first questions asked about a former president is whether he left the government in better or worse shape than he found it.

On this one, Bush has a rendezvous with a harsh destiny, particularly because of the government's much greater exposure—due to the forthcoming explosion of bills due in the aftermath of his presidency. Nearly ninety million people born just after World War II will retire and put unprecedented pressure on the twin pillars of the safety net for the elderly—Social Security and Medicare.

The judgment is likely to be especially harsh because the recent history of the country—especially since the first emergence of extreme budgetary pressures in the late 1960s—is replete with examples of presidents who bowed to the realities of arithmetic and refused to treat the Treasury as a bottomless piggy bank with no regard for the long-term consequences of irresponsibility.

After three years of trying to pay for both guns and butter (military and domestic programs) as the Vietnam War escalated, Lyndon Johnson eventually responded to reality as well as an international financial crisis. During the presidential election year of 1968, he successfully insisted that a Democratic Congress enact a 10 percent income tax surcharge to bring the budget closer to stability. In a political year of unprecedented turbulence, the tax increase was one more symbol of a country spinning out of control and probably aided Richard Nixon's election at the margins. But it was also necessary.

Going into the final year of a difficult presidency, Jimmy Carter also acted responsibly, as well as against his own and his party's interests, in the face of unprecedented double-digit inflation and double-digit interest rates. He reversed course, named a monetary policy hawk, New York's Paul A. Volcker, to chair the Federal Reserve, and inaugurated a policy of extremely tight money to wring the inflationary excesses out of the economy. The short-term impact was severe, including an actual downturn in economic output as the election year of 1980 began. Carter also pinned down his Democratic allies in Congress, negotiating for weeks over budget cuts to reduce a looming budget deficit that by today's standards was puny—$50 billion or so. None of this helped the hapless Carter politically, but Ronald Reagan as well as the country benefited for years from the longer-term effects of Carter's about-face.

Reagan himself was similarly aware that ideology and politics had their limits where responsible governance was concerned. After his astonishing success at winning approval of his income tax cuts and more during his first year in office, reality beckoned the following year. He had been unable to meet his pledge to combine the tax cuts with a large increase in Cold War military spending and spending cuts deep enough to produce a balanced budget in his first term; he also needed to persuade Volcker to loosen monetary policy as a severe recession (the worst in fifty years) dragged on into 1982, a congressional election year.

So Reagan made a budget deal, one that gave back one-third of the tax cuts he had won just the year before. He negotiated hard with Democratic congressional leaders, but it was this budget agreement, tax increases and all, that made an end to tight money possible and provided for the beginning of the strong if incomplete recovery that was central to the president's reelection in 1984.

Nor was Reagan through making deals. Faced with a harshly negative political reaction to a poorly conceived plan to reduce future Social Security benefits to early retirees, Reagan agreed to the appointment of a bipartisan commission with Alan Greenspan as chair. In 1983, the commission successfully pushed a compromise to stabilize the tottering system. It included both restraint on future benefits increases as well as a payroll tax increase. Indeed, there were tax increases of one kind or another for all but one of the remaining years of Reagan's presidency. None of this made him any less of a conservative; but his actions showed an awareness of the imperative of striking a balance between leading an ideological movement and successfully governing the country.

The first President Bush was no different, despite a rash promise in 1988 (the famous "read my lips" pledge) not to allow any tax increases of any kind if he were elected. The problem as Bush actually took office was that serious deficits had triggered a law Congress had enacted back in 1985. Named after its deficit hawk co-sponsors, Republican Senators Phil Gramm of Texas and Warren Rudman of New Hampshire, the Gramm-Rudman law dangled a sword in the form of automatic, virtually across-the-board spending cuts over the head of a reluctant government if certain deficit reduction targets were not met. Only benefit programs like Social Security and Medicare, as well as mandatory interest payments on the national debt, were exempted.

For nearly five years, nothing major happened because of various loopholes in the complex law that put off the day of reckoning. But that day loomed as Reagan's successor took office, and by early 1990 Bush Senior faced the prospect of slashes in military and domestic programs that were beyond the limits of acceptability.

So Bush, like Reagan, made a budget deal with the Democratic congressional leadership, this one much more painful for him than the one eight years before for Reagan. It included several new tools for enforcing spending discipline, but it also included income tax increases targeted on those with the highest earnings. The deal may have contributed to Republican losses in the 1990 congressional races, and the resulting conservative cries of apostasy certainly contributed to Bush's defeat in 1992. But this was the first major step toward the remarkable balancing of the federal budget later in the decade.

The next two steps were taken by Bill Clinton, and the first one also involved an abrupt switch in economic policy and considerable short-term political damage.

Clinton's famous campaign mantra throughout 1992 (It's the Economy, Stupid) represented a determination to hold Bush's father responsible for a virtually stagnant economy and to give that economy serious stimulus that would include a tax cut for Americans of moderate and modest means. Within weeks of his election, however, he was persuaded that the most important force holding the economy back was continued high long-term interest rates and that the quickest way to get them down was another major assault on the budget deficit.

This time, a president confronted the implacable hostility of every single member of the opposition Republicans in the House and Senate. It took him most of 1993 to painstakingly negotiate an agreement with his fellow Democrats, the vast majority of whom eventually decided to stick with him. The spending restrictions in the 1990 agreement former President Bush had negotiated were continued and in some cases tightened even further; and once again there were tax increases, focused on the top 2 percent of income-earners, but politically painful nonetheless. The economy did not immediately respond, though, and another sluggish 1994 contributed to the Republican revolution that fall. It was only later, after the political damage had been inflicted, that the advantages of this second bite at the deficit reduction apple became clear.

Even then, it took one more major deal to set the stage for the brief period of budget surpluses at the end of the decade. Following Clinton's reelection, the economy had begun to boom, at last producing the kinds of revenue gains capable of transforming well over three decades of red ink into black. Clinton and the congressional Republicans, however, agreed that the time had therefore finally arrived for the middle-income tax relief the president had promised back in 1992. The form it would take was the credit against taxes owed for each person under the age of eighteen in a household that was known as the child tax credit.

Making the tax cut work without returning the budget to perpetual deficit, however, required one last round of Clinton–congressional Republican negotiations on spending, focusing (too much, it turned out later) on government payments to doctors and other health care providers in the Medicare system.

With supreme confidence that he could succeed in getting all he wanted and, despite criticism at every stage that never budged him from the firm conviction he was doing the right thing, President Bush in effect spat in the face of this thirty-year tradition of deal-making and compromise. It was a tradition that continually put the soundness of the country's public finances ahead of the short-term and ideological concerns of individual presidents both Republican and Democratic. A month before the election in 2006 that repudiated him as much as it did Republicans in Congress, Bush actually celebrated a budget deficit of $248 billion.

"These budget numbers are proof that pro-growth economic policies work," he said. "By restraining spending in Washington and allowing Americans to keep more of what they earn, we're creating jobs, reducing the deficit, and making this nation prosperous for all our citizens."

But there was far more to this historic mess than rigidity, politics, ideology, and hubris. The record also shows that the president actively connived with his Republican enablers in Congress to play with the rules governing taxing and spending in order to get his ideas (at least temporarily) into law without regard to their impact on the deficit.

The best example involved one of the rules agreed upon back in 1990 to make it harder to cut taxes or increase spending without regard to the overall impact of such major changes on fiscal policy. In the patois of Washington, it was called PAYGO, short for pay as you go, and with an asterisk or two attached, it meant literally that.

Written into law as part of his father's deal with Congress, the rule required that any change in law that had the effect of increasing spending on benefits programs like Social Security had to be "paid for" by compensatory cutbacks in some other program or by revenue-raising measures. It also required that any change in law that had the effect of reducing revenue (tax cuts, in other words) also had to be covered by a compensatory increase in revenue from some other source or from a specified cutback in expenditures. And it contained a strict enforcement mechanism to make sure the rule was followed, requiring across-the-board cuts in specified benefits programs if the so-called offsets were not achieved. This—along with another major change that imposed restrictive limits, known as caps, on government programs subject to annual appropriations—was an effective limit on the government for the decade that followed. The surpluses that eventually showed up later could not have appeared without it.

When Bush took office, these rules stood in the way of his proposed initiatives—whether a conservative goal like slashing income tax rates or a compassionate conservative goal like setting up a limited market-oriented prescription drug insurance program for retired people. During his first year, he at least faced the issue squarely, winning votes in Congress that waived the rules for his proposed tax cuts. Those victories, though, came in an atmosphere suffused with the assumption in those days that an immense surplus loomed in the country's future and that there was thus no need to insist that PAYGO apply every year.

The following year, when everyone knew much better, subterfuge was used. The budget rules were due to expire at the end of 2002, and Bush simply worked with the Republican leadership to keep delaying requests for renewal votes until the clock ran out. With no rules restricting him, Bush was free to proceed with round two of his tax cuts and the prescription drug benefit as well, with no need for lip service to the budgetary consequences—legalized irresponsibility.

The president's cavalier actions could not obscure the danger in ignoring major problems or sweeping them under the rug: eventually they will emerge as even more serious problems. And presidents who don't act in the face of these dangers often lose the initiative to those who are prepared to, at the peril of all they were trying to accomplish in the first place.

That is precisely what happened after the congressional elections in 2006. The new Democratic majorities in the House and Senate are still finding their way in many areas, but on one issue they were quick and decisive—PAYGO returned in each chamber and several

Republicans joined their Democratic colleagues in supporting the rule's reinstatement.

Two other events transpired early in 2007. Summoning the supreme confidence only he can still summon, Bush declared victory in the fiscal wars—in the form of a budget officially projecting balance five years hence and three years after he will have left office. It took journalists and legislators about five minutes to discern just how the president had achieved this stupendous feat—for starters, by making no provision for any further reform of the dreaded Alternative Minimum Tax and by also making no provision for future costs of the seemingly endless conflicts in Iraq and Afghanistan.

The Democrats paid no attention to Bush's proposals as they began their own work on the year's congressional budget resolution. Like the president's, the essentially similar House and Senate versions contained their own fair share of smoke and mirrors, but they also projected a balanced budget in 2012 without ignoring the policy challenges immediately ahead. Each budget resolution contained the same hole, or contingency—a gap of roughly a half-trillion dollars that could be filled by the simple unwillingness of Congress to extend the life of roughly half the Bush tax cuts.

More than six years of unilateral budget-wrecking, enabled by a now defeated Republican Congress, had piled another $3 trillion on the national debt at just the wrong time. Pressing national needs from education to health care to the stalled cleanup after Hurricane Katrina had gone unmet. But that was about to change, and in the process Bush's unique mixture of arrogance and ineptitude had endangered the very conservative goals he had sought to accomplish. From the not-so-distant past, the index fingers of Presidents Johnson, Carter, Reagan, Bush I, and Clinton were wagging in stern disapproval of this failure.

9

THE THIRD RAIL

First, we must not change Social Security for those now retired, or nearing retirement. Let me put this plainly. For those on Social Security—or close to receiving it—nothing will change. Government has made a commitment, and you have made your plans. These promises will be honored. Yet, without reform, younger workers face a great risk—a lifetime of paying taxes for benefits they may never receive. The reforms I have in mind will actually increase their retirement income.

Second, all Social Security funds in the federal surplus must stay where they belong—dedicated to Social Security. In my economic plan, more than $2 trillion of the federal surplus is locked away for Social Security. For years, politicians in both parties have dipped into the trust fund to pay for more spending.

—Texas governor George W. Bush, May 15, 2000

IN THE MIDDLE of a long-ago budget war with Ronald Reagan, one of the late House Speaker Thomas P. "Tip" O'Neill's top aides came up with a phrase about the country's most important domestic program, which has thrived in politics for a generation.

Said Kirk O'Donnell about Social Security back in the summer of 1982, it is the "third rail of American politics." The message of the speaker's special counsel, himself now deceased, was that if you touch it alone you are going to get burned.

Reagan had done that in the heady, overconfident days of his first year in office. The burn was severe. No minor league politician he, Reagan never made that mistake again.

President George W. Bush touched that live third rail three times—as governor-candidate, as rookie president, and as reelected president. He never learned, he kept repeating the same mistake, the burn was much more severe, and his party and the conservative movement will be paying for his goofs for years to come.

Kirk O'Donnell's brilliant observation came with an underpublicized flip side. As he told journalists privately a year later—in the wake of a truly bipartisan compromise that has kept this vital safety net intact for more than twenty-five years—if that third rail is touched at the same moment by people of normally competing political parties, nothing bad happens. For something this huge, consensus is essential.

For all the right reasons, the unending wars in Iraq and Afghanistan overwhelmed the political and governmental scene as the country began to gear up for the pivotal presidential election in 2008. This understandable dominance, however, obscured the events that first unraveled Bush's political position after his reelection in 2004.

It started with Social Security, not the war. The morning after his narrow reelection victory over John Kerry (there hadn't been this narrow a reelection since Woodrow Wilson's in 1916), Bush chose to treat his win as if it were a landslide. He used the morning-after press conference to leave no doubt about his priorities—tax reform, meaning a simplification of the code he had done so much to make more complex; and his long-held goal of changing the Social Security system.

"We must show our leadership by strengthening Social Security for our children and our grandchildren," he said. "This is more than a problem to be solved; it is an opportunity to help millions of our fellow citizens find security and independence that comes from owning something, from ownership."

And then, the line that would be most remembered from the morning after the long night of waiting for the result from an all-night count in Ohio to be clear:

"Let me put it to you this way. I earned capital in the campaign, political capital, and now I intend to spend it."

Within six months, and by some analyses even sooner than that—and well before chagrin and fury over the course of the war in Iraq had become dominant in the country—this agenda was in tatters, even as the first stirrings of the revulsion over the course of the unending war began.

Despite Bush's hyped description of his standing in the days after the election, the fact is he never enjoyed anything resembling a honeymoon as he began his second term. In the *Washington Post*/ABC News polling that tracks his job approval ratings with the public, Bush peaked at the time of his inauguration with a 52 to 46 margin of approval over disapproval that, after giving allowance for statistical margins of error, may not have been any different from what prevailed on election day. By midsummer of 2005—just before the political jolt that Hurricane Katrina caused—the numbers had slightly more than reversed (in August, Bush's rating was 53 percent negative to 45 percent positive).

This steady slippage occurred despite a series of cross-country tours that resembled a political campaign. Both Bush and senior members of his administration fanned out across America. The subject, over and over again, was Social Security. At one point, the relentlessly hyper-political White House staged Social Security events somewhere in the country for sixty consecutive days. Each one of these appearances resembled every other one; the repetition became mind-numbing.

But the impact was consistent, unbroken by any other trend. The more the president traveled the country, the more he talked about changing Social Security, the more the public reacted negatively. There was a reason for this substantive and political fiasco, and it was the same reason Bush never got traction for his ideas as a candidate in 1999–2000 or as president after his first year in office.

Not once in all this time did Bush ever make a proposal in the sense that nearly everyone understands the word: here is how I would change the system, here is how it would affect payroll taxes and revenues, and here is how I would fund any added costs. Not once over six years did Bush ever go beyond a generalized description of what he consistently claimed was a serious problem facing the country. He gave only a generalized description of one major element in his thinking—the opportunity for people below the age of fifty to take 2 percentage points off their payroll tax each year and place the money in an investment account that would be managed until their retirement, in return for a lower monthly cash benefit.

There was, from the beginning, a certain method to his madness. Bush and his political advisers in 1999, and President Bush and his White House advisers after that, concluded that the best route to reform would be to get a serious process going in the Republican-led House of Representatives and then shape it as legislation moved forward.

But this never happened, not once, not even for a single day. Presidents often make strategic and tactical errors in trying to advance their agendas. Clinton's grand goof regarding health care in 1993–1994 comes to mind. But what makes Bush unique is that he kept repeating his mistake, over and over again, with no change whatsoever in the political impact or the legislative nonresult. Successful presidents are adaptive creatures; their switches in strategy and tactics are a constant reminder that in government the shortest distance between proposal and enactment of anything is rarely a straight line. But Bush on Social Security, not unlike Bush on the war in Iraq, was a model of pointless rigidity.

His purpose was anything but petty, and it had broad, deep support within the conservative movement.

Bush's thinking—and truth be told, there was thinking involved here—stretched back to the period after the primaries had ended in 2000 when he appeared to jump ahead of Vice President Al Gore, in part by reintroducing himself to the country via a series of speeches on important domestic issues (this is when he made his play, with much success, to claim the image of a compassionate conservative).

The Social Security speech came that May, and the setting chosen was perfect—Rancho Cucamonga, one of the fastest growing metropolitan areas in the country, the heart of California's swelling Inland Empire, and the upper-middle-class-dominated heart of San Bernardino County, no more than forty miles east of Los Angeles.

Philosophically, Bush at the time was arguing for a more traditionally Reagan-conservative position in favor of lower taxes and—at least back then—less intrusive, smaller government.

"There is a fundamental difference between my opponent and me," was how he phrased it. "He trusts the government to manage our retirement. I trust individual Americans. I trust Americans to make their own decision and manage their own money."

But in 2004, as the time for his reelection campaign neared, he and political/policy adviser Karl Rove had expanded that boilerplate concept considerably—in the direction of what Bush came to call the "ownership society."

Just as John Kerry was showing in February of 2004 that he was the likely Democratic Party nominee, Bush offered a first glimpse of his vision, not of Americans as beneficiaries of social insurance programs but as owners, not just of homes and small businesses, but of personalized health insurance and retirement plans of their own—stakeholders, if you will, in their own futures. He went on at some length:

> My administration understands the importance of ownership in our society. We've set a great goal. We want every worker in America to become a saver and an owner. And we have an agenda to meet this goal. We will help more people of every background to own their own homes and build their own savings. We will encourage more people to own their own small businesses. We'll help more people to own their own health care plans. We want younger workers to own and manage their own retirement under Social Security so that one day every worker can have the security of a personal account. When people have solid assets to call their own, they gain independence and

security and dignity and more control over their future. I believe in property so much, I want everyone in America to have some.

In shorter form, this material was inserted into Bush's acceptance speech at that summer's Republican National Convention. He used it on occasion throughout the campaign; and his intention to try again to partially privatize Social Security was also made clear from time to time. However, Bush never made this kind of rhetoric a constant. He was running for reelection in the post-9/11 atmosphere and for every reference to a domestic issue there were a hundred references to terrorism, and most specifically to the threat John Kerry allegedly posed to the country's safety.

Bush demonstrated the difference between putting a marker down on the campaign trail and actually leading a determined campaign to convince the country that a fundamental change in thinking was required, as well as fundamental changes in the basic safety net of social insurance—above all Social Security and Medicare. As it was, the polling data in both 2000 and 2004 consistently portrayed a country inclined to be suspicious of Bush's intentions, including many people who voted for him for other reasons, above all terrorism.

Social Security, after all, is a kitchen-table issue. It is one of those topics that get discussed within families trying to make plans and get by, and most people are already rather well informed on these kinds of topics. They also hardly need politicians, government officials, or even statistics to tell them how they are doing; they experience reality every day.

In occasionally dreaming of his ownership society, Bush again made the basic mistake of not confronting life as most Americans live it. In particular his rhetoric failed to address a major trend in public and private American life—the huge increases not so much in what people own as in how much (how very much) they owe.

It is true that some long-term favorable trends continued after 2000. The percentage of Americans owning their own residence continued inching toward 70 percent by the time Bush was re-elected. And the number of Americans owning mutual funds contin-ued to increase as well, surpassing 53 million by the time Bush was running for reelection, though the percentage of people with this most basic form of participation in the equity markets held basically steady at slightly less than half. At least when Bush was running for president the first time, the idea of investment accounts as an op-tional, partial replacement of Social Security benefits could appeal to younger workers because the markets were still enjoying the tech-nology boom; in fact, many people under the age of thirty had never experienced a downturn.

Nonetheless, for most American households the dominant reali-ties in the early years of the twenty-first century were relatively stag-nant wages and salaries and great piles of debt—their own, their employers', and their government's. The total of all the debt in the country had jumped from about $18 trillion in 2000 to nearly $23 trillion by mid-2004. Within households, the figure rose sharply from $7 trillion in 2000 to roughly $9.5 trillion four years later—including a jump in mortgage debt of more than 40 percent and in consumer debt of 20 percent.

Managing all this debt at the household level—where just one emergency, typically involving health care, could and did send mil-lions of additional families into foreclosure or bankruptcy—became a difficult and stressful task. At retirement, moreover, there is not all that much to fall back on except for Social Security. For two-thirds of today's more than forty million beneficiaries, Social Security (av-erage annual benefit: $12,000 and change) is their largest single source of income; for more than a third, Social Security provides at least 90 percent of all income; and for more than one in five, Social Security is all there is.

These numbers are not likely to change much in the future, espe-cially as traditional pensions in the private sector continue disap-pearing. At the time Bush sought the presidency, a revolution had occurred, one that largely replaced the so-called defined benefit system with one featuring defined contributions to investment accounts with some employer assistance, such as 401(k) plans. For those who regularly contribute to them—a minority of about forty million people—the average size had doubled in the first half of the new century's first decade to more than $100,000, but the median size (half above that, half below) was still barely $67,000.

In detail, this is what Kirk O'Donnell meant when he called Social Security the third rail of politics. Bush, however, all but jumped on it, and after he got his burns, he blithely kept repeating the same basic mistake.

On that long-ago day in Rancho Cucamonga, Bush's presentation was essentially in two parts, each more gauzy than fact-filled. His first major point was that Social Security was in trouble from the impending explosion in the number of beneficiaries compared to the number of workers and employers contributing payroll taxes. It would begin to run an operating deficit by the end of the century's second decade, and then would eventually go bust when reserves were exhausted sometime around mid-century.

Bush's second major point was his proposal—that workers below the age of fifty have the option of diverting 2 percentage points of their share of the payroll tax (workers and employers now split the 12.4 percent tab) to an investment account. In theory, the value of that account (there would be more than one investment package option, each of them very conservative) would increase more than enough over time to provide a basis for retirement income higher than if the worker had opted to stay in the current system. And accordingly, there would be a compensating drop in the worker's Social Security benefit.

Except for some rhetorical flourishes, that was it. Bush gambled that by leaving the details out—in fact by not even confronting a host of obvious questions about costs and benefits—he could rely on the prospect of the investment accounts to carry him politically in the campaign and then carry him into a legislative process that would deliver them. He was wrong in the campaign and he was dead wrong as president, but he never corrected his mistake.

The most obvious question about Bush's proposal, unanswered still, was the one that caused him grief as a candidate and that sank him as president. Social Security operates as a literal transfer of income from one generation to the next; each year's tax revenue pays for that year's benefits. If a worker can divert 2 percentage points of his taxes to his investment account, but the benefits under current law still have to be paid (and, needless to say, Bush promised every time he opened his mouth that benefits would never, ever be touched), the obvious question arose: how is the government supposed to fund the system during this presumably enormously expensive transition period?

There were scores of learned estimates, but a common one, which Bush and his advisers did not bother to try refuting, was that over ten years these transition costs from the depletion of revenue would amount to roughly $1 trillion. Bush has never answered the question of where the government was supposed to get a trillion dollars. In 2000, with the government flush and the official projections of a budget surplus reaching $5.6 trillion over the following ten years, Bush's exposure on this basic question was perhaps less costly. However, by the time he tried to jump-start the process after his reelection in 2004—with the surplus having completely disappeared, replaced by more oceans of deficits with no end in sight—the question was a substantive and political deal-breaker.

The other ongoing problem with Bush's proposal from the beginning was that the candidate and the president never confronted the alternatives—alternatives made politically and fiscally attractive both by a famous compromise back in 1983 and by the achievement under Bill Clinton of substantial budget surpluses at the end of the 1990s.

When Ronald Reagan touched the third rail in May of his first year in office, he floated a proposal to cut future benefits as one way of coming up with the money to balance the budget in the face of his tax cuts and increases in military spending. The proposal focused on future cuts in benefits for those retiring "early" at age sixty-two. The harshly negative reaction was the first moment when Reagan—until then a consistent winner with Congress and the public—lost his glow.

In the face of this reaction, and with a deep recession further raising the public's fears on the eve of a congressional election year, Reagan tried to stem the negative tide by agreeing at the end of 1981 to participate in a bipartisan commission that would not report until after the election. With the support of Reagan and the top congressional leaders of both parties, the commission (chaired by Alan Greenspan on his way to becoming chairman of the Federal Reserve four years later) surprised everyone including its own members by agreeing to a balanced set of revenue-raising and benefits-restraining measures that would put the system on a sound, as in surplus-producing, operating footing—amazingly enough—for a generation. Depending on the course of the economy, those operating surpluses were not expected to become deficits until 2015–2020.

Within five years, however, some participants in the great fix began crying foul—most notably the late Senator Daniel Patrick Moynihan of New York. Moynihan charged in the late 1980s that the government was in effect embezzling the annual Social Security surpluses by using them to mask the true size of the ongoing operating government budget deficits, and thus preventing the surpluses from being used to keep the system healthy and solvent far into the twenty-first century. Moynihan ignited an argument that often gets highly technical but his basic point was irrefutable.

The surpluses in Social Security typically approximated $150 billion annually and were used to purchase Treasury Department notes. Under the accounting concept that lumps all the government's activities together, however, these purchases had the effect of making the overall deficit seem that much lower. The proof that Moynihan was right was the fact that each year the government went borrowing to finance its deficit, and the amount it needed to borrow was the higher operating deficit figure, not the lower one incorporating the Social Security surplus that was more widely publicized.

Ten years later, Bill Clinton was the president who finally responded to Moynihan substantively. In his 1998 State of the Union speech, most famous because it was his first major public appearance after his ties to Monica Lewinsky were revealed, Clinton uttered four words to summarize his approach to the government—save Social Security first.

What he meant was that by balancing the budget, surpluses would accumulate that could be used to actually pay down and eventually eliminate the national debt—making the full financing of the baby boom generation's retirement with untouched benefits much easier. As surpluses in fact began to appear, official projections kept pushing back—well into the future—the dates when the system would begin to run out of resources.

It was into this increasingly hopeful climate that Bush charged, though more like a bull into a china shop. His ideas about a partially privatized Social Security system were provocative enough because of their ill-considered vagueness on fundamental questions; but they were also poorly matched for the alternatives then being proposed by Clinton and Al Gore.

The idea of helping working families save and accumulate wealth to supplement pension and Social Security income has been around since before the system was created under Franklin D. Roosevelt during the Depression. But with the prospect of budget surpluses in a growing economy, the idea at last became feasible on paper. Clinton and Gore, though their ideas differed in detail, were what are called "add-on" advocates—meaning they favored using tax credits and other subsidies to help workers set up investment accounts without touching the revenue stream provided by payroll taxes. By contrast, Bush was what is called a "carve-out" advocate—meaning he wanted to take revenue out of the system itself in order to finance accounts; eventually, participants would get smaller basic benefits, though these savings would not accumulate for years. In prosperous, surplus-producing 1999 and 2000, the Democrats had the better of the political argument.

Indeed, to cement his position, Gore promised repeatedly to sequester the Social Security surpluses so that they could never be used for any purpose outside of the system. This was the origin of his famous "lock box."

After the 2004 election, Bush was in the untenable position of advocating a new system, with a trillion-dollar hole in the middle of it, in far different economic and budgetary circumstances. To make matters worse, he was in a weak political position with two difficult wars on his hands, in a fifty–fifty, polarized country with a polarizing proposal to sell. To have any chance of even partial success, he needed the Republican House of Representatives—in an election cycle that is particularly dangerous for incumbents—to start the process.

But Bush, in his weakened position, got stiffed. With no overt backing from a relatively weak speaker, Dennis Hastert of Illinois, and a polarizing majority leader in Tom DeLay of Texas, the pivotal chairman of the Ways and Means Committee, California's Bill Thomas, was under no pressure to get out his rubber stamp, and so he didn't. Less than two months into Bush's second term, Thomas announced that his committee would be holding hearings into the entire group of complicated issues affecting retirement—including long-term health care, private pensions, and other elements of the national safety net not limited to Social Security. It was an elegant way of announcing that Bush's ideas weren't going anywhere as long as the president was unable to stick his neck out on behalf of a comprehensive proposal.

In the Senate, several Republicans tried to help, offering feelers and trial balloons on the unavoidable issue of financing transition costs. Some suggested it wouldn't literally be a tax rate increase if the so-called wage and salary cap (the limit on income subject to payroll taxes) was taken off. Others, unable to countenance any form of revenue-raising scheme, suggested deep cuts in other parts of the federal budget that were draconian to the extreme; they attracted little support from most legislators and none from the temporizing president.

With essentially no action under way in Congress during 2005, Bush was left to wander the country almost until he took his annual vacation in Texas that summer—arguing the issue in generalities before friendly White House–approved audiences, but presenting nothing that could serve as a basis for legislative work. After the novelty wore off, few of the sessions attracted much in the way of media attention because Bush rarely deviated from his rhetorical script.

Bush's flop on Social Security would be less significant if it simply represented a failure by a president to implement a grand goal of his administration—analogous, say, to Bill and Hillary Clinton's defeat on health care ten years before. But it was far more than that; by in effect wasting the better part of seven years in vague agitation for a vague vision of major change that he never came close to clarifying, and by wrecking the government's finances while he was at it, Bush has left Social Security in far worse shape than he found it, with the years of fiscal reckoning getting closer and no long-term stabilizing reform in sight.

He has also crippled earnest efforts by his fellow conservatives to reform the government's benefits programs—called entitlements. Their ideas may be controversial, but wiser and more competent conservatives than he have been working for decades on ideas to both rein in long-term expenditures and give privatization schemes a chance to work, at least on paper. After Bush, however, it will be years before conservatives are trusted again, through no real fault of their own.

The president had begun in 1999 as a competitive candidate on domestic issues; during his first year in office the public tended to be willing to give him an opportunity to perform; and in the early stages of his post-reelection campaign opinion on partial privatization was mixed, at least until Bush began to speak constantly about it. But by the fall of 2005, when Bush's Social Security fiasco had given way to other catastrophes, a *Washington Post*/ABC News opinion survey found voters trusting congressional Democrats over the president on the issue by a forbidding 56 to 33 percent margin. That is what Kirk O'Donnell meant by the third rail's impact.

Finally, Bush's fixation on Social Security turned out to be misplaced, at least to those for whom context and perspective are important. The government faces all kinds of problems and dilemmas in the future, including several involving entitlement programs that appear much more serious and pressing than Social Security.

According to the system's trustees, whose computers project future benefits and revenues for up to seventy-five years, the program's expenditures under current law exceed the financial resources also available under current law, and assuming a stable economy, by roughly $13.4 trillion.

That is not chump change. But the so-called unfunded liability of the new prescription drug insurance program enacted in 2003, and already beset by controversy and other problems, is estimated to be $16 trillion.

And the mother of all impending entitlements problems is represented by Medicare, whose crisis will be far larger and more pressing once the baby boomers start to need it. The latest estimate of Medicare's unfunded liability is more than $61 trillion.

10

MEDDLING

The case of Terri Schiavo raises complex issues. Yet in instances like this one, where there are serious questions and substantial doubts, our society, our laws, and our courts should have a presumption in favor of life. Those who live at the mercy of others deserve our special care and concern. It should be our goal as a nation to build a culture of life, where all Americans are valued, welcomed, and protected—and that culture of life must extend to individuals with disabilities.

—**President George W. Bush, March 17, 2005**

FOR THE THIRD major and, once again, self-inflicted wound in the disaster he made of his second term, President Bush acted in the middle of the night—not his best time of day.

It happened after an already frantic behind-the-scenes Palm Sunday in 2005 at his ranch in Texas, and culminated in a rash, poorly considered decision to fly back to Washington. He arrived after midnight to sign a piece of legislation that no one who had studied the issue it allegedly addressed believed had a prayer of surviving even casual court scrutiny.

And it didn't. In addition, the publicity stunt of his late-night flight exploded in his face politically—another widely predicted result. In a reckless violation of every principle of prudent conduct, Bush embarrassed himself, violated some of conservatism's fundamental tenets about the role of government, and weakened his office as well as the very cause he claimed to be championing.

Long after Terri Schiavo was laid to rest, the mystery remains how so many people with public duties could so completely lose control of themselves. It was the moral equivalent of a governmental riot. The person who could have prevented it, President Bush, instead was the cheerleader in chief—enabled not only by his political team but by two old pals from Texas who were used to helping him do what he wanted instead of offering the independent judgment their duties required—his new White House counsel, Harriet Miers, and his new attorney general, Alberto Gonzales. On Capitol Hill, Congress behaved even more badly, leaving both institutional wounds and a lingering impression of irresponsible incompetence that would have electoral consequences the following year.

The tragedy of Terri Schiavo's sudden heart failure and years of incapacitation in a vegetative state was a given. So was the compounding of that tragedy in the bitter legal and personal struggle between her husband and her parents over whether artificial means of keeping her technically alive should be continued. And so was the further compounding of the tragedy as a result of the decision by the president's brother Florida governor Jeb Bush (an extremely religious conservative) to use every tool in the state's legal arsenal to maintain her on a feeding tube.

But Congress? The president of the United States?

Both paid dearly for their recklessness, as well as quickly. The mess they created caused even more damage, moreover, because the Schiavo incident came to be seen as a metaphor for a government that was becoming an intrusive force in people's private lives in order to impose narrow religious values. Government was popping up where it wasn't wanted to comment on the teaching of evolution science, to proselytize about sex among unmarried young people, and eventually to threaten abortion rights. Instead of serving as a restraining force, Bush's often blind zealotry was increasingly transforming conservatism into the same kind of activist force it rose to prominence denouncing; it rode roughshod over the same powers of states and localities that conservatism had once championed. Instead of a

White House full of gates and gatekeepers, blocking impulses and blocking trouble, Bush's White House was crammed with enablers.

The public's verdict on Terri Schiavo was instant, vehement, sharply negative, and predictable, making Bush's behavior seem all the more irrational. According to a CBS News poll in the middle of the madness in late March, 78 percent of the public had very strong feelings about the massively publicized case.

To few political observers' surprise, moreover, an overwhelming 82 percent majority opposed the federal intervention in the case that Congress and Bush engineered—a figure that included two-thirds of those who described themselves as conservatives and evangelical Christians.

What is more, Bush and the congressional Republicans got no respect for even the courage of their convictions. Only 13 percent of those polled felt Bush and Congress had acted out of concern for Schiavo; nearly three-quarters smelled politics.

They had a point. Without denying the validity of everyone's concerns and emotions, political considerations were out in the open on Capitol Hill. A memorandum even surfaced from Republican Senate sources claiming that riding the issue would be a net plus, big-time, and that the "pro-life base will be excited by the issue." Written by a senior adviser to a junior member, freshman Mel Martinez from Florida, it also claimed that the Schiavo case could be used against the state's Democratic senator, Bill Nelson, who was up for reelection the following year. The author, one Brian Darling, confessed and resigned while claiming he had acted on his own, but his words fit the frenzied atmosphere perfectly.

The normal restraints that should have been operating in Congress, but weren't, similarly were just as absent within Bush's White House. The president can be forgiven for sharing the religious views of his brother who implored him to help. But Bush and his White House cannot be forgiven for ignoring the basic facts of the case that should have restrained a president from following his blindly interventionist instincts.

For one thing, the Shiavo legal case was as close to being open-and-shut as this kind of dispute can be. No court, no matter the political background of its judge, had ever ruled in favor of Schiavo's parents through nearly seven years of bitter litigation which included decisions after trial that she was in a persistent vegetative state, and that when she was healthy she had repeatedly expressed a desire not to exist that way. Between 1998 and 2003, she was maintained on the feeding tube (with one two-day exception early in 2001) while her parents appealed adverse rulings. It was the exhaustion of their state court remedies that brought Jeb Bush into the case, and it was his continuous defeat at the hands of Schiavo's husband in the courts that produced Governor Bush's appeals to Washington.

Intervention ignored one of conservative philosophy's most dearly held principles, that the federal government should not intervene in matters traditionally reserved to states and localities. According to one hard-liner, former Republican representative Bob Barr of Georgia, "To simply say that the culture of life or whatever you call it means that we don't have to pay attention to the principles of federalism or separation of powers is certainly not a conservative viewpoint."

And moderate Republican senator John Warner of Virginia summoned his customary grandiloquence to plead for restraint.

"That the misfortunes of life visited upon Theresa Marie Schiavo are a human tragedy, no one can deny," Warner said. "I said my prayers, as did many Americans, as we attended religious services this Palm Sunday. But I believe it unwise for the Congress to take from the state of Florida its constitutional responsibility to resolve the issue in this case."

Federalism—a bedrock conservative value, a legal doctrine at the core of the belief systems of so many of the people conservatives consider ideal for the federal bench—was simply swept aside in the rush by Washington to take over Schiavo's case. Federalism hardly insists that the national government ignore national considerations, even constitutional ones, that can arise because of state actions. But the concept does insist that there be a healthy respect for a state's legislative and legal processes that have run their course.

In rushing through the toll gates without pausing to consider ramifications and consequences—a fundamental, unforgivable goof by a president—Bush and his allies even ran roughshod over their own pasts in this area.

As the governor of Texas, during the year he began running for president, Bush had signed legislation that permitted doctors to remove life support systems from a patient's care, after approval by a facility's ethics committee, even in cases where the family wanted to continue with them. There was even a case where this happened, involving an infant, while he was governor. House Majority Leader Tom DeLay had joined with other members of his family back in 1988 in blocking extraordinary measures to keep his father alive after he was gravely injured in an accident; in the Schiavo case he said God had presented Congress with a great opportunity to take a stand. And the Senate majority leader, Bill Frist of Tennessee (the surgeon who would become infamous during the Schiavo melodrama for claiming, after seeing a video of her, that she showed signs of cognitive potential), had argued publicly as a physician to extend his state's definition of brain death to cover the kind of state in which Schiavo lingered.

The legislative work was a parody of sober consideration, with no regard to the disruptive potential of the precedent that might be set. It illustrated how in addition to functioning as little more than the president's rubber stamp when it was not shielding his policies from intense examination, the Congress and Bush at times pushed each other toward a fever pitch of extremism. The Schiavo case put Tom DeLay and Bill Frist, the key legislative players, on high-profile display, and the country instantly disliked what it saw.

The legislative parody was compounded by Bush's ill-considered decision to be passive on its specific content, again regardless of the consequences, as the publicity surrounding the case escalated. The process actually began with maneuvers to stage a faux hearing, with

Terri Schiavo as the summoned witness on the preposterous grounds that this stunt would require that she be kept "alive." The House version of the legislation that eventually began moving forward actually tried to deal with end-of-life issues generally; it would have permitted anyone who "cares about him or her" to have access to the federal courts after state courts had permitted or directed the withholding of nutrition in the absence of a living will directing otherwise. Despite the floodgates this bill would have opened, Bush took no position on it.

The Senate's bill, the one the president ultimately signed, was aimed specifically at the Schiavo situation—itself a mockery of the process since her condition and even the family dispute about it were hardly unique, and thus could subject future Congresses and presidents to a constant clamor for similar legal maneuvers.

Bush's post-midnight signature and hasty retreat to the silent seclusion of his ranch for more vacation time set the stage for exactly what most observers had assumed all along would happen—nothing. First a U.S. district court in Florida, and then the federal appeals court in Atlanta governing that circuit ruled without dissent the same way. Without her feeding tube, Terri Schiavo died peacefully at the end of the month. After her death, Bush's silence ended, but only for a canned statement he read in Washington:

> Today millions of Americans are saddened by the death of Terri Schiavo. Laura and I extend our condolences to Terri Schiavo's families. I appreciate the example of grace and dignity they have displayed at a difficult time.
>
> I urge all those who honor Terri Schiavo to continue to work to build a culture of life, where all Americans are welcomed and valued and protected, especially those who live at the mercy of others. The essence of civilization is that the strong have a duty to protect the weak. In questions where there are serious doubts and questions, the presumption should be in favor of life.

That is what they call spin in politics. After a drama as high-profile as this one, with opinion known already to be negative in the extreme, presidents are best advised to steer clear of spin because it only makes bad political situations worse. With these remarks Bush was speaking to a choir composed only of the roughly one in six Americans who favored the federal intervention; the other five only became more convinced he had taken leave of his senses.

Bush's statement deconstructs easily. There were no serious doubts and questions. The professionals who had examined the patient over fifteen long years had all reached the same conclusion—persistent vegetative state. Her parents can easily be forgiven their mixture of hope and fervent belief that she was anything other than what the professionals said she was. But not so Bill Frist, the video doctor, and certainly not politicians like Republican senator George Allen of Virginia (who would go down to defeat the following year), who said he could easily dismiss all the state court decisions in the case, adding, "When I see the videotape of Terri Schiavo it is clear she is conscious and has feelings."

She wasn't and she didn't, but the ardor of people like Bush and Allen evoked a sharp reaction from elsewhere in the conservative movement, which is anything but a monolithic entity. Some focus on promoting economic growth through the tax and regulatory relief, others are most interested in states' and individuals' rights, and still others emphasize social and religious values that at times require an activist government to promote and protect.

The Schiavo case exposed the fissures inside this coalition, first assembled to help make Ronald Reagan president in 1980. As an alleged leader, Bush never did anything to smooth the fissures. Indeed, as other issues came down the pike during his presidency he managed to make them worse, all the while further eroding conservatism's, as well as his own, attractiveness to the Americans who don't consider themselves partisan or ideological.

Abortion rights is the classic example. Notwithstanding the

shouting match that proponents and opponents have been conducting ever since the Supreme Court ruled in 1973, the politics, the personal emotions, and even the substantive details of the issue are rarely simple. And for decades, the Bush family has been the perfect example of abortion's often twisted politics and many contradictions.

The president's grandfather, Prescott Bush, was the archetype of the Yankee pol when he represented Connecticut in the Senate. Shortly before his election in 1952, he actually held a leadership role in the Planned Parenthood Federation's first national capital campaign, not long after its name was changed (softened) from the original Birth Control Federation of America (back when advocating that could get you arrested). Bush's father and mother continued the family tradition right through the elder Bush's election to Congress in the 1960s. It was as he began to position himself to run for president that what politicians like to call an "evolution" occurred. Bush's first step was to support a ban on the use of federal money to pay for abortions not needed to save a pregnant woman's life or in cases where pregnancy was the result of rape or incest.

His complete transformation in 1980 was less subtle. Bush's Faustian bargain to go on Reagan's ticket required he support an amendment to the Constitution outlawing all abortions. He caved quickly, and he never looked back. His son had no record of involvement with the issue until he ran for governor of Texas in 1994.

The current Bush has often twisted himself into a pretzel on the issue—mouthing the language of the right-to-life movement but also seeking to convey the impression that he would not do anything directly to try to overturn *Roe v. Wade*—a goal assisted by the occasional acknowledgment of his mother and his wife, who are pro-choice. Instead, he bought into two efforts by the right-to-life movement to get at *Roe* by indirection.

One of them involved linking the long-standing conservative campaign to find "strict constructionists" to nominate to the federal bench to the movement's goals, without overtly seeking people with long paper trails of opposition to abortion rights. Bush's father had a mixed record, but to date the son has appeared to succeed with Chief Justice John Roberts and Justice Samuel Alito.

The main reason involves the second effort—a campaign dating to the mid-1990s ostensibly to outlaw a specific abortion procedure, named "partial birth abortion" by political advisers, but to do so in ways that chipped away at two key elements of the *Roe* decision. The first is the division of pregnancy for regulation purposes into three trimesters, and the second is the provision that abortion restrictions may not endanger a woman's health, including her ability to have children in the future.

This campaign finally succeeded in 2007 once Justice Alito had replaced Sandra Day O'Connor, with a 5–4 Supreme Court decision. However, that still left untouched the basic constitutional right to choose abortion. In all the years since Reagan's election, despite having three sympathetic presidents, the right-to-life-movement has never been able to affect the pace of abortion in the United States. With the prospect of a majority of like-minded Supreme Court justices, some elements of the movement decided to try a test case.

The guinea pig was South Dakota, which enacted a law in 2006 outlawing all abortions except those needed to save a woman's life. But instead of becoming a test case in the presumably friendlier courts, the law's passage awakened the citizens of South Dakota. Signatures for a referendum were collected quickly and a vigorous campaign ensued. The result was not close; pro-choice voters overturned the statute by a 55 to 45 percent margin.

The South Dakota law put President Bush on the spot and in wiggling furiously he managed to satisfy no one. Previously, abortion rights had been more of a theoretical issue because the prospects of something actually happening were so remote; the changed composition of the Supreme Court combined with the South Dakota challenge changed all that. But the best Bush could manage was a series of comments to the effect that the issue was properly a state matter, but that he had always favored exceptions for rape and incest that the state statute lacked.

Bush's inability to speak clearly on abortion, stretching all the way back to his first presidential campaign, has been compounded by his inability to resolve the long-standing federalism contradiction in the right-to-life position. On one level, there is a widely held view among conservatives that abortion is an issue properly left in the hands of the states. But on the other, there is the fervent belief, driven by religious conservatives, that what they call "human life" begins at the instant of conception. If that were the case, God would not presumably like to see abortion legal in California but completely illegal in Louisiana and illegal with exceptions somewhere else.

This is why the Republican Party since Reagan has always included a no-exceptions amendment to the Constitution banning abortion in its platform, and nominees from Reagan forward have given it lip service. Until Bush, however, this issue has seemed almost academic. The president, however, has made it much less so, while giving every pro-choice person in the country a reason to be alarmed. Were *Roe* to be overturned, the resulting political and state legislative firestorm would seriously threaten the fortunes of conservatives trying to walk the fine line between states' rights and their conviction that abortion is murder—a point often made by Republican political consultants.

By contrast, Bush has been more willing to face the contradiction between strict federalism and conservative values on another hot-button issue—whether gay people should be allowed to get married. Here the politics are much more favorable to conservatives. Indeed, Bush's reelection campaign actually linked up in 2004 with religious conservatives in several states (most notably in pivotal Ohio) that were sponsoring state constitutional amendment referendums to ban gay marriage and, in some cases, civil unions as well.

After the election, however, the trend began to move in the opposite direction. Four of New England's six states now have laws allowing either actual marriage (Massachusetts) or civil unions (Connecticut, Vermont, and New Hampshire). In addition, a civil union statute has been enacted in New Jersey and major attempts in this direction were under way in megastates New York and California as well.

From a national perspective, conservative religious organizations have long sensed the societal momentum. And their sense of it has also been informed by their realization that even in the states with their own bans, there is the small matter of the U.S. Constitution and its language, which in effect forbids overt discrimination. This coalition of religious organizations went to Bush early in 2004 looking for a response to two looming possibilities—that a federal judge will someday rule state laws banning gay marriage unconstitutional, or that so many other states will permit it or its civil equivalent that a national trend will take hold.

The president took the easy way out, endorsing what politics keeps him from endorsing on abortion—a U.S. constitutional amendment. Bush never worked the issue very hard, and his stance immediately split his own party between the values of conservatives who agreed with him and the hard-line federalists who didn't. Given that split, the amendment never came close to clearing Congress in 2004 and there is no current prospect of that happening in the foreseeable future.

On one level, it is easy for Bush to mouth the boilerplate rhetoric of the movement—stating a generalized belief, presumably religion-based, that marriage "is between a man and a woman" and that such an arrangement should be considered "sanctified" or "sacred."

But on another level, Bush's relentless effort to have it both ways on social issues is losing the respect of true-believing conservatives, and turning off everyone else while solving nothing in the meantime. His efforts to avoid clear choices and clear commitments have had utility in the short run, but now he faces long-term damage, as does the conservative movement, precisely because he has appeared to focus almost exclusively on the politics.

As Bush's political position deteriorated during his second term, his standing with America's all-important middle deteriorated even faster. When his job approval hovers around 30 percent, he is not just losing Democrats; he is losing independents and people who consider their views moderate by nearly the same margin. He is also facing defections from up to 20 percent of his conservative base.

Clearly, Iraq dominates the stage. However, at least a sizable portion of the centrist disgust and the conservative erosion is the result of a Bush-fed view that he would countenance an intrusive governmental presence in people's private lives in order to advance a narrow social policy agenda, but that this agenda never manages to advance very far. That's the worst of both worlds.

11

DISASTER

Tonight so many victims of the hurricane and the flood are far from home and friends and familiar things. You need to know that our whole nation cares about you, and in the journey ahead you're not alone. To all who carry a burden of loss, I extend the deepest sympathy of our country. To every person who has served and sacrificed in this emergency, I offer the gratitude of our country. And tonight I also offer this pledge of the American people: Throughout the area hit by the hurricane, we will do what it takes, we will stay as long as it takes, to help citizens rebuild their communities and their lives. And all who question the future of the Crescent City need to know there is no way to imagine America without New Orleans, and this great city will rise again. The work of rescue is largely finished; the work of recovery is moving forward.

—President George W. Bush, September 15, 2005

EVEN WITH A monster of a hurricane bearing down on the Gulf Coast, nothing was going to keep President George Bush's White House from what it does best—marketing strenuously to triumph in each day's news cycle by staying "on message."

For the week straddling the end of August and the beginning of September 2005, the message was marginally Freudian and familiar: the decisive president had learned from the biggest mistakes of his father. In the case of the huge storm named Katrina, that meant he was taking firm hold of the government and avoiding the passivity that plagued President George H. W. Bush after another catastrophe named Andrew had laid waste to southern Florida thirteen years before.

As the hurricane slammed ashore, the marketing found some takers. In the *Chicago Tribune* on September 1, for example (three days after landfall), there was this quote from Joe Allbaugh—Bush's campaign manager in 2000 and his first director of the alleged coordinator of national response, the Federal Emergency Management Agency (FEMA): "I think all of them are rising to the occasion," said Allbaugh of his White House friends and former colleagues, "starting with the President. He understands that one of the principal roles is to become that hands-on CEO at a time of disaster."

There had even been an event just the day before, which the article cited to show just how hands-on the president was in this crisis.

"To punctuate that point," it said, "Bush made a national address from the Rose Garden on Wednesday, encircled by Cabinet secretaries as he outlined a broad-based plan for relief. And the President plans a ground-level inspection of the storm-stricken region Friday or Saturday."

As it turned out, it was on Friday—famous for Bush's gusher of a compliment to Michael Brown, Allbaugh's former deputy and successor, who, the president said, was doing a "heckuva job."

The link to the Bush family past that the White House was determined not to repeat turned out to be chief of staff Andrew Card, who had been dispatched by the first President Bush to South Florida to do damage control after the initial response to Andrew bordered on the nonexistent. This time, the article noted, things were different, with Card running things "for a President who is personally taking the reins of relief."

There was just one problem, of course. While the typically arrogant and self-promoting White House was crowing, more than a thousand people had been killed, the Gulf Coast was a moonscape from the Texas to the Florida borders, New Orleans had drowned, thousands of people were stranded in the flood, and tens of thousands were penned inside the fetid confines of the New Orleans

Superdome and the Convention Center with no relief or even drinking water in sight. And this was just the beginning of what would stretch into two years of halfhearted responses to an ongoing crisis of biblical proportions.

The Bush administration is unusual in many, many respects, but nowhere more so than in its trademark combination of arrogance and ineptitude. The truth is that no one had learned anything of consequence from Hurricane Andrew, no one in authority had followed any of the clear signals of approaching catastrophe in the form of Katrina, and the response to the storm's aftermath had all the trappings of post-invasion Iraq. It was not one huge screw-up; that might have made it easier to fix.

Instead, this was a whole series of screw-ups beginning well before and continuing well after the hurricane hit. It marked the reappearance of the familiar deadly Bush sins of ineptitude, inattentiveness, hubris, cronyism, public relations spin, ideological rigidity, old-fashioned stubbornness, and know-it-all-ism at a highest-profile moment when the country is looking for results. Looked at from a distance, the Bush administration's response to Katrina resembles panic as much as a monumental failure.

Katrina is Andrew's bookend, two huge storms deep into two Bush presidencies that illustrated a government neither in touch nor in charge. But Katrina is also Iraq's bookend, a tragic opportunity for Americans to see some of what was going terribly wrong right here—as well as thousands of miles away.

When Katrina hit, the Bush presidency was already in a serious decline that was becoming increasingly obvious as the second term unfolded. A completely botched Social Security initiative, the ham-handed and inept intervention in the Terri Schiavo case, and then the fresh realization that there appeared no way out of an increasingly deadly and costly quagmire in Iraq had all combined by the late summer to make Bush a decidedly unpopular president. Job approval ratings were in the mid-40s on his best days and support was sharply declining from the all-important middle of the political spectrum.

Katrina was the exclamation point. It was the disastrous response to the hurricane that drove Bush's approval numbers into the 30s for the first time. It was Katrina that first introduced concepts like embarrassment and shame to the discussion of his tenure, symbolized perhaps by the offers of people and money that came from other countries in the midst of the administration's paralysis. And it was in the aftermath of Katrina that the adjective "incompetent" began to be used on a large scale in analyses of Bush's ineffectual governance. Before Katrina, Bush was in serious trouble; after Katrina, his administration was in tatters.

The hurricane's devastation was so enormous and so vast that symbols often illuminate more than numbers. Where Bush is concerned, panic was the response to the immediate failure to act after Katrina hit. It soon morphed into something worse. A need to assure clamorous fellow Republicans of his alleged decisiveness prompted Bush to float a couple of trial balloons to convey the impression that someone was actually in charge. As the president prepared to address the nation from New Orleans' fabled Jackson Square more than two weeks into the crisis, a cry went up for a "czar" to take charge of the entire federal response, in place of the at times comically ineffectual Michael Brown. The first trial balloon was that the so-called czar would be recently retired General Tommy Franks, just at the time the extent of his careerist acquiescence in leading an inadequate force into Iraq was becoming public. After that failed to fly, the second trial balloon, almost on the eve of Bush's speech, was that the response and reconstruction effort would be overseen by Karl Rove. Within a month, the White House was denying that ever happened. And it was not until fully two months later that someone was finally appointed—a Texas banker and old Bush pal named Donald Powell, then running the Federal Deposit Insurance Corporation, was appointed bureaucrat-in-charge.

For the president's nationally televised address, electric power was restored at least in the parts of the ravaged city where Bush himself appeared. The lighting in Jackson Square was simply gorgeous, and gone shortly after he spoke. The president's motorcade route included streets in the warehouse district near the Mississippi River; about a half-hour before he passed through the lights came on as if it were a normal September 15 evening, save for the fact there were no people on the streets; within an hour afterward, the area was pitch-black once more.

The casual cruelty and political indifference of the government was at times astonishing. In disasters, it is common for the federal government to send money early to pay the salaries of local police officers, firefighters, and the like because of the havoc often wreaked on property tax bases; there were grants after 9/11, and foreign aid to Iraq takes the form of grants; but after Katrina there was instead a $750 million loan. Within days, the administration had also decided in effect to cut the pay of everyone who would be working on cleanup and reconstruction, by suspending a seventy-year-old statutory requirement that "prevailing" wages be paid; not even the Republican Congress would countenance that. And of course, there were no-bid contracts galore, the first one (worth $29.8 million for general cleanup) went to Halliburton.

Just as cronies and other hacks with no relevant background in the work to be done abounded in post-invasion Baghdad, they proliferated in pre-Katrina FEMA. In addition to Allbaugh and then Brown, a majority of the senior staff at the agency had come directly from event planning and media posts in the Bush campaign, supplemented by someone who had been lieutenant governor of Nebraska and someone else who had advised on political affairs at the U.S. Chamber of Commerce.

In politicizing what had been evolving in the direction of a professional agency, Bush was ignoring one of the central lessons of Hurricane Andrew and other natural disaster flops that occurred under his father. The first President Bush, an often indifferent chief executive in domestic affairs, had delegated disaster relief to his chief of staff, the abrasive former governor of New Hampshire and architect of Bush's rescue there in the closing days of the 1988 primary campaign, John Sununu. And Sununu had sprinkled loyal campaign operatives throughout the agency, starting at the top with his old friend and neighbor, Wallace Stickney. Unlike most agencies, FEMA has a famously high percentage of its positions open for political appointees and Sununu and Stickney created a patronage heaven on their watch.

The results when Andrew hit were catastrophic. Literally nothing happened following this Category 5 hurricane for three days, and the most famous pictures immediately thereafter were of the lines that snaked literally for miles at hastily assembled relief centers where inadequate amounts of water and other necessities were distributed. Ironically, it was the dispatch of Andrew Card, formerly Sununu's deputy and then the secretary of transportation, that began to turn the chaotic situation around.

One person who learned the lessons of Andrew was Bill Clinton. His FEMA choice was also an old pal and crony, but he was also an experienced handler of natural disasters as well as the operator of his own construction company. James Lee Witt professionalized the agency, winning from Clinton the power to interview every job applicant (thus making hacks harder to place via the White House) and focusing FEMA on the task of using its relatively small size (not much more than four thousand people) to maximum effect by emphasizing meticulous planning for quick emergency responses. The results were dramatically apparent just a year after Andrew during the huge Mississippi River flood, the Northridge earthquake near Los Angeles the year after that, and the Oklahoma City terror bombing in 1995 (when Witt's advance team was on the site within six hours of the explosion).

The second Bush administration was in most respects worse than the first, largely a consequence of inattention in the wake of 9/11. After wasting a year fighting a rearguard action against congressional calls for a separate department to concentrate on protecting vulnerable infrastructure and managing immigration, Bush's sudden lurch—dispatching Card and just a few aides to draw up the blueprint for what became the Homeland Security Department—had horrid consequences. Almost cavalierly, FEMA was folded into the new, gigantic bureaucracy as what amounted to a stepchild.

When the agency was created under Jimmy Carter in the late 1970s, the essence of its separate charter was the direct link between its director and the president in times of natural disaster. That link was broken by Bush. There was an understandable preoccupation with terrorism, but presidents are paid $400,000 a year to think through their moves, and there is no evidence that any thought was given to the consequences of a neutered FEMA.

At any rate, the budget cuts and the loss of scores of key people with rich experience soon followed, aided by Allbaugh's ill-considered attitude that states shouldn't view disaster relief as another entitlement program and that volunteer groups, including churches, should play a bigger role after natural disasters. Allbaugh's decision to cash in, his replacement by Michael Brown, and the replacement of a former governor (Tom Ridge of Pennsylvania) as Homeland Security secretary by a former Justice Department official and federal appellate judge whose experience with natural disasters was nil (Michael Chertoff)—symbolized FEMA's decline.

The budget cut in 2004 alone approached $200 million; the administration had also slashed away at the Army Corps of Engineers, whose New Orleans district that same year had to absorb its biggest budget cut ever. The inevitable departure of talented professionals was itself a flood. By the time Katrina hit, nine of FEMA's regional directors were "acting," and three of five division heads' offices concerned with natural disaster response were vacant. Overall, some five hundred positions at the agency had been eliminated by the summer of 2005, requiring the jettisoning of one of FEMA's three emergency management teams, the groups that do the day-in, day-out job of coordinating the governmental responses to natural disasters.

This was the factual context for the federal government's nonresponse to the actual assault by the hurricane. Behind it lie some fundamental truths about the operation of an effective presidency. The thunderous impact of the 9/11 attacks is as undeniable as it is understandable. The emergence of a gigantic subject (terrorism), however worthy of the kind of massive focus that can become pre-occupation, is never an excuse for ignoring all the other topics com-peting for a president's attention, especially those that matter to ordinary Americans. Bush's decision in 2002 to reverse a year of op-position and support the creation of what became the Department of Homeland Security hardly justifies the near-evisceration of FEMA that accompanied it.

In a narrow political sense, Bush's desire to keep very secret his intention to flip-flop on the new department is understandable, but this is an excellent example of how secrecy preoccupied him and how obsessive secrecy produces major mistakes. While chief of staff Andrew Card and a handful of assistants were laboring furi-ously behind the scenes, moving boxes around on an evolving or-ganizational chart, the kind of elementary consultation and idea-testing that might have produced a well-considered proposal was rejected in the small-minded interest of springing a surprise.

The best evidence that this is so is the fact that the status of FEMA in Bush's Department of Homeland Security scheme was pointed out almost immediately, and was the reason some Demo-crats opposed the reorganization when it was before Congress in 2002. Listen to veteran congresswoman Marcy Kaptur of Ohio, speaking just a week after Katrina hit:

> It has been quite painful for me as a member of Congress who served on the FEMA oversight committee for a number of years, to witness the constant failures of judgment by this team. It started with the President himself, when he took office and, importantly, early on in his administration when he hollowed out FEMA, taking away its Cabinet status, saying that it should no longer be an independent agency that reported directly to the President, instead rolling it into

the gargantuan Department of Homeland Security and tasking that with eliminating terrorism.

FEMA is tucked three levels down in this lumbering, massive bureaucracy of 170,000 people which still cannot figure out how to answer a letter. I voted No on that reorganization.

That reorganization, however, was the occasion for the flagrant display of the partisan proclivities of the Bush presidency, proclivities that often trumped policy considerations, even where terrorism was concerned. Once the administration had put down on a marker in February of 2002 that the response to the 9/11 attacks was to be a key feature of that year's congressional election campaigns, it was no giant step for Karl Rove to manufacture a made-for-television issue out of the substantive differences that emerged as the new department was being created. In that kind of atmosphere, policy wonks like Marcy Kaptur, even partisan ones, were simply ignored.

It was this new department that embarrassed the country when the massive hurricane reached the Gulf Coast. In a memo to Secretary Chertoff on the day it hit, FEMA director Brown called the storm a "near-catastrophic event" and avoided any other words lending urgency to the region's needs. It was not until the day after that, Chertoff later admitted, that he became aware that the famously weak levees protecting New Orleans had been breached in three places, flooding the city. More preposterously, Brown proposed holding off on the dispatch of a thousand FEMA workers to the area for another two days, on the grounds that they needed special training, and suggested in the same memo that perhaps another two thousand could be sent in a week.

It is a fact that the disaster was in very large part the result of decades of poor planning and poor policies at the federal, state, and local levels; the poor condition of the levees, in particular, had been widely known for years. However, it is also a fact that federal agencies had received an ominous, updated, and detailed description of just how exposed the city was only the year before, as well as in 2001. For five days in the summer of 2004 FEMA had presided over a simulated emergency—imagining for planning purposes that "Hurricane Pam" struck southern Louisiana with 120 miles per hour winds and with rain and storm surge sufficient to cause water to flow over the top of the New Orleans area's levees. In such a situation—a Category 3 hurricane that was somewhat less powerful than Katrina actually was—the simulation foresaw the evacuation of more than one million residents and the destruction of more than a half million buildings. That should have served as a wake-up call. But there is no evidence that the government took any significant action to beef up its readiness over the following year. The Gulf Coast was both physically and governmentally naked in front of the monster that attacked it the very next summer.

But despite the wealth of the evidence, the Bush White House's relentless fixation on the politics of the situation produced a familiar excuse. Within a week of the hurricane's landfall and the colossal shame of the nonresponse to the initial horror, it became the official mantra that no one could have foreseen that a huge storm would both hit the Gulf Coast head-on and strike with a force that would cause levees to fail. Michael Brown used it; Chertoff used it; and even Bush himself used it.

Students of the administration will recognize the formulation— which had its origin in the response in the spring of 2002 to the first reports of the warnings about impending terrorist attacks that had filled the intelligence community's in-boxes in the months prior to the 9/11 attacks. Beginning with National Security Advisor Condoleezza Rice and continuing with other security officials, including the president himself, the refrain then had been that "no one could have foreseen" that a group of terrorists would hijack airplanes and fly them into buildings inside the United States. The refutation, of course, was that a surprisingly large number of people had foreseen precisely that and that evidence of plotting (the infamous dots that were never connected) had been uncovered.

Similarly, the assertion that the Gulf Coast disaster, epitomized by the flooding of New Orleans and parishes (counties) to the south and east, was something no one could have foreseen is contradicted by the wealth of information that once again a great many people had indeed foreseen it. The 9/11 formulation worked politically for a while; in the case of Hurricane Katrina it failed from the beginning and was soon abandoned as a politically viable excuse. The White House had more luck helping to focus criticism on Louisiana Democrats like New Orleans mayor Ray Nagin and Governor Kathleen Babineaux Blanco (in part because their responses had been widely criticized locally and nationally). However, Bush's behavior was a classic illustration of the truism that a presidency excessively focused on the politics of huge problems will end up with worse problems and even more political damage.

Within a year of the hurricane, the public's largely disgusted reaction mirrored the president's low standing overall in the polls as the congressional election neared. According to a *Newsweek* survey in August of 2006, the public by a five-to-three margin believed Bush had not followed through on his commitments to the Gulf Coast. And the fundamental approve/disapprove question in a CNN/Gallup survey the same month found that the public was disapproving by a 64 to 34 percent margin of Bush's handling of the storm's aftermath.

Public opinion basically got it right. Within weeks of the hurricane, and then stretching out indefinitely, it had become clear that the administration was consistently a day late and a dollar short in its policy responses. With tens of thousands of people stranded in motels all over the country, with unused FEMA trailers filling vacant land in nearby states, and with the littered, abandoned landscape throughout the region an unchanging symbol of what was not happening, the images of post-Katrina were omnipresent and stark.

Behind the images, moreover, was a series of policy goofs that were largely responsible for the disturbing pictures. There were at least three major ones.

In the first place, the administration continued to break with the record of past federal responses, delivering major chunks of assistance in the form of loans instead of grants. In the past, federal law recognized that some communities and even states could be so devastated after a disaster that loan repayment by jurisdictions that were not getting any revenue could be an unmanageable burden; there were specific provisions enabling the forgiveness of these loans. But for the first time ever, the Republican Congress in 2005 specifically forbade the forgiveness of loans made to communities devastated financially as well as physically by Katrina and the storm that followed it (Rita); and Bush signed their mean-spirited work product into law.

This attitude extended to the treatment of individuals, where it bordered on cruelty. For two years after the storm, stories abounded of people who had lost everything, received a small amount of assistance via FEMA to replace some of their losses, and then been pestered by the agency to almost immediately repay it. A vivid illustration, recounted in early 2007 in the pages of the indefatigable *New Orleans Times-Picayune,* involved a student at Dillard University in New Orleans. The flood had ruined all her possessions, so she applied to FEMA and received $9,500 to replace her belongings, not realizing that within months FEMA would be on her back to repay the paltry sum, threatening to take her to court.

In the vacuum of leadership even decisive action was penalized. At one congressional hearing, military officials told of a situation at a building outside the central city where soldiers fanned out in adjacent neighborhoods to assist in rebuilding, only to be slapped by FEMA officials with a 30 percent "penalty" on top of their labor and material costs because the work had been "unauthorized."

Secondly, in a particularly noxious act, the Bush administration pointedly refused to use statutory powers to waive another requirement in federal law that roughly 10 percent of the disaster aid provided by FEMA be matched by the recipient community or state. As a consequence, scores of projects in the affected region were delayed or never started while local governments scrambled to come up with money they didn't have—projects including the rebuilding of a prison destroyed south of New Orleans, a public school administration building in the suburbs, and a hospital on the western Louisiana coast. Not until 2007, with a new Congress in office, did the process of relieving localities of this burden get a boost from legislation introduced by Senators Mary Landrieu (D-La.) and Ted Stevens (R-Alaska).

Nothing, however, held a candle to the third major mistake—failing to provide housing. More than eighteen months after the storm, for example, a $6.9 billion program to help homeowners repair their damaged dwellings had been swamped by claims from tens of thousands of homeowners. At a minimum, the claims appeared to exceed the allotted budget for the effort by roughly $3 billion. This huge snafu, moreover, engulfed a program that was not even operating until the summer of 2006 because of delays and wrangling between state and federal officials. According to one audit of the program, as of May 2007, there had been more than 130,000 applicants but only 16,000 actual disbursements of money.

Often, localities found themselves caught in catch-22 situations between wrangling or paralyzed federal agencies. On one devastated New Orleans street, for example, construction could not commence, FEMA had ruled, until a nearby seawall and pier had been rebuilt—a project budgeted at less than $1.5 million. Nothing, however, happened for more than a year because the agency responsibile for the flood control work in the area, the Army Corps of Engineers, had neglected to ask for the required congressional appropriation.

Meanwhile, in a photogenic display of the underlying misfeasance, thousands of FEMA trailers stood empty, parked by the hundreds on available vacant land in nearby states, needed desperately but unused for months. Katrina's horror cried out for a hands-on president—the competent CEO—with key officials reporting directly to him. The problems are so immense, the bureaucratic confusion so enormous, that only a president can cut through it all. But Bush was consistently hands-off, and it showed.

After his massively hyped vows to personally take charge of the complex effort to repair and rebuild, President Bush gradually backpedaled. His return visits to the region became less frequent, and as a final insult his State of the Union address at the beginning of 2007 included not a single mention of the worst hurricane in the country's history—one that overwhelmed the president and became as potent a symbol of his administration's multiple breakdowns as the ongoing mess in Iraq.

For the record, the headline on that richly ironic *Chicago Tribune* story was: "President Learns from Father's Mistake After Andrew."

12

POLITICAL SECURITY

Our methods for fighting this war at home are very different from those we use abroad, yet our strategy is the same: We're on the offensive against terror. We're determined to stop the enemy before they can strike our people.

Every morning I am briefed from the latest information on the threats to our country, and those threats are real. The enemy is wounded, but still resourceful and actively recruiting, and still dangerous. We cannot afford a moment of complacency. Yet, as you know, we've taken extraordinary measures these past two years to protect America. And we're making progress. There are solid results that we can report to the American people.

—President George W. Bush, September 10, 2003

ON MARCH 8, 2006, the administrative officer for George Bush's White House, Andrew Card, told the president that after more than five years, it was time for him to leave his position as chief of staff.

Not coincidentally, this was the same day the House Appropriations Committee voted to block the pending acquisition of an international corporation based in Britain—the Peninsular and Oriental Steam Navigation Company—by another international corporation based in one of the United Arab Emirates along the Persian Gulf—Dubai Ports World. Included most prominently in the assets the Dubai outfit was seeking to acquire just happened to be the licenses to operate six of the largest commercial ports in the United States east of the Mississippi River, from New York all the way around Miami to New Orleans.

The committee's vote was by a stunning 62–2 margin, a stinging rebuke of the administration by its Republican allies in Congress—who included by the time the vote was taken, both the House speaker, Dennis Hastert, and the Senate majority leader, Bill Frist. The president's Democratic foes were also aboard this freight train, but compared to the significance of the desertion by Bush's fellow Republicans, their role was ancillary.

After five years of bumbling, special interest favors, and the flagrant politicization of homeland security issues, the president had all but asked for this rejection. His government had not seen the Dubai deal controversy coming, it had almost comically mismanaged the political controversy it subsequently ignited, and then as a final incompetent indignity, Bush had personally inflated the vote's significance by repeatedly threatening to veto any congressional action seeking to block the merger despite the fact he had never attracted enough support to sustain such an action.

The Dubai Ports fiasco is a perfect window on the Bush administration and the president's long slide from approval and popularity. Polls are ordinarily a poor yardstick on national security issues involving terrorism for the simple reason that there is much the public doesn't and shouldn't know. But they are useful in a case like this one, because one of government's obvious functions in a dangerous new world is to reassure the public that the authorities are doing all they can to protect the country.

In early 2002, when memories of the September 11 attacks were still painfully fresh and the administration was still hyperactive in seeking to appear "tough" on the issue, roughly 70 percent of the public said they just about always or mostly trusted the administration's handling of national security and terrorism matters. Later that year, an ABC News poll found approval of the administration's campaign against terrorism by a whopping 78 to 21 percent margin.

But barely three years later, that margin—the last major element of policy where Bush could lay claim to public support—had disappeared. Just as the furor over the ports deal was climaxing, the same ABC survey found approval had shrunk to 52 to 46 percent, right at the poll's 3-point margin for statistical error. The same survey found just 22 percent of the public feeling "much safer" than it did after the 2001 attacks. Another 33 percent said they only felt "somewhat" safer and fully 35 percent said they were less safe. By February of 2007, this inexorable slide in the same survey had produced a negative 52 to 46 percent rating.

Another reason the Dubai deal fiasco is such a perfect metaphor is that it doesn't matter what your views on the merits of the issue are. You can believe that it was a perfectly straightforward commercial transaction with a now friendly Arab government, an ally in combating terrorism. You can believe it was probably a sensible transaction but deserved very careful scrutiny in a new environment, especially given the fact that two of the nineteen hijackers on September 11 were from Dubai, that banks in the emirate had handled some of the terrorists' money transfers, that its sprawling ports had helped transship technology to Libya and Iran traceable to the infamous proliferator-for-profit, Pakistan's A. Q. Khan, and that the Emirates were, until the 2001 attacks, one of the handful of governments in the world to recognize the rogue Taliban regime in Afghanistan that had sheltered Osama bin Laden for five years. Or you can believe that in this new and dangerous environment it is simply not prudent to allow any foreign firm, much less firms owned by Arab governments, to have anything to do with the operation of U.S. port facilities.

It doesn't matter. Whatever your point of view, Bush's handling of this mess was inept from start to finish, the real reason it ultimately collapsed. It was also part of a disturbing pattern of government failures that stretched back to the months before the terrorists attacked and then forward to the present. This pattern didn't just affect homeland security, anti-terrorism efforts, and the wars in Iraq and Afghanistan; it affected nearly every aspect of the Bush presidency.

The government has been charged with watching foreign acquisitions of American companies for more than thirty years. The system that exists today dates to an executive order issued by Gerald Ford in 1975 at a time when concerns were raised about the recycling of petrodollars in the wake of the first energy crisis, but it has since been codified and amended in statutes that established something called the Committee on Foreign Investments in the United States, or CFIUS, which bureaucrats on the inside pronounce as if it were a word. It is one of scores of statutory bodies comprised of several different government agencies that carry out regulatory functions.

The underlying law gives a president considerable leeway, including the power to block a transaction, subject to congressional override, if there is credible evidence a foreign entity might take actions threatening national security and if blocking the merger is the only way to protect the country. The CFIUS operation has elaborate rules about notification, protection of data supplied by corporate applicants, and timelines for action. In general, it provides for relatively cursory examinations of a proposed acquisition (no more than thirty days) and more intensive ones (no more than forty-five days), triggered by a formal statement of concern by one or more federal agencies.

In practice, however, the committee's history strongly suggests it wields a rubber stamp. That, at any rate, had been the conclusion in a 2005 report by the Government Accountability Office issued just before the chain of events in the ports controversy began. The report concluded that the committee's record showed an extremely narrow interpretation of the law—no more than twenty-five full investigations into some 1,600 transactions over the years.

That had been, in effect, a pre-9/11 mentality, to use the phrase favored by White House political guru Karl Rove as an attack line against supposedly "weak" Democrats. What the country had a right to expect was that this would have changed after the terrorist attacks and that extra vigilance would be the practice throughout the government.

But nothing changed, because where business interests were concerned, Bush had a bad habit of going soft, before and after 9/11.

In late October of 2005, the Dubai company contacted CFIUS and sent a representative to brief its staff at the end of the month. A pro forma assessment from intelligence agencies was requested in early November. The formal notice triggering the timeline was received in early December, a cursory letter of security "assurances" was negotiated in early January, and the green light was officially flashed in mid-January, whereupon all hell broke loose on Capitol Hill.

None of the twelve agencies objected, although the Coast Guard registered concerns that were kept short of the formal notice that would have produced a deeper probe. Politically and substantively, the Bush Bubble—hermetically sealed compartments ruled by pro-business ideology and know-it-all attitudes—produced the worst possible outcome.

The best way to avoid political trouble is to consult outside the bubble. There is even a provision in the CFIUS law making it crystal clear that "nothing" in the sections governing the privacy of information in the approval process is to be "construed to prevent disclosure to either House of Congress or to any duly authorized committee or subcommittee" of something worrisome that is coming down the pike. Airing that something out ahead of time should be almost automatic.

But it wasn't. Nominally, the CFIUS operation's twelve participating agencies are represented by their top people; in practice, staff members run the show, but the extent to which they keep their bosses informed, especially about potential problems, is determined by the atmosphere that is established from the top. When that atmosphere is business as usual, notification up the chain becomes perfunctory.

In this case, that meant that no red flag went up about an obvious conflict of interest. The new head of the Maritime Administration, David Sanborn, had run operations for Dubai Ports World in Europe and Los Angeles, and before that had been with the transportation giant CSX Corp., from whose ranks Bush had selected his second treasury secretary, John Snow. And it was from CSX that the Dubai company acquired other port terminal facilities in 2004.

As a practical matter, CFIUS is nominally run by each agency's number two person and is thus chaired by the deputy treasury secretary, in this case a former Washington lawyer named Robert Kimmitt, who took office in 2005 with ambitions to succeed Snow. Kimmitt's one previous brush with notoriety had come in 1992, when he was assigned by his mentor, none other than former Reagan and George H. W. Bush guru James Baker, to vet the background of Dan Quayle—the vice presidential pick of Bush's father—and failed to ask him about how he got into the National Guard during the Vietnam War. This time around, Kimmitt actually claimed he didn't even know about the Dubai Ports World acquisition until after the committee he nominally chaired had approved it and members of Congress had begun to complain.

With the president already greatly weakened after a year of avoidable messes at home and at war, his response to the controversy was initially ineffectual and feckless (he attributed objections to anti-Arab and anti-Muslim bias) and then made the situation worse (he threatened to veto any congressional measure rejecting the deal). Bush, however, could at least be forgiven for turning to his prized White House political machine in distress because it had produced so many short-term successes after the 9/11 attacks.

The key phrase there is "short-term." The United States had been attacked suddenly and dramatically on a day that rivaled Pearl Harbor in both casualties and impact. After 1941, the country really did unite under Franklin Roosevelt to fight the world war the Japanese sneak attack finally provoked the United States to join. After 9/11, the initial unity was fractured in less than six months by President Bush's actions that politicized the aftermath. Given the national trauma, the initial response was reassuring, but political success only lasts if the underlying reality complements it. All the calibrated rhetoric and cute moves can work for a while, they can even help a politician get reelected. But eventually, the facts on the ground (whether in Iraq or inside the government) rule, as Bush ultimately discovered to his regret.

One of the best observations of the Bush team was provided in 2003 by the wife of one of the most experienced of the White House counterterrorism officials, Rand Beers, who served as Richard Clarke's deputy well into 2003. It was temporarily easy for Bush's political operatives to dismiss Rand Beers as a serious critic because he almost immediately signed on as Democratic candidate John Kerry's foreign policy adviser, but the truth is that if the government had approached the terrorist threat more seriously and competently, with less regard for short-term politics, he would probably still be on duty. He is a Marine Corps veteran with more than thirty years of experience in government, including a stint in Ronald Reagan's White House when he was assigned to the sensitive desk just vacated by the disgraced operative Oliver North.

This is what his wife, Bonnie, told *The Washington Post,* in the late spring of 2003, in comments eerily reminiscent of John DiIulio's damning observations nearly two years before: "It's a very closed, small, controlled group. This is an administration that determines what it thinks and then sets about to prove it. There's almost a religious kind of certainty. There's no curiosity about opposing points of view. It's very scary. There's kind of a ghost agenda."

In the immediate aftermath of the 9/11 attacks, that agenda included the continual support of industry groups trying to block congressional action to require a major upgrading of security around the most important elements of the country's industrial and commercial infrastructure—including ports, chemical and nuclear power plants, large shopping malls, and major rail routes and junctions. One of the defining characteristics of the Bush administration from the beginning has been an astonishing degree of attentiveness to the agendas of its business community supporters. This behavior illustrated what can go wrong—politically and substantively—when that attentiveness becomes slavish.

It has long been considered a fact that the exception, also from the beginning, involved the system attacked successfully on 9/11—the airlines. It is true that the security changes since then have probably made the system safe from would-be hijackers armed with sharp box cutters. However, it took the exposure of a plot based in Britain in the summer of 2006—involving a revival with alterations of a decade-old al Qaeda plan to blow up a significant number of airplanes in flight simultaneously—to expose a glaring weakness the administration had not addressed for nearly five years. It was still possible for someone to board an airplane, mix two undetectable liquids, and detonate the result with a simple electronic device.

A fresh round of restrictions of carry-on materials followed, but the hue and cry about bottled water, toothpaste, and iPods could not obscure some disturbing facts about the new Department of Homeland Security. It turned out that not only had research on the obviously vital task of detecting explosives gone essentially nowhere, but that money supposedly set aside for countermeasures against such threats had been diverted, Congress belatedly learned, to pay for budgetary needs elsewhere in the sprawling department, including paying the salaries of the growing army of passenger screeners.

That inconvenient truth—a vivid illustration of the worst kind of policymaking that robs from protection against well-known threats to pay for current underfunded operations—surfaced late in Bush's sixth year in office. In fact, business-influenced fights over homeland security issues had been a fact of Washington life since the immediate aftermath of the 9/11 attacks, and in no area was the squabbling more constant and draining than over security at the country's ports.

Barely two months into the new war on terrorism, there was an innocuous-seeming attempt in the Senate to include roughly $15 billion for beefed-up security operations in a budget bill, about one-fifth of it for transportation-related items, including airports and seaports. Bush opposed it and lobbied all Senate Republicans to keep the money out of the bill, which they promptly did. It might surprise those familiar with the partisan hothouse Washington has become, but there is nothing Democratic or Republican, liberal or conservative about protecting ports from the special danger presented by the millions of unopened metal containers delivered to the country's shores each year. Among port security professionals, there has long been consensus that smugglers as well as terrorists will be effectively deterred if it is known that at least 10 percent of these containers are going to be inspected. In fact, however, the actual percentage has rarely gone above half that, largely because port operators and the largest companies (often huge retailers) on the receiving end lobbied to keep their costs down, their profits up, and their delivery time short. It was not until the summer of 2006, after repeated rebuffed attempts in the intervening years, that a budgetary add-on for port security was finally approved. It was in the context of all this special interest politics that the furor over the Dubai Ports deal added a dramatic climax.

In the meantime, Bush compounded his errors by committing a cardinal security sin—making claims about protection programs that were demonstrably false. To compensate politically for the small percentage of container inspections, Bush had begun what the administration called its Container Security Initiative, designed to identify through intelligence collection and industry and foreign government cooperation those cargoes that could be deemed "suspicious." The logic—inspecting containers before they are ever shipped—seemed sound, but the implementation was spotty and inept on its best days. Four years after the terrorist attacks, Congress's Government Accountability Office concluded that just two out of three containers headed for high-priority ports were even being assessed and that barely seven in ten of those identified as dangerous were being inspected.

If it is possible, the self-inflicted wounds regarding another area of huge concern—chemical manufacturing plants—were even more serious. As accidents around the world, including in the United States, have demonstrated, chemical plants pose a very high risk to the surrounding population even in the absence of threats from terrorism. According to the Environmental Protection Agency, supported by industry studies, two dozen states contain more than one hundred facilities that individually put more than a million people in danger from explosions or other accidental releases of highly toxic gases.

The most prevalent is chlorine, an omnipresent additive at waste treatment plants, but one of the principal ingredients in plastics is a nerve gas and products containing cyanide are used to make nylon, and concentrated ammonia helps make fertilizer. For environmental reasons, the Clean Air Act since 1990 has required chemical plants to assess their risks and accident histories, but they have never been required to consider using manufacturing compounds that are less dangerous.

The 9/11 attacks obviously increased the threat's urgency—everywhere but in the chemical industry and its too accommodating friends in the Bush administration. Within weeks of the terrorist attacks, legislation requiring substitution of safer ingredients where possible was introduced by Senator Jon Corzine of New Jersey (now the state's governor) and was immediately opposed by the American Chemical Council and other industry groups. It was none other than political adviser Karl Rove who was designated to receive a delegation of chemical manufacturers supporting toothless substitute legislation. No vote in Congress was ever even taken and the squabbling over chemical plant security continued for another four years, underlining the extent to which interest group politics was trumping security considerations.

The lobbying over chemical plant security was just as intense from transportation interests seeking to block tighter regulation of the more than sixty thousand tank cars that carry hazardous material by rail. Existing law makes such regulation possible but no major step has been taken since the 9/11 attacks. Anyone who has ever stopped at a railroad crossing and watched tank cars on a freight train pass carrying spray-painted messages like "Jimmy Loves Mary" can understand the vulnerability of this dangerous cargo.

But nothing exceeds the noxious mixture of ineptitude and politics than the creation of the new Department of Homeland Security itself. The idea of putting all the security-related functions of the government under one cabinet-level roof had surfaced in Congress very soon after the 9/11 attacks. In Bush's insular world that made it instantly suspect, and with the added impetus of ideology, the idea was opposed as both unnecessary and a wasteful expansion of the federal government. Time passed, however, and the administration began to lose both the argument and the initiative in early 2002.

Rather than fight a losing battle, the White House political operation prepared secretly to engineer a complete flip-flop. Chief of staff Andrew Card was dispatched to prepare with just a handful of assistants a plan for the department the president's spokesmen continued to oppose. As always happens in government, secrecy and insularity make for very bad policy. And eventually, the entire country would see the results of the decision to fold the once independent Federal Emergency Management Agency deep inside this new department. An operation that proved in the 1990s it could respond with speed and effectiveness to natural disaster, if led by dedicated professionals, lost its zeal, a lot of its money, and a lot of its best people. The results were on graphic display in the horrific aftermath of Hurricane Katrina three years later.

In the short term, however, the new department represented the triumph of politics, and not just with color-coded warnings to the public. The abrupt end to the era of united feelings after 9/11 was signaled by a hubris-drenched speech Bush permitted Karl Rove to give to the Republican National Committee early in 2002, in which he declared that the struggle against terrorism would be the foundation of the party's campaign message in that year's congressional elections, with the Democrats assigned their traditional role of weak-kneed obstructionists.

The initial trouble with Rove's message, though, was that for months the White House lacked an issue around which its most dedicated supporters could be mobilized. If anything, the Democrats were pushing for stronger homeland security measures than Bush was willing to support. The White House's opportunity finally came over what initially appeared to be almost a technical dispute—over labor-management relations inside the Department of Homeland Security, and how much authority managers would have to transfer people and set pay levels outside normal collective bargaining channels.

The White House had its issue when the final passage of the legislation establishing the new department was held up over the matter. Within weeks, television commercials had appeared all over the country slamming Democrats as opponents in the struggle against terrorism and even morphing images of their candidates into the ominous visage of Osama bin Laden himself. It worked; the Republicans regained control of the Senate and strengthened their slender majority in the House of Representatives.

In a supreme irony, it became clear four years later that the so-called fight had all been about nothing. Federal courts routinely started tossing out the department's labor relations rules for the obvious violations of basic labor law they were, and the ordered changes hardly hurt the fight against terrorism. It was a classic example of how Bush's fixation on the politics of security in the short term ended up dividing the country in wartime, and in the long term undermined his credibility.

The truth is that the atmosphere and the screw-ups that produced the Dubai Ports World fiasco, and the much more damaging bungling of homeland security issues in general, had been there all along; before the 9/11 attacks, immediately after them, and they are present still—the bubble, the ideology, the certainty, the cronyism, the special interests. The Bush administration has never been soft on terrorism, has never failed to take it seriously and earnestly, and deserves credit for the absence of follow-up attacks on American soil well into 2007; but it has been consistently myopic, often concerned with other priorities, and therefore frequently wrongheaded. Its dogmatic vision of the forest obscured its vision of the individual trees that are specific threats; that vision also sharply divided along partisan and ideological lines what was, briefly, a united nation.

The USS *Cole* was bombed at anchor in Yemen by al Qaeda terrorists, directly supervised by Osama bin Laden himself, twenty-five days before the presidential election in 2000. Within weeks, the evidence was more than sufficient to justify a "preliminary" intelligence community assessment of the responsibility. The word "preliminary" was used solely for legal reasons. In fact, there was evidence that the *Cole* attack was an al Qaeda operation, and the pile of such evidence kept accumulating.

The White House counterterrorism coordinator, Richard Clarke, had a response outlined and recommended it to President Clinton weeks before he left office. Terrorism in general and al Qaeda in particular were at the top of the foreign policy subjects discussed with senior officials of the incoming administration, including Dick Cheney and Bush himself. All new administrations are famously imbued with a strong sense of fresh-faced omniscience; but what was unusual about the Bush team was its willful failure to treat al Qaeda with the urgency that the *Cole* attack (coming on the heels of bin Laden actions throughout the preceding decade) demanded. Not only did the new president resist entreaties to formally pin the *Cole* incident on al Qaeda and order a response, he also decided to embark on a longer range plan to confront the organization, which had a lower priority than other foreign policy matters during his first year in office, and put off officials who were urging a quick response to specific threats.

Even before the *Cole* incident, Bush had been personally briefed by CIA officials as a candidate. One of them, Ben Bonk of the agency's Counterterrorism Center, told him flat out that more Americans were going to die during the next president's term. Clarke's alarms were more detailed and more frequent, starting in the period before Bush took office and continuing through the summer of 2001.

Beginning in the spring, in the eventually famous words of CIA director George Tenet, "The system was blinking red." What the intelligence agencies generated was a series of "dots," another eventually famous word, that were communicated to very high levels of the administration. In the absence of an alerted officialdom these dots were never connected.

For all the attempts to find sources of inside information about this period, it is easy to forget what the Bush administration was doing and saying in public. Every year, the government is required to issue a formal report on international terrorism, an exercise that necessarily involves top officials and gobs of lower-level documents and meetings, with the secretary of state designated as the spokesman. The first such document produced by the Bush administration was published at the end of April in 2001 over Colin Powell's signature, and it reflects the administration's underlying focus on matters other than terrorism. In its key summary section, the report said:

> While the threat continues, 2000 saw the international community's commitment to counterterrorism cooperation and ability to mobilize its resources grow stronger than ever. As a result, state sponsored terrorism has continued to decline, international isolation of terrorist groups and countries has increased, and terrorists are being brought to justice. Indeed, the vigilance of all members of the international community is central to limiting the mobility and capability of terrorists throughout the world, and both we and the terrorists know it.

Behind the scenes, of course, the dots were beginning to proliferate. These dots were anything but minor tidbits of information. In the intensive investigations that followed the attack on the *Cole,* the

CIA established a clear link between a known Osama bin Laden operative and a man named Khalid al-Mihdhar, who had already been in California and would return for good after a visit to Yemen on July 4, 2001—to become one of the 9/11 hijackers. By May of 2001, the CIA had assembled cables from the previous year that showed Mihdhar had a visa for travel to America and that a known associate, another hijacker-to-be, had arrived in Los Angeles in January of 2000. Partly as a result, there was a meeting of counter-terrorism officials in New York that triggered a low-level and low-intensity search for the two men. In early July, an agent in the FBI's Phoenix office sent a memorandum to headquarters noting "an inordinate number of individuals of investigative interest" who had been at civil aviation schools and raising the possibility of al Qaeda involvement. Had it not been ignored, the memo might have helped the government understand the potential significance of the detention the following month in Minnesota of Zacarias Moussaoui, whose laptop computer contained evidence of contacts, including money transfers, with one of al Qaeda's most important operatives, Ramzi Binalshibh. Moussaoui's detainers did not alert the FBI's top officials in Washington, but the case was known within the CIA (a memo described him as possibly a "suicide hijacker"), including Director Tenet. And finally, by July, CIA research had established that an al Qaeda bigshot known as "Khaled," reliably reported to be recruiting agents to link up inside the United States, was in fact Khalid Sheikh Mohammed, already under indictment for his role in a plot to blow up commercial airliners that had been hatched in the Philippines in the mid-1990s.

President Bush himself had inquired that spring and summer whether the large spike in threat-reporting might involve the United States. Those inquiries are what produced, in the written daily intelligence briefings he preferred, the famous memo in August with the headline "Bin Ladin Determined to Strike in US," which produced no follow-up activity directed from the top whatsoever.

Richard Clarke's informed agitation was the exception, despite a quasi-demotion that denied him regular access to Bush but nonetheless had him in constant contact with National Security Advisor Condoleezza Rice and her deputy, Stephen Hadley. The paper trail, extensive and alarmist, began in the administration's first week with a request Clarke called "urgent" for a meeting of the top foreign and security officials to fix responsibility for the *Cole* attack and authorize a response—a first cousin to the mixture of Special Forces and aid to the anti-Taliban Northern Alliance in Afghanistan to destroy al Qaeda's sanctuary that was ordered after 9/11.

The meeting, an essentially inconclusive affair, did not take place until September 4. Before it convened, Clarke sent Rice a prophetic note, arguing that the first decision needing to be made was whether the administration considered al Qaeda "a big deal" or not. It continued:

> Decision makers should imagine themselves on a future day when the [administration] has not succeeded in stopping Al Qaeda attacks and hundreds of Americans lay dead in several countries, including the US. What would those decision makers wish that they had done earlier? That future day could happen at any time.

The case of the pre-9/11 hard information that was never acted upon despite very high-level awareness of the threat is quite different from farcical foul-ups like the bungled, abortive Dubai Ports World deal, despite the display of similar characteristics of Bush's governance: know-it-all-ism, hubris, secrecy inside a politically impervious bubble, willful ignorance of risks, genetic aversion to changing course on the basis of changed information . . . just for starters.

At the time, no one outside Bush's government knew what was happening and not happening. The first hints of pre-9/11 blunders began to emerge about nine months after the attacks; there was much more in 2003, and then a gusher of damning information in

2004 as the bipartisan 9/11 Commission, whose formation Bush had opposed strenuously and whose investigative work he tried to block repeatedly, first held public hearings and then wrote its unanimous narrative and analysis of the fiasco.

With some of the best minds in the conservative political movement in his employ, the president was able, to an extent, to deflect the disclosures. And with the same people at work, Bush was narrowly reelected in 2004—in very large part because of the ongoing public fears about terrorism, fears that his political team helped stoke. That, however, was then.

George Bush is Exhibit A for the proposition that an American presidency never stops being a work in progress. Election or reelection success never guarantees a single governmental accomplishment; political tactics that work in the short run can backfire spectacularly later, to the country's lasting damage but also to the long-term reputation of the administration in question. The behavior of Bush, Cheney, and the administration's most senior security officials is best seen as a series of time bombs.

When they began to explode—and the mere passage of time guaranteed that they would—every short-term maneuver that kept certain details secret or appeared to explain away others only added to the explosive power. By the end of his sixth year in office, Bush had largely squandered his most important political asset in the wake of the 9/11 attacks—the impression in the country that he was a strong and decisive wartime leader who made big decisions based on facts and principles and presided over a tough and effective program to protect the American homeland.

Shortly after the Dubai Ports mess erupted, two examples surfaced of how such transactions can be handled competently. It turned out that in January of 2006, another firm based in Great Britain with extensive operations in some two hundred port cities around the world, including the Middle East and more than twenty U.S. facilities, had been purchased for nearly $300 million by still another concern owned by the United Arab Emirates. The company, Inchcape Shipping Services, even had a $50 million contract to provide services for the U.S. Navy.

In addition, approval was given for the acquisition by a Dubai-based government entity, for more than $1 billion, of yet another British firm, Doncasters Group Ltd., with even more sensitive operations—including nine manufacturing plants in the United States that among other specialties constituted the Pentagon's only source of the blades used in turbine engines.

In the case of the shipping services deal, the companies' attorneys had contacted the interagency committee months before and had been told in cursory fashion that no approval was required. In the case of the Doncasters transaction, early contact with the interagency committee was followed by detailed briefings of key members of Congress to deal with potential problems at the beginning of the process. In the end, Bush approved the acquisitions with hardly a peep of political protest. The difference involved all-important appearances. In the Dubai Ports deal that caused all the trouble, there was no record indicating a careful check to make sure no detailed probe was needed. In the other acquisitions, by total contrast, attention to the basics of good politics (putting administration and congressional key people on notice, being available for questions, even anticipating and resolving a possible issue or two) ensured they were treated with dispatch.

Much too little, and way too late.

13

ENEMIES

Our war on terror begins with al Qaeda, but it does not end there. It will not end until every terrorist group of global reach has been found, stopped and defeated. Americans are asking, why do they hate us? They hate what we see right here in this chamber—a democratically elected government. Their leaders are self-appointed. They hate our freedoms—our freedom of religion, our freedom of speech, our freedom to vote and assemble and disagree with each other. They want to overthrow existing governments in many Muslim countries, such as Egypt, Saudi Arabia, and Jordan. They want to drive Israel out of the Middle East. They want to drive Christians and Jews out of vast regions of Asia and Africa. These terrorists kill not merely to end lives, but to disrupt and end a way of life. With every atrocity, they hope that America grows fearful, retreating from the world and forsaking our friends. They stand against us, because we stand in their way.

—President George W. Bush, September 20, 2001

HE WAS ALMOST instantly infamous. He was one of the first villains of what was already in late 2001 being called the global war on terror. But only five years later, he was languishing in near-anonymity—not so much forgotten as pushed aside in his prison cell, an inconvenient reminder that things have rarely been as they first seemed in the new world ushered in by the 9/11 attacks and all that followed.

After bombing and then fighting began in Afghanistan, John Walker Lindh—first with a haggard, emaciated face and a few words that made little sense—seemed to fit the bill for a living, breathing symbol of the new enemy. After all, he was an American, a willing fighter for the Taliban movement that had transformed a country battered by its violent history into a rogue state, one that had compounded its sins by providing al Qaeda with assistance and sanctuary.

From the top echelons of the Bush administration, to Democratic and Republican politicians in Congress, and to the merchants of shout on cable television and talk radio, there was almost a competition to find the roughest words to describe the twenty-year-old Californian who was captured on a remote battlefield in Afghanistan's northern territory. "Traitor" was a mild example, and "treason" was a common word used to define his crimes.

Within months, however, the Justice Department would quietly make a plea bargain with the young man, shipping him off to federal prison for twenty years and gaining his attorneys' acceptance of a provision in the agreement preventing them from raising issues associated with his treatment between capture and guilty plea to providing assistance to the Taliban regime.

That was in 2002. Within two years, however, large portions of the real story began to emerge, suggesting that John Walker Lindh was in very large part a guinea pig for many of the most self-defeating and embarrassing practices that have stained the country's reputation, that probably made the fight against the most dangerous enemies harder to wage, and that severely injured the Bush administration's reputation with the American people as the trustworthy and competent prosecutor of a complex and deadly conflict.

From the young man's capture and interrogation—under conditions that meet the definition of torture—through his plea bargain and imprisonment, there is evidence illuminating the administration's most serious self-inflicted wounds: secret overseas prisons, an offshore facility in Cuba's Guantánamo Bay, the use of marginal coercive interrogation techniques, the evolution of an extreme interpretation of near-absolute presidential power over individuals (foreigners and citizens alike), and the ruthless suppression of internal dissent from security and legal professionals inside the government.

John Walker Lindh's case is both symbolic as well as important, because its key decisions were made at the highest levels of Bush's White House, the Justice Department and the Pentagon. From those decisions flowed a series of policies and practices that became routine; Lindh's case turned out to be much more a harbinger than a fluke.

Even while Lindh was being interrogated—often while hourly reports of his answers were being faxed to senior officials' offices in Washington—the administration was embarking on other extreme interpretations of law and presidential power. It detained Americans by the hundreds, and foreigners in this country by the thousands, under conditions that denied them access to lawyers, and spied and eavesdropped on countless others on the flimsiest of investigative excuses. At every stage, government professionals, who urged more traditional and by-the-lawbook approaches to terrorism-related cases in the interest of both greater success and fewer problems down the road, were ignored. It was a classic case of fear and zeal trumping judgment.

From the beginning, there was a passionate debate—initially behind closed government doors, but eventually in full view of the American public and the world—about the legitimacy of these practices and these claims about the government's power over individuals, whether U.S. citizens, legal residents, or people caught up in the war on terrorism's machinery abroad. The debate is still going on and probably will go on forever.

The debate, however, skips over an equally important threshold question—whether all these secret, brutal tactics and all these envelope-pushing claims of unchecked power were wise. The record, from the beginning, is devoid of evidence that the consequences of these tactics were seriously considered. It is at these pivotal moments that governments led and staffed by adults are expected to think through actions, asking the most basic questions—"what if what I'm doing becomes public," "what if what I'm doing inflames domestic or international opinion," "what if the most extreme claims of executive power are rejected in the inevitable clashes in the courts," and "what might be the consequences to the effectiveness of the worldwide struggle itself."

When officials don't do their jobs properly, when instead they yield to a frenzied atmosphere no matter how potentially threatening, they are going to screw up—and that is precisely what happened at the street level of the fight against terrorism in this country and abroad. One can either support Bush's arguments for unchecked authority to declare people enemies and spirit them away to secret detention and even torture; or one can vehemently oppose them. The first step should be to consider whether tactics and strategies are truly essential, that there is no other way to proceed, if they will undercut political support for a long war in this country and abroad, and whether they can survive public scrutiny at the unavoidable moment when secrecy breaks down.

In the case of John Walker Lindh, every red flag, every time bomb that ultimately exploded, was present at the outset. And he was just the first.

Twenty years old at the time, and a teenaged convert to Islam while growing up in Northern California, Lindh had journeyed to Afghanistan, embraced its Taliban regime, and trained in its camps where would-be terrorists were also given instruction. He had also taken up arms (a rifle) against the indigenous fighting force, the Northern Alliance, that the United States used as proxies for the assault on Afghanistan's capital, Kabul. Lindh was captured with scores of other armed men on the battlefield by Northern Alliance fighters and taken to the town of Mazar-i-Sharif, and turned over to two Central Intelligence agents once his identity was learned.

The agents used a video camera in their initial interrogation of Lindh, and used a threat of imminent death to try to get him to start talking, which he did not. Even at this initial stage, the agents were communicating with their superiors, who passed on information to senior officials in the Defense and Justice departments as well as the White House. The interrogation, however, was soon interrupted by a prisoner uprising, during which one of the agents, Johnny "Mike" Spann, was killed under horrific conditions, becoming the first American to die in combat in the war and naturally inflaming American passions even more.

The uprising was quickly quelled and Lindh was recaptured as well as shot in the leg. Shortly thereafter, his status became publicly known and a media cause célèbre. Lindh's father retained a lawyer in California who was told by a Pentagon official that the young man's wound was being attended to and that he was being treated not only decently but in full accord with the protections of the Geneva Conventions for prisoners of war.

Actually, within minutes of the commencement of the second round of interrogation, the now larger contingent of agents and soldiers had checked with the senior officer overseeing operations in the town (an admiral) and were told that Pentagon general counsel William J. Haynes had authorized them to "take the gloves off" in questioning Lindh.

Once it was clear his wound was not serious, it was ignored. Lindh was stripped naked, bound tightly to a stretcher, propped up, denied food for days, kept from sleeping for more than a few moments at a time, and threatened with death. This treatment lasted for nearly two months—in an Afghan school building being used as a detention facility, at one of the military's first bases in the country, and eventually on board a naval vessel; all before he was provided any legal assistance, or even learned that a lawyer had been retained for him in America.

During his period of secret confinement and torture, in still another harbinger of things to come in the war on terror, soldiers and agents involved in handling Lindh posed for still photographs and video recordings standing next to his naked body. During this time no one ever developed a shred of evidence that Lindh had any special status in his Taliban unit, or even knew anything of consequence about terrorism in general or al Qaeda in particular; that he was nothing more than a grunt with a rifle, just an American who had committed a serious crime at the worst possible moment.

The Geneva Conventions do not mince words when it comes to the treatment of prisoners. At a minimum, they are supposed to be clothed and fed, given medical attention as needed, and allowed to rest. Humiliation is also forbidden.

Far from raising any alarms among the Bush administration officials aware—in graphic detail—of what was going on, the Lindh case instead prompted top-level discussions of how to handle the rapidly growing number of people getting snared in the new war's dragnet. As it turned out, at the end of 2001 as well as far into 2006, there was a premium on maximizing power and secrecy; and the all-important distinction between a John Walker Lindh and a true terrorist disappeared.

The first memo traffic dates from the end of 2001, when the evidence surfaced of a plan to hold captured individuals outside the United States (Guantánamo was recommended very early), presumably so that the location was beyond the reach of the federal courts, allowing interrogation techniques that constituted torture, and arguing that a president's "inherent" power as commander in chief of the armed forces permitted both the designation of an individual (citizen or not) as an enemy combatant and his indefinite incarceration. So-called aggressive interrogation was permitted because the Geneva Conventions did not apply to members of nongovernment organizations using terrorism; the conventions were, in the famous dismissive word used in writing by then White House counsel Alberto Gonzales, "quaint."

The record shows that the few red flags raised at the time were almost casually brushed aside, showing the extent to which ideology and hubris and secrecy were defining Bush administration traits. The only top-level official to object occasionally, and not always forcefully, was Secretary of State Colin Powell, who had been both a chairman of the Joint Chiefs of Staff and a White House national security advisor in his long career in government. At least for the record, he warned early on (as he would argue much later as a private citizen) that Bush's approach to prisoners "will reverse over a century of U.S. policy and practices in supporting the Geneva Conventions and undermine the protections of the law of war for our troops, both in this context and in general."

Even one of the true-believing senior officials—then a deputy assistant attorney general under John Ashcroft (his name was John Yoo)—felt obliged to note prophetically in one of his memos that detention outside the United States meant detention ostensibly beyond the federal courts' reach, but that "there remains some litigation risk that a district court might reach the opposite result."

More telling is the story of what happened to one young lawyer in the Justice Department who directly challenged her political superiors. Jesselyn Radack was on duty one day in December of 2001, while Lindh was in secret custody, and was asked by a prosecutor about the propriety of permitting an FBI agent to interrogate him. As a matter of ethics, and with a criminal inquiry then fully under way, Radack said that Lindh should not be seen outside the presence of his lawyer.

Her advice was ignored. Furthermore, she was told that an unfavorable job performance report would go into her personnel file if she didn't leave the government. That is what she did, joining a law firm in Washington and then providing Lindh case documents to the press. When the department retaliated by opening a criminal investigation of her and telling her new employer of it, she was dismissed.

As it became more and more clear that Lindh did not even qualify as a small fish in the struggle with terrorism, the Bush administration decided not to send him to Guantánamo, which would mean indefinite incarceration, more interrogation, and more publicity. Instead, it sought to quickly plead him out in California federal court, and given the white-hot public passions of the moment, his guilty plea and twenty-year sentence for aiding the Taliban in Afghanistan made sense at the time, though the provision in his deal that he not publicly discuss the circumstances of his brutal interrogation should have been a red flag.

Another early case of a U.S. citizen captured in Afghanistan at the same time lent even more perspective. He, too, was a Taliban grunt with a gun, but there was no other evidence to suggest he might have been a terrorist. Yaser Hamdi was technically a citizen; he had been born in Louisiana to Saudi parents but had returned to their country as a child.

Unlike Lindh, Hamdi was an early export to the fledgling prison in Cuba, where he was held under the Bush claim that people could be detained indefinitely and denied access to both a lawyer and a court to judge the propriety of their detention. As the rules and procedures became better understood and human rights lawyers used his case and another to challenge them, Hamdi was moved to the naval brig in Charleston, South Carolina, where he was held incommunicado after the summer of 2003 while his case worked its way through the courts.

Before the Supreme Court, Hamdi won, showing that John Yoo's muted warning that the house of cards represented by the administration's approach to "enemy combatants" was indeed vulnerable to judicial challenge. The Court did not deny a president's power to declare someone an enemy, but it upheld every person's right to challenge his detention in some kind of hearing.

Confronted with the need to go through a formal process and produce evidence (which didn't exist) to justify his detention, the administration simply caved. By the summer of 2004, Hamdi was back home in Saudi Arabia living with his family. To justify all the bother and expense, the U.S. government made him renounce his citizenship, report all travel to the Saudi authorities for fifteen years, and agree never to travel to Afghanistan, Iraq, Syria, and Israel or any of its occupied territories.

Caught under the same circumstances but amidst huge prejudicial publicity, John Walker Lindh was tortured and sent off to prison for twenty years. More quietly, Yaser Hamdi walked.

There was still another guinea pig in this new war—his detention case was also an early example of the Bush policies in divisive, ineffectual action—but the proper perspective for this bizarre, ugly saga involves the first big al Qaeda fish landed after the 9/11 attacks, Abu Zubaydah. Just how big a fish remains a matter of some dispute among the FBI, intelligence agencies, and the more detached 9/11 Commission. But at the time he fell badly wounded during a raid on his Pakistan hideout roughly six months after the al Qaeda attacks, no more senior figure in the terrorist network had been taken alive. At a minimum he had handled logistical details involving actual al Qaeda terrorists, facilitating transportation into and out of Afghanistan as well as communications with operatives who had been sent on missions abroad, including the 9/11 attacks.

The question was what to do with him and where. Transported in secrecy to Thailand, Zubaydah was initially questioned by FBI agents with the assistance of intelligence operatives, using the conventional techniques that had proved their value in the thorough investigations that followed the terrorist assaults on the World Trade Center in New York in 1993, the American embassies in Tanzania and Kenya five years later, and the USS *Cole* in 2000. His wounds were attended to and agents attempted a mixture of rapport with him along with a (false) sense that they were simply trying to get him to confirm information they already possessed.

At first, there was success. All sides in what eventually degenerated into an FBI-CIA feud agreed that Zubaydah, among other tidbits, had identified Khalid Sheikh Mohammed from a picture the Americans had—an important step on the road to the 9/11 mastermind's eventual capture. Shortly after his interrogation began, however, CIA officials reported that Zubaydah had begun to clam up, and so they sought approval from superiors (over FBI objections) to switch to what amounted to torture. After Bush himself had signed a secret directive following the 9/11 attacks, the CIA was authorized to send a team from its Counterterrorism Center in Washington to take over the interrogation. These CIA members told their FBI counterparts that their interrogation techniques had been approved by the White House.

Shortly after their arrival on the scene, Zubaydah's treatment changed. He was stripped naked and all furniture removed from his cell. Still not fully recovered from his wounds, he was prevented from sleeping for long stretches, in part by subjecting him to loud rock 'n' roll music, and the temperature in his room was lowered sharply as well.

There is no assertion yet on public record that the quantity or quality of the information he provided improved as a result of this mistreatment, but there is evidence that the government ignored some of Zubaydah's early attempts to steer FBI agents away from potential suspects he considered inconsequential figures.

The best known of these is another person, also a U.S. citizen, whose detainment without rules was challenged (this time unsuccessfully, but under circumstances that exposed the handling of the matter as a sham) before the Supreme Court. His name is Jose Padilla.

In May of 2002, waiting federal agents detained Padilla on arrival in Chicago from overseas, carrying more than $10,000 in cash, a cell phone, and e-mail addresses of known al Qaeda operatives. In June, the day after his transfer to military custody as an "enemy combatant" was approved, Attorney General Ashcroft made his detention public while on a trip to Russia. He dramatically announced that Padilla was suspected of planning an attack in the United States using explosives mixed with radioactive isotopes—the so-called dirty bomb long feared in the counterterrorism community.

As a citizen Padilla was ordered held incommunicado in the same South Carolina brig as Hamdi, and human rights lawyers again began filing motions on his behalf, testing the government's ability to hold individuals without charges and without access to a lawyer or the courts. As it turned out, Padilla would not actually see an attorney until two years after his original detention, but his case nonethe-less proceeded through the system with mixed results. One appeals court decision ordering that he be tried as a criminal and not in any military-run system was overturned on a technicality by the Supreme Court in 2004.

A second case produced another appeals court ruling upholding the government's power over him, but just days before a Supreme Court hearing on the case in November of 2005, the government abruptly changed strategies. Out went the allegedly ominous dirty bomb plot, and in came a sudden indictment by a Miami grand jury on charges that Padilla had conspired with others to commit acts of terrorism outside the country.

That paved the way for a divided Supreme Court to rule that his case should not be heard under these altered circumstances, though it also produced an unusually sharp rebuke from a senior appeals court judge. Said well-known conservative jurist J. Michael Luttig (whom Bush considered for both Supreme Court vacancies that oc-curred in 2005), the government's gamesmanship had risked its credibility in the judicial process and left the impressions that Padilla's military detention had all been a mistake. Of course, it had been.

Padilla is a onetime gang member from Chicago who converted to Islam in prison, and subsequently to violent radicalism. There is considerable evidence that he was in Pakistan in early 2002, where many of al Qaeda's most important figures had escaped just weeks before. There is also evidence that he at least talked about attacks with Khalid Sheikh Mohammed and others, including the potential use of radioactive explosives. The charges against him in Florida are anything but frivolous and carry a life sentence upon conviction for good reason. Nonetheless, as he faced weeks on trial for conspiring to support terrorism and to murder people abroad, Padilla was anything but the infamous dirty bomber of John Ashcroft's hyped announce-ment years before. Instead he looks more like one of nearly three hundred people Justice Department attorneys have won convictions against for "terrorism-related" offenses. Still, there have been three times that many investigations and only eighty-one people by the late spring of 2007 had received sentences of five years or more in federal prison.

There is also evidence that Padilla was somewhere between a blowhard and an idiot. One source of this information turns out to be Abu Zubaydah himself, long before Padilla's detention and long before Ashcroft's hyped announcement.

According to several accounts, Zubaydah mocked Padilla's intelligence, ability, and even commitment to much more than self-glorification and said that others in the organization shared his assessment. He gave an illustration of Padilla the Plotter in action. Zubaydah described his own knowledge of critical nuclear weapons technology involving centrifuges to separate out weapons-grade material from uranium. In an example of low-tech enthusiasm, he said Padilla claimed he could get usable material by dissolving uranium in a bucketful of liquid and then twirling it in a rapid circle using his arm.

Meanwhile, Padilla sat in South Carolina and Zubaydah was abused and then secreted along with dozens of the government's "high-value" prisoners in CIA-run facilities abroad. The new war on terror began employing a new weapon—secretly grabbing people off the street and transporting them in small jets to countries where torture is routine—mainly Egypt, but on occasion Morocco, Syria (a war on terrorism ally for the first year), and Jordan. To date, there has not been one confirmed case where this practice had anything substantial to do with the detention of a big-time terrorist or the thwarting of a truly serious plot. But there has been a huge pile of evidence that it has significantly undercut America's reputation in the world, severely exacerbated relations with would-be allies, and ultimately made more difficult the very struggle it was intended to assist. The few early warnings behind the scenes hinted this practice would cause more trouble than it avoided. They were, as usual, ignored.

The one significant exception involved an al Qaeda operative (his name is Ibn al-Sheikh al-Libi) who had been in charge of one of the terrorists' training camps in Afghanistan. Early in the war, and with the FBI again objecting, the CIA shipped him off for what the bureaucrats call "aggressive interrogation" in Egypt. Not surprisingly, Libi turned out to be the exception who proved the rule that torture usually produces unreliable intelligence. He was the original source of a claim often parroted by top administration officials, including Colin Powell in his presentation to the United Nations shortly before the invasion of Iraq, that Saddam Hussein had offered to train al Qaeda agents in the use of chemical or biological weapons. Not only did subsequent investigation show the claim was false, as were all suggestions of an operational relationship between Iraq and Osama bin Laden's organization, but Libi himself eventually recanted.

The problem is perfectly posed in the government's preferred term for what amounts to kidnapping—"extraordinary rendition," a classic Orwellian euphemism. Rendition is a federal legal term involving sending a person in one jurisdiction to the one where he has been charged with something; in state proceedings it is known by its more commonly used term "extradition." The adjective "extraordinary" has no meaning, but it falsely implies necessity.

On an extremely limited basis, beginning in the mid-1990s and involving at most a handful of cases, people U.S. agents suspected of significant involvement with terrorism were transported to countries that either had outstanding warrants of their own against the suspects or had already convicted them in absentia. Most of the suspects involved were wanted in Egypt after having participated in violent movements there. It was a nasty business, but using a large loophole in the United Nations Convention Against Torture (ratified by Congress in 1994), it was legally defensible.

After the 9/11 attacks, in the panic to search for additional plots, White House counsel Gonzales began talking of a "new paradigm" in handling terrorism cases, and Vice President Cheney famously said that the United States would have to be prepared to inhabit "the dark side" of counterterrorist operations.

Almost immediately, the criteria changed; there was no more requirement for an outstanding warrant or conviction in a torturing country, merely a pro forma "assurance" that of course the receiving country would not use torture on the "rendered" suspect. From the outset, Bush himself declared that "torture is never acceptable nor do we hand over people to be tortured"—a flat-out falsehood from the beginning. Suspects were grabbed on five continents, nearly two hundred in all, and shipped off to their horrid fates, weeks and often months before their families had any idea where they were or what had happened to them.

As was predicted, it didn't take long for reports of secret U.S. flights to begin appearing, and of jets either owned outright by the U.S. government or through easily identified dummy corporations. The outcries, especially from abroad and within the Muslim world that the United States was ostensibly trying to woo, never let up. Undeterred by these self-inflicted wounds, Defense Secretary Rumsfeld even added a distant cousin of this program in war-torn Iraq, personally ordering that as many as a hundred suspected insurgents be held secretly with no formal notification of their capture to agencies like the Red Crescent while they were "aggressively" interrogated.

There was one more terrorism time bomb waiting patiently to explode, and it detonated to the administration's embarrassment and dismay in the summer of 2006. Even as suspects once called by Donald Rumsfeld the worst of the worst were arriving in jumpsuits, blindfolds, and chains at Guantánamo nearly five years before, Bush had announced plans to try them (his preferred phrase was "bring them to justice") using military commissions entirely of his own creation. For months and then years, however, nothing actually happened. First John Walker Lindh and then Jose Padilla had their cases switched to normal civilian courts, as did several cases involving people in the United States of varying (usually very low) degrees of seriousness and no imminent threats.

As with the issue of detainment without counsel, Bush's decision to establish what became known as military commissions was criticized by human and civil rights advocates and quickly became the object of lawsuits. Once the rules Bush was proposing to govern the activity of these commissions became known, they were severely criticized from within the military itself by the Pentagon's large and experienced staff of attorneys in the Judge Advocate General's Corps. The criticism and the warnings about the program took on two forms. The proposed rules would have made it possible to admit hearsay evidence in eventual trials, which would disclose secret intelligence information to commission officials that remained secret from the accused. It would liberally permit evidence developed through what ordinary people call torture, and in the process would unilaterally alter the terms of U.S. compliance with the binding requirements of both the Geneva Conventions and the U.S. Uniform Code of Military Justice.

The administration was advised by the military lawyers that its plans not only risked similar extralegal treatment of American servicemen and agents captured in the future but also would cause severe political and image problems. They also said that the federal courts were very likely to block the administration's plans. In the late spring of 2006, a divided Supreme Court did exactly that, decisively, thus throwing more than four years of work out the window and requiring a legislative scramble that fall to provide the necessary authority for trials to proceed. By mid-2007, nearly six years after the 9/11 attacks, not a single trial had begun.

The legal, political, and foreign policy mess made of the war on terror abroad was only compounded—again needlessly—at home. In the frantic, near-panic atmosphere after the attacks, legitimately fearing more assaults might be coming, President Bush committed the cardinal government sin: overreaction and a gross misapplication of resources.

The most precious of those resources, beyond the country's obvious economic and security strengths, were the anger and instantly selfless instincts for a unity of purpose felt among nearly all Americans in the immediate aftermath of the attacks. Like most people, Bush had a shaky, uncertain beginning as the scope of the unprecedented assault became clear. But the president found himself, and his voice, at a National Cathedral memorial service three days later and again on the heartbreaking pile of debris at the southern tip of Manhattan.

Almost immediately, however, he began making decisions that appear in retrospect to have been more impulsive than carefully considered, and which slowly but surely polarized a once unified nation. The basic reaction, encapsulated in his famous instruction to John Ashcroft to never let this happen again, was entirely understandable. In operation, though, it revealed a fundamental, conceptual error, as if the entire country and everyone in it could be methodically sifted until threats and would-be attackers were discovered.

At first, hardly anyone noticed; at most a few peeps of protest, albeit prophetic, from the left and the libertarian right as a new era of intense domestic security operations commenced. The highly visual measures to deny would-be attackers access to airports and airplanes, at least until it was discovered nearly five years later that virtually nothing had been done to protect Americans from easily assembled liquid explosive bombs, was a factor. So, too, were the initial successes abroad in toppling the hated Taliban regime and even the ease with which Saddam Hussein's dictatorship in Iraq disintegrated.

When the war in Iraq turned into a murderous mess, when a violent insurgency sank fresh roots in Afghanistan, Americans began to look more critically at their domestic security and increasingly found fault with it.

Its most vivid example involved that colossal mistake in judgment when Bush unleashed his campaign boss, Karl Rove, to tell the Republican National Committee that the defining issue of the 2002 elections would be security, with his guys on the strong side and the aimless Democrats on the weak side. The second mistake was to take a minor dispute over labor relations in the new Homeland

Security Department and use it to frame the alleged difference. Both tactics worked beautifully in the short term, buttressed by yahoo politics on social issues like whether gay people should be allowed to marry. And Bush won narrow reelection two years later.

In America, however, elections are rarely defining events. More often they are way stations, referendums on the status quo whose very mandate is subject to debate the minute they end. At the national level, presidents still have to get their programs enacted and their policies established and then administer them competently and effectively. Actions and campaign-like statements that work in the short run lose their magic when they boomerang in the end.

Inside this country, the fear and anger after 9/11 inevitably produced a climate that both justified and supported stern measures to assist counterterrorism operations. But by overreacting and politicizing his policies, Bush undercut their effectiveness, and ultimately replaced that climate of consensus with virtually nonstop controversy. Consider:

- One of the first responses was an effort to update the country's laws concerning terrorism and related crimes, known as the Patriot Act. With only one dissenting vote in the Senate (Democrat Russ Feingold of Wisconsin), it made a major change that had overwhelming support across party lines, permitting information directly relating to terrorist activity uncovered by intelligence agencies (primarily through eavesdropping) abroad to be used in criminal investigations and prosecutions. However, by letting his guard down and allowing investigative agencies as well as legislators to pack the measure with what amounted to policy wish lists, Bush sowed the seeds of controversy and division down the road. The most publicized example was a provision (almost never used, it turned out) permitting the FBI to inspect the library activity of Americans. By the time the act was up for renewal, the administration's excesses had spawned a coalition of conservatives and liberals that actually blocked final passage for several weeks at the end of 2005 while changes were negotiated.

- In the frantic near-panic after 9/11, Bush also approved a flagrant misuse of a basic feature of criminal law that severely injured relations with the country's Muslim minority and also produced needless controversy. Witnesses in criminal cases, under a law passed in 1984, who are determined by the authorities to be likely to flee, can be detained; they are called material witnesses. But Bush permitted the abuse of this law as a pretext for locking up people in order to investigate their activities further. Virtually all the proceedings were initially held in secret, with sealed records, and thus secret evidence, often no lawyers were involved, and family members remained in terrified ignorance of what was happening to loved ones. People were typically held incommunicado for weeks and in one eventually highly publicized case (in a federal facility in Brooklyn) were beaten and abused by guards. In the inevitable publicity this abuse of power received, it was revealed that nearly a hundred people had been detained this way, more than half of them were released with no charges at all, and nearly all the rest faced nothing more than common violations of immigration rules.

- In another overreaction, the president too quickly signed off on a proposal by the National Security Agency, the country's electronic intelligence super-bureaucracy, to use computers to mine telephone records in search of communication between suspected al Qaeda members overseas and people inside the United States. Despite the 1978 law already streamlining procedures for quickly securing secret surveillance warrants from a special court, Bush and Vice President Cheney swiftly approved the new proposal. They did so without either firmly establishing their legal authority or making sure that a warrant-free program was even necessary—much less thinking through the consequences of the inevitable public disclosure of such a large program (which occurred four years later).

- In the unavoidable numbers game surrounding counterterrorism operations in America, the undeniable fact that the country remains at serious risk of another attack and will be so indefinitely has been buried in a blizzard of near-trivia. For each of the few cases of actual threat (the fingerprint of a young Jordanian man denied entry into this country in 2003 turned up on what was left of a suicide bomber in Iraq two years later), there have been scores of people who did not even rise to the level of a John Walker Lindh. One study of actual prosecutions of individuals classified as terrorism-related (including purely domestic non–al Qaeda crimes) found that nearly all of the more than four hundred people charged with violations had committed immigration-related offenses. Of some forty cases called terrorism-related, many involved "plots" that had barely progressed beyond the talking stage, usually in the presence of an undercover FBI agent and occasionally what amounted to a paid provocateur. The administration has an unassailable case that after 9/11 nothing should be ignored, but publicizing and politicizing routine actions takes an inevitable toll on public support and vigilance. Few Americans have forgotten that an actual second attack—the mailing of weaponized anthrax spores to media and political figures shortly after 9/11 that killed six people—remains an unsolved mystery deep into 2006.

Begun in outrage and tragedy, the war on terror had the complete support of a country unified in sorrow and anger. That unity has since disintegrated, not because the feelings are any less intense but because of the way the war was prosecuted. And what was once an overwhelming natural advantage for President Bush and his political party has now become at best a marginal asset.

In the spring of 2007, John Walker Lindh's parents began a media campaign to prepare the way for a legal effort to get the twenty-year sentence for the "American Taliban" reduced. They acted after an Australian, David Hicks, detained under similar circumstances in late 2001 was let out of confinement at Guantánamo Bay and sent home after he acknowledged his responsibility for training in Afghanistan and supporting the Taliban regime.

Hicks had also been captured by the Northern Alliance after Kabul had fallen, but had never been charged with any specific terrorist act or plan. Without the frenzied atmosphere that had accompanied Lindh's detainment, there was not a murmur of protest when Hicks was released.

14

PRELUDE TO CATASTROPHE

Another argument holds that opposing Saddam Hussein would cause even greater troubles in that part of the world, and interfere with the larger war against terror. I believe the opposite is true. Regime change in Iraq would bring about a number of benefits to the region. When the gravest of threats are eliminated, the freedom-loving peoples of the region will have a chance to promote the values that can bring lasting peace. As for the reaction of the Arab "street," the Middle East expert Professor Fouad Ajami predicts that after liberation, the streets in Basra and Baghdad are "sure to erupt in joy in the same way the throngs in Kabul greeted the Americans." Extremists in the region would have to rethink their strategy of Jihad. Moderates throughout the region would take heart. And our ability to advance the Israeli-Palestinian peace process would be enhanced, just as it was following the liberation of Kuwait in 1991.

—**Vice President Dick Cheney, August 26, 2002**

NOT LONG AFTER the United States invaded Iraq in March of 2003, an oddly revealing parlor game sprang up among political junkies and foreign policy types in Washington. It revolved around what in ordinary circumstances would have seemed a simple question: precisely when did President Bush decide to do it?

There were many competing answers, none of them even remotely resembling certainty, and all of them hinting at a revealing ultimate answer: namely, that no one had a clue about the definitive moment.

The favored answers were all over the lot. The defense secretary, Donald Rumsfeld, had clearly begun updating on-the-shelf Pentagon war plans by December of 2001. There were reports that high-level Saudi guests had emerged from the White House in January of 2002 to reveal that Bush himself had said an invasion was coming. By the spring, when Bush had begun publicly to make demands that the Iraqi regime start complying with the letter of United Nations arms inspection resolutions, a few prominent legislators with regular White House invitations, notably Senator Joseph Biden (the Democrats' ranking person on the Foreign Relations Committee), had begun passing the word that invading Iraq was an assumed given among top officials. Around that time, a member of the Senate Intelligence Committee said that U.S. troops would be in Baghdad by the spring of 2003. And also around that time, with Osama bin Laden and a few top surviving members of al Qaeda still at large somewhere and with a nascent, weak regime anything but secure in Afghanistan, reports first surfaced of Special Forces and other military and intelligence assets being transferred for possible use against Iraq. These types of actions had to have followed a distinct decision to move against Saddam Hussein.

All of these nominees for the answer to the parlor game's question make a powerful point about how a president can make a world-class mistake. The point has nothing to do with a policy choice that may turn out horribly wrong because of flaws in execution or unforeseen developments that cause a carefully constructed plan to disintegrate. This world-class mistake with gigantic consequences did not stem from a policy choice that could have gone either way; it stemmed from a much more basic flaw in this presidency.

In modern government, a truly major decision cannot come merely after isolated consideration of the merits alone. Given the complexities of the country and the world, there are very few things a sensible president can decide to do that aren't inextricably connected to considerations of how, why, when, and with what foreseeable consequences. Each of those considerations, by definition, must have the potential of reversing the "whether" decision or else that government simply is not doing its basic job.

The Bush administration, however, contained all the ingredients for a perfect storm, a screw-up that would cost thousands of lives and hundreds of billions of dollars, severely weaken America's position in the world, profoundly affect the larger struggle with terrorism and Islamic extremism, and in the process wreck the president's standing with his own citizens. It is a lethal, possibly unique combination—strong, mutually reinforcing officials certain of their judgments after long experience, operating in a tiny, almost hermetically sealed bubble of secrecy and isolation, cherry-picking supportive information from favored sources inside and outside the government, and wrapping them all in a package that was sold to the public by a first-rate public relations team richly experienced in the short-term skills of winning election campaigns in an atmosphere still defined by the deep and festering wounds of the 9/11 attacks.

What was missing—because it was carefully and methodically suppressed by a combination of arrogance, hubris, and finely honed skills in the black arts of bureaucratic infighting—were some of the most important resources a president in competent command of his office needs. The careful airing of alternatives (through the press via trial balloons and privately with politicians who don't work directly for him) is one way presidents avoid serious goofs. That process, complete with passionate devil's advocates, is supposed to be institutionalized inside a competent administration and White House. And the need for extreme, organized care in execution is even more necessary when the idea under consideration is the invasion of another country.

Contrary to myths sometimes popular on the political left, Bush did not order the invasion of Iraq simply because many of his closest advisers came from a school of thought that for years had favored the destruction of Iraq's dangerous dictatorship as part of a larger dream of a transformed Middle East, or to gain control over huge reserves of crude oil. The invasion is unthinkable without the context of the 9/11 attacks, and the only evidence that has ever surfaced about the administration prior to them is that Iraq and the danger posed by al Qaeda were well down its list of foreign policy priorities until that horrid September morning. Except for a few impulsive words in the immediate aftermath of the attacks, moreover, the available evidence is that conquering Iraq was not a serious option then, either; the first decisions all involved plans primarily put together within the Central Intelligence Agency to topple the Taliban regime in Afghanistan quickly, protect the United States from further attack, and hunt al Qaeda members worldwide.

Instead, serious planning for the invasion of Iraq followed an event that turned out to be something quite different from what it was made to appear at the time—the furious final assault on al Qaeda from the air and on the ground near the end of 2001. The bombing was massive, and as a force of Afghan fighters moved into the mountains, the atmosphere created in the press was climactic, as if any moment bin Laden himself would turn up dead or in chains. In the area as well were several hundred highly skilled American fighters, but the Bush administration (at the top, not at the operational level on the scene) decided to withhold them from the battle. Instead, they relied on the Afghan surrogates hiding in the mountains near the border with Pakistan, as the United States had done in the initial assault on the Taliban regime. It was one of those decisions that in microcosm reflected blind faith in Donald Rumsfeld's obsession with avoiding traditional commitments of massive, overwhelming force and relying instead on smaller, more mobile, and faster forces that could use local fighters backed by massive airpower to achieve objectives with minimal casualties. It was an intriguing theory, a compelling alternative to Colin Powell's doctrine of overwhelming force that had been applied in the first Gulf War in the 1991 campaign to toss the Iraqi invaders out of Kuwait. There is, however, no more basic mistake in government than blind adherence to any doctrine. This was, potentially, the endgame for al Qaeda;

its fighters and what remained of its top leadership were trapped in the mountains and subjected to massive bombardment; a minimal commitment was all that was needed to complete an assault on al Qaeda in its Afghanistan sanctuary and with it an initial response to the 9/11 attacks that had the support of virtually the entire country.

And then, after at least some communication between the two groups of fighters about a possible surrender, bin Laden and his battered band simply vanished. Operating in secrecy, the facts about what had transpired did not emerge immediately from the Bush administration. The Tora Bora episode, however, was a quick course in a basic rule of politics and government: suppressing information is a short-term tactic that will eventually backfire when the information inevitably emerges. By the spring of 2002, the hyped battle of Tora Bora had become, politically and strategically, the first significant setback for Bush in the post-9/11 worldwide confrontation with international terrorism.

The reaction to it could only have occurred inside a bubble, populated by a few headstrong, arrogant, isolated know-it-alls. At first, Bush continued to concentrate on the remote tribal territories on either side of the Afghanistan-Pakistan border. A successor operation, code-named Anaconda, and accompanied by as much publicity as the assault on Tora Bora, battered al Qaeda and Taliban remnants for weeks with assistance from the NATO force that had by then become part of operations in Afghanistan. Eventually, however, the attack lost steam without producing the hoped-for results.

But instead of focusing on the eminently soluble problem— scattered, depleted, and poorly armed fighters, a nascent regime in Kabul facing gigantic economic and reconstruction problems after more than twenty years of fighting as well as an uncertain security situation—Bush switched gears. The public face of the abrupt shift was the sudden halt to his bin Laden–fixated rhetoric. From idle, silly chatter about wanting him dead or alive, Bush began to speak dismissively of the 9/11 mastermind and eventually not to speak of him at all. The secret face, though it did not stay secret for very long because too many people were involved, consisted of a significant transfer of people and assets from Afghanistan to bases and staging areas in the Persian Gulf.

Even before the shift was fully under way, Bush began to talk about the new war in very different terms. What had begun shortly after 9/11—backed by a virtually unanimous congressional resolution—as an all-out assault on international terrorism with the overt support of more than ninety nations, designed to crush al Qaeda and confront countries that harbored its members—suddenly morphed into a much grander set of goals and targets, among which Saddam Hussein's regime in Iraq was in the center.

There was dissent from this new formulation of a doctrine of preemptive war, from abroad and inside the United States even within the administration and the U.S. military.

Among the tiny band of policymakers, however, there is no evidence all these years later of the occurrence of any serious debate, of that most basic of governmental processes—serious consideration of a serious position, complete with detailed assessments of pros, cons, consequences, and alternatives. Instead, there were pronouncements, which for the most part passed through a stenographic, as opposed to critical, news media to a public still justifiably astir after the 9/11 attacks and almost instinctively willing to trust its mobilizing government.

Bush's first State of the Union address after the attacks, in late January of 2002, is famous for its surprise description of an "axis of evil" in the world, specifically said by the president to include Iraq, Iran, and North Korea.

Less well remembered, but equally surprising in its sudden change of policy, was the full quote: "States like these and their terrorist allies constitute an axis of evil, arming to threaten the peace of the world. We'll be deliberate, yet time is not on our side. I will not wait on events while dangers gather. I will not stand by as peril draws closer and closer. The United States of America will not permit the world's most dangerous regimes to threaten us with the world's most destructive weapons."

This first whiff of a doctrine known as preemption got much more flesh on its bones as the year unfolded. For the elites, for the rest of the world, and for the rest of the government, there was a new foreign policy document, prepared by National Security Advisor Condoleezza Rice, augustly entitled the National Security Strategy of the United States. It broke new ground by defining an aggressive American involvement in the world that would seek "a new balance of power that favors human freedom" through economic leverage and diplomacy if possible, but through the use of force if necessary. What is more, the document directly challenged the role of international institutions in the post-9/11 world by paying lip service to them but stating a new determination to act alone or with "coalitions of the willing" if considered necessary.

For the public, Bush packaged his new doctrine in a commencement address that June at the United States Military Academy. Up to the moment of his arrival at West Point, the American tradition had been to go to war with countries that attacked us or committed massive aggression first, and the exceptions involving Mexico, Spain, and Vietnam in our history if anything reinforced that tradition. But in his speech, which would be repeated in different form and forums for months, the message was that the United States would not wait.

Or, as Bush put it, "We must take the battle to the enemy, disrupt his plans and confront the worse threats before they emerge. If we wait for threats to fully materialize, we will have waited too long."

The enemy was not the radical regime that was assumed already to have made a nuclear weapon and was active in smuggling missile systems and other elements of technology abroad (North Korea); nor was it the radical regime that already had an active nuclear program under way in secret and was on the verge of being able to enrich uranium to weapons-grade material (Iran).

Instead, it was Iraq. As Bush proceeded from his true starting point, most likely very early in 2002, he displayed a classic example of what happens when the question of whether is allowed by a president to take precedence over the equally important why, when, and how.

During the 2000 presidential campaign, Iraq was not a central concern of Bush, nor was it one during his pre-9/11 first year or in the immediate aftermath of the attacks when the decisions about al Qaeda and the Taliban regime in Afghanistan were being made. Instead, it appears to have emerged out of the cloudy atmosphere of the frustrating end of the first phase of the fighting in Afghanistan, with remnants of al Qaeda and the Taliban still alive and functioning, and therefore with the potential to grow stronger.

Invading Iraq as a means of "shocking" Islamic extremists and regimes that either harbored or tolerated terrorists proceeded at the very least because Saddam Hussein's regime was so weak and that an invasion could be mounted comparatively quickly and at tolerably minimal costs, at least in theory. That impulse was in turn fed by several crosscurrents of thinking at the top of the impulsive administration: a replacement government, especially if it were democratic, would transform the Middle East; it could be a catalyst for a move to moderation that eventually might help produce a just final settlement of the never-ending strife between Israel and the Palestinians in its occupied territories.

Yet to date, no evidence exists beyond the administration's increasingly strident rhetoric as 2002 unfolded to indicate that Iraq was viewed as a serious threat to the United States or as a serious player in international terrorism in al Qaeda's league. The oft-quoted Downing Street Memo, which contained a summary of mid-2002 conversations between Bush and British prime minister Tony Blair, simply treated the decision to invade as a given; the largely phony and conjectural intelligence claims about unconventional weapons was merely a politically useful peg on which to hang that decision.

Long after the invasion, one of the policy's principal architects, Deputy Defense Secretary Paul Wolfowitz, "explained" that the administration's public obsession with the alleged danger posed by Iraq's alleged weapons of mass destruction was chosen because it was the "reason" around which the entire administration could mobilize. A political campaign to build support for an invasion that emphasized keeping the world's second largest reserves of petroleum out of unfriendly hands would have elicited dissent as an unworthy objective; so would a public relations offensive designed to convince Americans that conquering Iraq and replacing its regime with one friendly to the United States and allied in the struggle against terrorism was worth the costs of war. But raising fears about chemical, biological, and above all nuclear weapons was a tactic that could get the entire administration on the same political page, a decision that had nothing to do with veracity.

That mind-set set the stage for a blunder of epic proportions, whether one thinks conquering Iraq was a sound idea or a moral obscenity. Politics suffuses the presidency by definition. Common sense, however, restrains occupants of the White House from telling enormous whoppers even in the middle of intense political fighting, for the simple reason that the disaster that ensues when you are caught lying will obliterate whatever short-term success comes from the assertion of a falsehood. The Bush administration, however, was so trapped in its own sealed world that this common sense was marginalized in the policymaking clique and suppressed by an outside army of enablers and sycophants. The prewar propaganda was also bolstered by a security-obsessed and intimidated news media that served as a megaphone instead of a filter, and by an equally intimidated and cheerleading Congress.

The drumbeat started very early. The first example occurred in late December of 2001, about the time the internal mobilization for war was beginning. As would be the case so often for the next fifteen months, the occasion was a story in *The New York Times* by the veteran security affairs correspondent Judith Miller. It was fed by a network of Iraqi exile groups promoting invasion and their own ambitions for postwar Iraq and the supportive Bush administration officials in the White House and Defense Department who were giving the exile groups millions of dollars and promoting their cause.

Miller's story was single-sourced, from a defector being promoted by the principal exile group—the Iraqi National Congress and its well-connected leader, Ahmed Chalabi. The defector was identified as one Ihsan Saeed al-Haideri, who said he was an engineer by trade. The man claimed to have worked on nuclear, biological, and chemical weapons programs in at least twenty secret locations in the country, in underground facilities beneath hospitals and on the grounds of Saddam Hussein's famous network of palaces.

The story, not a word of which was accurate, had all the advantages that would assist the people inside the administration in their political campaign to mobilize support for an invasion: it had specificity. It filled the wide information gap that had existed ever since Saddam Hussein expelled United Nations weapons inspectors in 1998, and it was irrefutable precisely because the intelligence community had so little hard information and because from late 2001 for almost a year the weapons inspectors were still barred from the country. For months, these advantages were emphasized through a succession of disturbing tidbits—that Iraq had received shipments of tubes made out of aluminum that could be used in the elaborate centrifuges that enrich uranium to weapons-grade; that Iraq had gone shopping for a uranium source called yellow cake in the African nation of Niger; that trailers containing small laboratories in which biological and chemical agents were weaponized were being hauled around the country in secret; that Iraq had developed unmanned aircraft that could be shipped close to the American coast and from which biological agents could be sprayed.

The campaign was managed by many of the same people who were part of modern conservatism's awesome election-winning machine. Truth was beside the point; the goal was building public support for invasion. The most important argument in support of invasion was actually the product of President Bush's chief speechwriter, Michael Gerson, who over the summer of 2002 came up with a line to counter the obvious point that none of the propaganda for a war of choice as opposed to a war of necessity constituted a smoking gun, much less rock-solid evidence. "If we wait," he wrote, "the smoking gun could appear in the form of a mushroom cloud." The line, world-class by political standards, was first tested in public by the person whose role was often to try out catchy phrases during the critical period before the invasion—National Security Advisor Condoleezza Rice.

In a competently managed administration the first job of the national security advisor is to make sure that a president has the chance to seriously consider every conceivable option in foreign policy, to make sure that no information gets to him that has not been ruthlessly vetted, and to make sure that all the gears of the American military and diplomatic machine mesh. In a major break with tradition as well as prudence, she instead functioned as the chief enabler of Bush and his tight inner circle that formulated the policies dominated by Rumsfeld and Cheney.

In the tension and legitimate fear that consumed the country in the months after the 9/11 attacks, a weird form of circular reasoning trumped sober, mature judgment. Ambitious Iraqi exiles proffered unverified information that was accepted by officials because they were running a public relations campaign, not a rigorous search for truth. The most obvious danger to the president's credibility—that Iraq could be invaded and then found to contain nothing more dangerous than its weakened dictator—was just as easily ignored by more circular reasoning. The invasion would succeed, Iraq would stabilize and democratize successfully, the impact in the region would be dramatic, and thus any ultimate lack of unconventional weapons would be a mere footnote to a far more important and rewarding history.

The needs of short-term politics always trumped the need for equal consideration to possible effects down the road. So the White House got support for a Congressional resolution authorizing the use of force and then a companion resolution in the United Nations

Security Council—only to short-circuit the same weapons inspectors the resolutions were designed to empower. The bizarre campaign to use weapons of mass destruction as the political justification for an invasion, like the more sinister effort to suggest ties between Iraq and al Queda and even with the 9/11 attacks, was a tollgate through which the runaway vehicle that was the Bush administration smashed.

But there were two more important considerations—in addition to concern of the long-term effects of war, where the politics of wishful thinking and opinion manipulation triumphed over reason—the vital questions of how much a war would cost, and how large a force would be required to conquer and stabilize Iraq.

Imagine if President Bush had chosen to level with the country during the frantic preliminary to Congress's lopsided vote authorizing the use of force in Iraq in the early fall of 2002.

What a prudent president could have told the country prior to a planned invasion with multiple, understandable postwar uncertainties was that the up-front costs would be substantial but bearable, and that there was no reason to think a quick conquering of Iraq would pose any serious threat to a slowly growing American economy. In fact, at least one of Bush's top officials said basically that in a newspaper interview, but, instead of winning praise for helpful candor, the official was first shunned and then fired, drawing still more attention to Bush's prewar comments, to the substantial discredit of the administration.

The official was Lawrence B. Lindsey, Bush's economics adviser; the originator of his tax cut proposals; a full-time adviser since Bush's presidential campaign began in earnest in 1999; and an economist with lengthy loyal service to the Bush family and a more than decent reputation in his profession.

In an interview in *The Wall Street Journal* in mid-September of 2002, Lindsey was careful to stay in economics-speak, estimating that the cost of an invasion and brief aftermath, using at most half of the 500,000 troops sent to the first Gulf War in 1991, would be roughly 1 to 2 percent of the economy's total output. Stressing this was the "upper bound" of his estimate, that projection translated to $100 billion to $200 billion. Lindsey also said that there would be offsets to that number, including assets inside Iraq that could be applied to the cost (like its huge oil industry and even dollars Saddam Hussein had stolen from his people). He predicted that a stable postwar nation would lead to lower world oil prices and a corresponding boost to the U.S. economy.

All the politics-crazed Bush team saw was the $100–200 billion headline, and assumed both Lindsey's disloyalty and danger to its propaganda campaign. In fact, there has never been a shred of evidence that Lindsey's hedged comments had the slightest impact on the lopsided congressional majorities of that October as America rushed to war.

Indeed, in the days that followed Lindsey's comments, administration budget director Mitch Daniels offered up the lower end of the cost projections, perhaps $50–60 billion in direct costs for a year or so, an estimate not appreciably different from one floated at the same time by the Democratic staff on the House Budget Committee. These numbers were not grabbed out of thin air; they were straightforward projections of direct costs without a long occupation and roughly in line with calculations coming from nongovernment budget specialists.

If short-term politics produced the blunder months before the invasion, it was the remarkable, arrogant certainty inside the policy bubble that compounded it in the weeks just before the shooting started. The administration's secretive certainty, as usual, produced another round of self-defeating circular reasoning: the invasion would be quick and painless, the aftermath would be a minor irritant in the face of welcoming Iraqi millions and the shock and awe evoked by the invasion, and the net cost to the United States would be kept minuscule by a rapidly expanding Iraqi oil industry. As with every element of this fiasco, there were in fact hints and indications of contrary views and very different facts and assumptions both inside and outside the administration's closed circle (on everything from aluminum tubes to cost estimates). The sad combination of a go-along news media and a timorous political opposition, however, blocked the kind of serious debate and recalculation that is vital to a functional democracy.

A month before the invasion, the administration was predicting that oil money and other Iraqi assets would produce at least $50 billion and more likely up to $100 billion in funds to support post-invasion reconstruction and social programs. The war's leading policy architect, Wolfowitz, told a congressional hearing (after the invasion was under way) that Iraqi oil would be producing up to $18 billion in revenue for reconstruction programs annually, adding confidently that "we're dealing with a country that can really finance its own reconstruction, and relatively soon."

Almost on the eve of the invasion, the ultimate in intentionally low estimates was offered by an official with key overall responsibilities for helping put Iraq on its own feet. According to administrator Anthony Natsios of the State Department's Agency for International Development, the net cost to the United States from invasion, occupation, and reconstruction would not exceed $1.7 billion. By the time the statue of Saddam Hussein was toppled, Bush had requested only $2.5 billion for the war's aftermath.

As it turned out, roughly $500 billion had been appropriated for Iraq and even more for the ongoing conflict in Afghanistan by mid-2007. According to the Congressional Budget Office, the direct costs of the invasion and aftermath will exceed $500 billion based on the assumption that all activity has ceased before the end of the decade; factoring in unavoidable future costs (to treat the disabilities of thousands of veterans and pay additional interest on a swollen national debt) the true bill is likely to exceed $2 trillion. For the minor short-term benefit of suppressed doubts and suppressed facts, Bush left himself open to disaster when reality intruded.

In addition to Larry Lindsey, the other government official who spoke candidly prior to the invasion and suffered for his trouble was a military man. Nearing the end of a distinguished career, Army

General Eric Shinseki, the service's secretary at the time, had quietly participated in one of the strangest debates in America's military history, all of which occurred behind the Bush administration's typically closed doors. It concerned a fairly basic question, namely how large a force was necessary to conquer Iraq and oversee its stabilization. No more important issue is imaginable, and yet the weird intra-administration conversation (it was more like a negotiation between the minimalist policymakers inside the Bush Bubble and traditional, conservative military minds) produced possibly the most egregious of all the administration's scores of screw-ups, one that cost more than three thousand American lives.

At one of the hitherto perfunctory Senate hearings just before the invasion, Shinseki was asked by Democratic senator Carl Levin of Michigan how large the invading force should be and what it would take to efficiently secure Iraq in the aftermath of universally presumed success. Contrary to subsequent headline summaries, Shinseki did not blurt out an arresting answer. Instead, he was cautious and explained himself:

> I would say that what's been mobilized to this point—something on the order of several hundred thousand soldiers are probably, you know, a figure that would be required. We're talking about posthostilities control over a piece of geography that's fairly significant, with the kinds of ethnic tensions that could lead to other problems. And so it takes a significant ground-force presence to maintain a safe and secure environment to ensure that people are fed, that water is distributed, all the normal responsibilities that go along with administering a situation like this.

They call it nation-building, and Bush had campaigned for the presidency in open contempt of it, until even he saw its unavoidability after wars of choice, either invasions or interventions.

As with the discussion of the war's potential cost, Shinseki was not talking through his hat. The prudent sizing of forces had been a topic of intense study among defense intellectuals in and out of the military for years. In one important report on post–World War II situations by the RAND Corporation, researchers found that from Germany and Japan through Bosnia and Kosovo, the typical post-conflict occupying force had never had fewer than one solider for every fifty inhabitants of the occupied nation.

In the case of Iraq, with nearly 25 million inhabitants, that suggested a force of roughly the 400,000 servicemen that Shinseki in fact referred to in a separate private hearing. He was not alone. When General Anthony Zinni retired well before the invasion as the boss at CENTCOM, the United States–based command that oversaw operations in the region—he left behind a contingency war plan for Iraq that envisioned roughly 375,000 invading and occupying troops. Others could imagine that figure reduced by 50,000 to 75,000 on the sensible assumption that far fewer would be needed in the much more stable Iraqi region of Kurdistan. This thinking flowed directly from Colin Powell's insistence a decade earlier that a force of 500,000 soldiers attack the Iraqis occupying Kuwait. This debate had also dominated several conferences of specialists outside the Bush Bubble that occurred prior to the invasion but were largely ignored by the high-profile news media.

What is more, Shinseki's comment had been preceded by a review of the past by military historians and was informed both by his analysis of war games the previous year that had been used to test various scenarios, as well as his concern (his prophetic concern) that a United States–led occupation would attract Islamic extremists to Iraq from all over the region and especially from the al Qaeda network.

As befits an administration whose first instinct in response to criticism is to counterattack and demonize, a campaign to marginalize Shinseki began immediately. Aided by a war-frenzied news media that in the main went no further than a he-said, he-said battle of short quotes, Paul Wolfowitz was quickly mobilized to pronounce Shinseki's estimate "unduly off the mark." Without elaboration that might have provoked a more serious debate, he oozed confidence that within three months or so of a successful invasion the U.S. force could be reduced to no more than thirty thousand occupiers.

And, dripping arrogant sarcasm about Shinseki's analogy with the Balkans, Wolfowitz said the following before the same Senate Armed Services Committee in a cavalier comment that summarizes the sorry record of the administration's know-it-all hubris: "There has been none of the record in Iraq of ethnic militias fighting one another that produced so much bloodshed and permanent scars in Bosnia."

Indeed.

As it turned out, the invasion's top commander, General Tommy Franks (who caved in to Donald Rumsfeld's insistence on negotiating down from General Zinni's original planning figure), crossed the border with roughly 140,000 troops, a figure improvidently slashed at the last minute when Turkey refused to be the staging area for the Army division that was to invade from the north.

It may be a hackneyed expression, but if President Bush wanted to conquer Iraq in the worst way, he proceeded to do precisely that.

The ultimate responsibility of a president making a serious security decision is to make triply certain that he has seen and considered every conceivable option that might apply. One reason the Cuban Missile Crisis ended without full-scale war in 1962 was that President Kennedy was looking at a complete list of choices, each fully developed, for responding to the secret placement of Soviet missiles on the island—from invasion to diplomacy to an idea rescued from the contingency planning bowels of the Pentagon, a naval blockade.

By contrast, George W. Bush's corporate administration, with its top-down hierarchy and tight decision-making circle, was uniquely handicapped to carefully consider alternatives. His national security office, designed for the Cold War to keep the decision-making process flooded with realistic options, instead functioned as an enabler under Condoleezza Rice for what bordered on a snap decision. For much of 2002, a grand illusion was created that careful consideration and planning was occurring for a war that would be a choice of last resort to deal with a grave security threat—first in the Congress and then at the United Nations.

The benefits were all short-term—a manufactured public drumbeat for war, easy approval of a congressional resolution authorizing the use of force, a narrow Republican Party victory in the midterm elections, and then a unanimous United Nations Security Council resolution demanding that Iraq reopen itself to intrusive weapons inspections. But the costs were longer-range and much more damaging to the country and to the administration—a growing division of opinion in the United States, as well as a steady collapse of what had been an international united front against terrorism after the 9/11 attacks—even before the invasion's epically mishandled aftermath produced a deadly quagmire.

The broadest agreement in 2002 was in favor of bringing the infuriating situation in Iraq to a climactic head, on the grounds that after al Qaeda's criminal spectacular it was intolerable to permit a rogue state to flout years of U.N. resolutions that contained no clear consequences for noncompliance.

Instead of having been developed inside a thorough administration, the obvious alternatives came from the outside, from Americans and foreign diplomats easily demonized as peaceniks, but whose ideas and words are the ones that have stood the test of time and were eerily prophetic.

In the summer of 2002, in a speech that was all but buried as the propaganda campaign began to rage, Senator Edward Kennedy proposed that instead of a blank check from Congress, the administration should win a new resolution at the United Nations (tougher even than the one ultimately adopted in November) that clearly set the stage for a multilateral use of force in the event of defiance. This is part of what Kennedy said, and it is worth emphasizing that this was nearly a year before the invasion took place:

> It is an open secret in Washington that the nation's uniformed military leadership is skeptical about the wisdom of war with Iraq. They

share the concern that it may adversely affect the ongoing war against Al Qaeda and the continuing effort in Afghanistan by draining resources and armed forces already stretched so thin that many reservists have been called for a second year of duty and record numbers of service members have been kept on active duty beyond their obligated service.

Ironically, Kennedy was introduced that September day at Johns Hopkins University by Francis Fukuyama, the first prominent conservative intellectual to question blind commitment to preemptive war in the aftermath of 9/11. Fukuyama's prescient argument before the war, during the occupation in a series of lectures, and then in an important book, *America at the Crossroads,* was that conservatism had been hijacked by Bush from its Cold War foundation and been morphed into a wrongheaded doctrine of unilateral military adventurism whose reach far exceeded its grasp and whose concept of the threat posed by Islamic extremism was unrealistically apocalyptic.

Indeed, of all those who should be most angered by the massive deception that preceded the invasion and the sophomoric bungling that followed it, the first in line should be those who most wanted to promote Saddam Hussein's demise and a decent aftermath with international support.

Just before the invasion, there was a barely noticed development that epitomized the manipulated rush to war. Another report surfaced from an Iraqi defector who had been trumpeted by the administration. Placed in its "Periscope" section and not picked up by any other publication during the final month of pre-invasion hysteria, *Newsweek* magazine reported the defector had told U.N. weapons inspectors as well as U.S. and British intelligence eight years before that all of Iraq's unconventional weapons and associated material had been destroyed after the first Gulf War.

The defector was Saddam Hussein's son-in-law General Hussein Kamel, who had been in charge of the regime's secret defiance of U.N. weapons resolutions. When he returned to Iraq, Saddam Hussein had him killed. Kamel had already surfaced in the press for his exposure of the extent to which Iraq's program, especially in the area of biological and chemical weapons, had advanced at the time of the first Gulf War. Obviously, nothing was known for sure about what had happened since his defection and Kamel had said records and blueprints were secretly retained against the day when inspections might cease and Iraq could try again. But his information (supported by another Iraqi military man who defected with him) surfaced at a time when renewed U.N. weapons inspections were failing to turn up anything.

The records of Kamel's debriefings had been kept secret, which provided the cover behind which the Bush administration continued using him during the run-up to the invasion. It was a classic bit of public deception, arguing that Kamel had shown the extent of Iraq's perfidy while covering up the relevant fact that he had also reported the weapons were destroyed. The fiction was peddled by all the top people—Bush himself, Dick Cheney, Colin Powell in his prewar slide show at the United Nations, and Deputy National Security Advisor Stephen Hadley.

For interested members of Congress about to vote on the resolution authorizing military force, this maneuver was the perfect counterpart to the hyped National Intelligence Estimate raising the specter of mass destruction. Aware that few members would bother to read the secret document beyond its ominous summary, the document included numerous references to the widespread dissents about whether the claims were supported by solid evidence.

In exchange for short-term political advantage what Bush had actually done was plant a time bomb certain to detonate eventually. As it happened, the detonation came surprisingly quickly, and with devastating force.

15

CATASTROPHE

Having broken the Baathist regime, we face a remnant of violent Saddam
supporters. Men who ran away from our troops in battle are now dispersed and
attack from the shadows. These killers, joined by foreign terrorists, are a
serious, continuing danger. Yet we're making progress against them. The once all-
powerful ruler of Iraq was found in a hole, and now sits in a prison cell. Of the
top 55 officials of the former regime, we have captured or killed 45. Our forces
are on the offensive, leading over 1,600 patrols a day and conducting an
average of 180 raids a week. We are dealing with these thugs in Iraq, just as
surely as we dealt with Saddam Hussein's evil regime.

—**President George W. Bush, January 20, 2004**

COMPLETELY MESSING UP the affairs of a conquered
and occupied country is no simple task for a president of the United
States.

Completely messing up a war that evolves from that screw-up is
even more difficult, especially for the leader of the most powerful
nation in the history of the world.

Almost by definition, a foul-up of these historic dimensions is
much more than a mistake of the one-dimensional, "oops," variety.

To produce the murderous mess in Iraq for which President Bush
is directly responsible, in fact takes a long series of interconnected
mistakes, each contributive to the next one and compounding it.
Along the way, for something like what happened in Iraq to unfold,
a president must almost intentionally ignore the previous mistakes

he has made, in the face of dramatic evidence of them, in order for the ground to be properly prepared for the next big one.

The damage Bush did to his country is gigantic and will take years to repair. The list is horrifyingly long, even when restricted to large-scale unintended consequences: roughly four thousand dead Americans; more than forty thousand injuries and wounds; unknown tens of thousands of dead Iraqis; more than $500 billion spent already; the biggest refugee crisis in the region in sixty years, and in the world since World War II; a shattering of America's standing in an interdependent world where standing matters more than standing armies; a sharp deterioration in the security situation throughout the Middle East; no lessening, and in fact an intensification, of the pressure by international terrorists globally; a serious weakening of the U.S. hand in dealing with serious threats elsewhere, including Iran, Lebanon, northern Africa, and North Korea; and a military tattered from misuse to such an extent that rebuilding adequate forces, from the National Guard to elite combat teams, will take a decade.

Political and communications skills, above all maintaining a rhetorical link between the conflict in Iraq and the struggle against terrorism, helped Bush limp to reelection with a Republican Congress in 2004 without the customary discipline of accountability. But all those missteps claimed their price as reality in Iraq gradually overtook spin in Washington—with a vengeance. In addition to lives and treasure, the president also sacrificed his own credibility and seriously wounded his office.

And instead of the ninety-day wonder he originally planned, the wars in Iraq and Afghanistan exceeded the time the United States spent as a combatant in World War II.

The administration's signature, relentless reliance on politics to shore up its disintegrating position, was continually successful on its own short-term terms. But the eventual cost was a steady disintegration of public support for open-ended involvement in the wars that followed 9/11, a steady souring of Bush's own reputation and political standing in the country (not to mention the steady isolation of the United States in an increasingly critical and then hostile region and world), a steady decline in the broader and far more important (to the United States as well as to the world) struggle with Islamic extremism and terrorism, and finally, on one day in November of 2006, the loss of his Republican majorities in Congress that had been so important to keeping critics of his failed policies at bay.

If every detail of the invasion and occupation of Afghanistan and Iraq had gone according to plan (dream is a more accurate word), Bush might have been hailed as a visionary with an epic achievement in a dangerous part of the world where success is typically measured in inches. However, among the many fatal flaws in his scheme was a myopic refusal to plan for things to go wrong (much less horribly wrong) along the way and to be prepared to make adjustments as needed. For that reason, the Americans most aggrieved by a misadventure that already ranks with Vietnam are those who believed most passionately in the original mission: attempting to overthrow two of the most dangerous regimes in the world at the time of the 9/11 attacks—Afghanistan and Iraq; and to help implant, with international support, a stable, bordering on democratic, regime in the heart of the violent Middle East. It is conservatives and neoconservatives who had a rare opportunity after 2000 to build a long-term political hegemony, and who had to watch their dream crumble amidst the rubble of Bush's policies and administration. It is they who most need to study what went so horribly wrong.

Nothing defines this kind of failure more starkly than the willful failure to consider serious alternatives to the almost entirely American-British invasion of Iraq itself. Bush managed to mismanage world opinion so that unanimity in the United Nations Security Council in November of 2002 had mutated into politically internecine sniping on the eve of the invasion, inside this country as well as abroad.

Political memories are short, but the refusal to even consider the views of others, most notably the successfully demonized French, is an instructive moment for anyone seeking to understand the origins of the debacle. Colin Powell's telegenic display of what turned out to be mostly false information about Iraq's unconventional weapons got nearly all the headlines during the first week of February 2003. But it was the approach of France's foreign minister at the time, Dominique de Villepin, that has stood the test of time.

In insisting that a second U.N. resolution precede combat, de Villepin not only argued that weapons inspectors and the work of the International Atomic Energy Agency were producing "tangible results," he urged that the numbers of those performing intrusive inspections be increased exponentially, even throwing out the near-invasion-sized number of thirty thousand backed by a credible threat of force in the event of resistance.

De Villepin's point was that international near-unanimity was an essential precondition to the success of the all-important aftermath of any toppling of Saddam Hussein's dictatorship, whether by internal coup or external invasion.

"Given the choice between military intervention and an inspections regime that is inadequate because of a failure to cooperate on Iraq's part we must choose the decisive reinforcement of the means of inspection," he said on February 6.

The Bush machine's political response was devastatingly effective, symbolized by the childish substitution of Freedom Fries for French Fries on the menu in the House of Representatives' dining room. Bush was equally effective for the short term in selling the proposition that the inspections could never succeed, making war seemingly the only option.

Looking back, however, de Villepin's words on the eve of war are both prophetic and instructive in the dangers of blind refusals by presidents to seriously consider alternatives to their impulses.

He insisted that no country by itself, not even the United States, possessed the means to manage Iraq's future, adding, "To those who think that the scourge of terrorism will be eradicated through the action in Iraq, we say they run the risk of failing in their objective. The eruption of force in this area which is so unstable can only exacerbate tensions and divisions on which the terrorists feed."

The French minister's word's complemented an even more telling observation that same month from Edward Kennedy, who had offered a competing set of ideas months before: "If inspections work we avoid war. If they don't we will gain the cooperation of the international community in fighting the war and in winning the peace."

Even before the first bomb fell, Bush had committed three of the most basic mistakes a president can make—failing even to consider expert advice on the size of the invasion and occupying force, failing even to consider alternatives to essentially unilateral invasion in the face of growing international opposition, and failing to plan seriously for anything more than a brief transitional occupation.

The worst, of course, was yet to come.

During the month or so while Iraq was being conquered and occupied with predictable, though dizzying, speed, Americans got a few hints that something might be amiss, though they were mostly covered up by the fog of war.

The most publicized was a fiasco involving a thirty-three-member supply unit that made a wrong turn off the road of advance and was attacked, with twenty-seven of its soldiers killed, wounded, or captured. What made the incident the most widely known, after the fact, were the injuries sustained by one of the unit's members who was held captive and then rescued under highly publicized circumstances, Jessica Lynch.

The entire advance toward Baghdad, moreover, was completely stalled for three days near the end of March, during which the adequacy of the force's size briefly became a subject of public debate. It ended as suddenly as it began when the invading army quickly reached the Iraqi capital's outskirts and Saddam Hussein's dictatorship collapsed.

Americans were treated to live televised reports from correspondents placed in individual advancing units as they raced north against no appreciable resistance, and then enjoyed the symbolic scene of a

Saddam Hussein statue being pulled from its foundation. But far less attention was paid to developments that were not so visible. One was the almost complete absence of large Iraqi military units surrendering to their advancing enemies; instead they seemed to have simply melted away.

The other development was the occasional, but worrisome, reports of brief attacks on the U.S. and British forces by guerrilla units, often riding in nothing more than pickup trucks, out of uniform, and firing nothing more than automatic weapons and grenade launchers. These strongly suggested the presence of organized Iraqis who were prepared to fight an irregular war against the coalition armies.

Presidents, whether fighting wars, occupying countries, or confronting domestic problems, are meant to be the most adaptable of creatures. They lurch and shift, fire people, hire others, and tack left and right, fully aware that at their level of responsibility the most navigable distance between two points is rarely a straight line.

President Bush has been uniquely different, a truly special example of stubborn persistence and resistance to holding himself or those closest to him responsible for egregious mistakes that stands as a lasting model of what not to emulate. As the invasion became an occupation (far more than a liberation), this transformation produced resistance with popular roots going well beyond al Qaeda and remnants of the dictatorship's Baath Party cadres.

Two events symbolized Bush's dogmatic insistence on a pre-fixed course in Iraq, one political, the other involving the security of both Americans and Iraqis. Unlike most of the stories about homeland security, or the international and domestic efforts to defeat terrorism, or the propaganda-fed buildup to the invasion, these were not time bombs that exploded months or years after the fact.

Iraq became a deadly quagmire in real time.

Even as the television cameras were broadcasting live the toppling of Saddam Hussein's statue other cameras had begun broadcasting fresh images of Iraqis looting the country's administrative and public services buildings (hospitals included), and even its national museum. The looting occurred on a massive scale all over the country, and the images quickly replaced the gung ho scenes of the American military on the march as cable network staples. This was as damaging inside Iraq and the up-for-grabs Arab world as it was in America. With U.S. troops literally standing aside as this wholesale larceny unfolded, the clear impression was that the invaders could have cared less. And the U.S. inability to respond decisively was a public dramatization of the fact that there were nowhere near enough soldiers to guard important choke points and intersections or even large supplies of weapons and explosives, much less visibly patrol populated communities.

The response from the top in Washington was almost exclusively political at the cost of addressing the underlying problems. This emphasis on short-term politics and imagery was what produced Rumsfeld's astonishingly dismissive comment that "stuff happens" as well as a broader campaign against the broadcast media's new focus.

Behind the scenes, the looting at least accelerated, if not produced, a decision to replace the leadership of the occupation. The switch came in early May of 2003 from a retired Army general, who had for months been the symbol of Rumsfeld's bureaucratic coup taking over control of the postwar reconstruction of the country from people who actually knew something about the complex process, to a veteran diplomat who had gone into the private sector. It is beside the point whether a personnel switch like this had always been contemplated. It is a bit more relevant that Jay Garner, the Army general, had aroused the ire of the Iraqi exile still joined at the hip to the White House and Pentagon, Ahmed Chalabi, whose continuing status had been dramatized by a decision to airlift him and a couple hundred of his Iraqi National Congress supporters into the country as the invasion was still proceeding.

This was not merely a lurch in the choice of top personnel, itself a symptom of presidential confusions and lack of purpose. The postwar planning may have been abysmal, but the sudden switch in the leadership of the occupation just as it was beginning deepened the chaos and facilitated the flagrant politics, incompetence, and outright corruption that were the occupation's distinguishing characteristics for a year as valuable time was lost, security compromised, and the vacuum created into which a full-blown insurgency gradually moved.

What is irrefutable is that L. Paul Bremer III had no idea of his impending appointment until after the invasion had succeeded and he was contacted by Paul Wolfowitz and a top aide to Vice President Cheney. His abrupt arrival put an exclamation point after the fact that the prewar planning for the post-invasion period had been sketchy on its best days—and almost entirely based on the assumption that the occupation and reconstruction of Iraq would be virtually self-financing, with at most a residual force of thirty thousand Americans after three months, and without anything resembling a contingency plan if the assumption proved absurd.

Effective governments attack mistakes; the Bush administration's hallmark is compounding them. Within days of Bremer's arrival with a mandate from Rumsfeld and Bush himself to run the country, decisions were announced that contradicted other high-level decisions made weeks earlier. But, worse, they raised the profile of the Americans as all-powerful occupiers, and weakened the capacity of Iraqis to begin participating significantly in the administration of their own country.

The first decision was a move to eliminate from government and other public service all senior and many relatively junior officials of the Baath Party, the Nazi-like institution out of which Saddam Hussein had originally emerged and to which thousands of Iraqis belonged simply in order to have jobs and future prospects. The second decision, which had also been discussed secretly with Bremer by top officials before he left, was to completely disband the Iraqi armed forces that had all but melted away rather than seriously engage the invasion force.

The so-called de-Baathification orders, going far beyond previous administration discussions, threw forty thousand freshly disgruntled Iraqis out of work and also gravely injured what was left of Iraq's self-governing potential—from important cabinet departments to basic public services like education and health care. The disbanding of the military added another 400,000 to the pile, plus another 300,000 from the former dictatorship's internal security forces, with no immediate prospect of viable replacements.

These were not ideological decisions; they were massive mistakes by people who combined know-it-all inflexibility with hubris inside their bubble and did not consider consequences and plan accordingly. These impulsive acts by officials unmoved from their uninformed faith in a quick and easy transition in fact created much of the disgruntled sea in which insurgents ultimately swam.

The insurgency, however, was anything but spontaneous. Instead of chemical, biological, or nuclear weapons, what the invading force did discover was gobs of documentary material, confirmed by defecting and captured officials, showing that Saddam Hussein himself had helped foment the insurgency prior to the invasion. Military units that faded away frequently hid large quantities of weapons and explosives all over the country, in addition to the large known stockpiles that were looted after stretched-thin U.S. forces failed to secure them. The first fighters from outside Iraq, including suicide-bombers-to-be, were actually imported and trained at a secret site prior to the invasion. The ultimate proof of Saddam's intention to take his movement underground in anticipation of a successful United States–led attack surfaced three years later in the form of video of the dictator and his high command being shown and demonstrating the lowest-tech weapons of guerrilla war—Molotov cocktails and even slingshots.

The essence of this, and much of the supportive detail, was communicated to senior U.S. officials in numerous analyses from the intelligence community prior to the invasion, and backed by several military officers reporting anecdotal evidence during the attack itself. It was all ignored or, worse, misused. The Iraqi camp south of

Baghdad, training the first groups of foreign fighters to battle the invading forces, was actually used politically by the Bush administration officials as evidence of a tie between the Iraqi regime and al Qaeda. They used this as one more justification for the invasion; but in fact, CIA officials knew its actual purpose was to help prepare for a guerrilla war after Iraq's inevitable occupation by a superior armed force. Believing its own propaganda, the United States trained extensively to operate on a battlefield polluted by deadly chemical agents, but it trained not at all for what its military actually faced—a fanatically committed insurgency operating amidst hundreds of thousands of unnecessarily demoralized and disgruntled Iraqis.

The key antidote to post-invasion chaos was to have been the reconstruction of a society shattered by three decades of inept dictatorship and war, to give it an economic infrastructure that Bush himself pledged would be second to none in the region, while in the process providing massive employment opportunities to help rebuild shattered lives and provide alternatives to insurgency. In fact, well into 2007, a combination of bumbling and corruption had left Iraq not much different than it had been before the war, but missing up to two million of its best-trained citizens who had the financial means to leave the deadly mess that emerged (another two million people were displaced inside Iraq). In the process, tens of billions of dollars were flushed down the toilet, stolen, missing, and misspent. There has never been anything like this massive failure, compounded by a parallel failure to rebuild Iraqi military and domestic security forces to a level of minimal competence and capability. For every dedicated American civil servant trying his best to oversee this colossal waste, there was at least one junior varsity political appointee either abetting the corruption or wasting time and money on a mission to apply some snippet of right-wing doctrine to some uncomprehending snippet of Iraqi life.

Not one dollar of this colossal mess is attributable to a failure of conservative or neoconservative ideas. There is neither a progressive nor a right-of-center way to effectively help a failed state revive.

There is simply a right way and a wrong way. At the root of the Bush administration's historic failure in Iraq is the ignorance of a fundamental concept of good governance—accountability and responsibility. In business, CEO heads would roll within months of the kinds of shenanigans and outright criminality that unfolded in post-invasion Iraq. But in the politics-obsessed president's world, denial and spin were the continuous rule. In shielding themselves from the consequences of their ineptitude and worse, Bush and his most senior officials were aided in the short term by what amounted to a pliant, rubber-stamp Republican Congress. They kept the pressure off to such an extent that the only significant hearings into the corrupt mess of reconstruction were conducted by an arm of the Senate Democratic minority, which produced some interesting whistle-blowers but lacked the authority to summon responsible officials. The voters, however, took care of that problem in November of 2006; the cost of cover-up was a loss of the very majorities that shielded the administration from scrutiny, with exit polls showing concern over "corruption" as the second most important factor in the congressional elections after the fouled-up war itself.

The very first contract from the Pentagon for the postwar period was granted four months before the invasion to a subsidiary of Halliburton—the firm Dick Cheney had run in the late 1990s—to plan work on Iraq's oil production system. A contract worth $7 billion was then awarded in early March of 2003. For all that money, oil output in the fall of 2006, at 2.4 million barrels daily, was still running slightly below the daily average prior to the invasion, more than a half-million barrels below the prewar projection for postwar production. The country's electrical generating capacity remained a half-megawatt below prewar levels. Barely half the planned water projects had been completed more than three years after the invasion, only twenty of a planned 142 new health clinics had been opened, and but forty-nine of a planned 136 sanitation projects were finished. In three years the $20.9 billion appropriated to the postwar Iraq Relief and Reconstruction Fund was spent, and one-fourth of that had been siphoned off to fund security needs as the violence in the country escalated.

In part, this was a case of bungling a vital job that had not been even minimally planned properly, and then doing nothing to correct the resulting mess, a certain route to a steady deterioration of public support. But in part, the massive diversion also reflected what amounted to a decision to partially privatize security in Iraq. Private contractors flooded into Iraq by the thousands. According to a subsequent Government Accountability Office audit, just one of these contractors cost the government nearly a half-million dollars a year in pay, benefits, and expenses.

The administration also sowed the seeds of deteriorating public support by conniving in the mal-administration (to use a polite word) of high-profile construction contracts, as opposed to confronting the problem. The sorry saga began with the very first oil production contract awarded without competitive bidding and under "emergency" conditions to Halliburton. Even before it was awarded the deal had been questioned by the Army Corps of Engineers' top procurement officer, a twenty-year veteran named Bunnatine Greenhouse. The eventually publicized paper trail, from the outset, included her incredulity that a multibillion-dollar deal should be awarded under these circumstances and that "emergency" conditions could prevail over a contract life of up to five years. As the inevitable problems and questionable payments began to surface, her ire focused on one case of potential overbilling for fuel costs that amounted to more than $60 million.

Any competently run administration would recognize both the likely merit of Greenhouse's detailed findings and the fact that she epitomized a ticking time bomb legally as well as politically. She also represented an easily presented, compelling story—a top federal executive who had come from next to nothing in segregation-era Louisiana and who presented her findings with a modulated disgust that television cameras would love, and eventually did. But instead of dealing with her findings, the administration ignored her and then demoted her—virtually guaranteeing an eventual explosion. It came within a year. The resulting lawsuits and the disclosures they in turn triggered became a symbol for the reconstruction that never really happened—all of it preventable.

Short-term politics covering up deep-seated problems and goofs that inevitably came to light, however, was the guiding hand of post-invasion Iraq. In the narrowest of terms, the conservative political machine that had so regularly been successful since Ronald Reagan's victory in 1980 could produce a narrow reelection of President Bush in 2004 while the broader public concern about terrorism was still fresh and strong. But it could not deal with the underlying messes that inevitably came to light and just as inevitably helped wreck the prospects for Bush's second term and his reputation, not to mention Iraq. From the original looting to the horrifying, endless violence and death, the response was consistently a resort to expediency and policies that simply postponed collisions with reality.

In the short term, the administration could deal with the consequences of a severely overstretched American military by raiding the National Guard and Reserves. It could also deal with them by lengthening deployments (ultimately to fifteen months) and by sending people back to the war zone three and four times. But over the long run, these stopgap measures were unsustainable. The size of the armed forces was simply not adequate to support the policy in Iraq to which Bush stubbornly clung.

In the short term, the administration could deflect the concern about a growing insurgency with dismissive talk about isolated terrorists and "dead enders" from Saddam Hussein's most intense followers; Bush himself could even goad the gathering forces with a remark of such enormous silliness—Bring 'em on!—that even he recognized his goof two years later. But over the long run, reality that is ignored or ineptly confronted inevitably triumphs over spin. It turned out the various elements of the initial insurgency, foreign fighters as well as men from Saddam Hussein's Sunni minority, showed astonishing discipline in using terrorism to provoke the majority Shiites into armed responses that eventually ignited a civil war right under the noses of some 150,000 poorly commanded American troops.

But nothing epitomized the gap between the administration's relentlessly short-term politics and reality more than the false benchmarks that for a time appeared to mark "progress" in Iraq, but that in fact deflected efforts to examine the lack of progress, and thereby to learn and change.

The first benchmark was the capture of the disheveled and on-the-run Saddam Hussein near the end of 2003. Almost on the eve of the Iowa caucuses, Democratic front-runner Howard Dean may have been impolitic when he observed that the heralded capture had nothing to do with making Americans any safer from terrorism in the world; but he was right.

Meanwhile, the benchmarks for Iraq were reached and then found to have been inconsequential because the underlying failure was never confronted either with a massive infusion of armed force or a decision to withdraw gradually and leave the challenge of internal security to the people who had more than enough guns, but very little of the will, to provide it.

The benchmarks did, however, provide the backdrop for a novel political technique as the war spread and escalated in the ruined country. Instead of focusing on a larger and potentially elusive concept like success or victory, the White House tried to focus attention on a series of shorter-term benchmarks. As each was met and the results trumpeted triumphantly—the transfer of sovereignty in 2004, for example, or the string of elections and referendums that followed it—attention was then fixed on the next one, and so on.

Eventually, as the public caught on, Bush lurched in the opposite direction. With public support and public approval of his handling of the war in free fall as 2005 unfolded, the president suddenly began insisting that "victory" was his goal in a noble cause. In an address at the Naval Academy in December of that grim year, Bush used the word "victory" no fewer than fifteen times. Reflecting attention to the politics of the war at the expense of a sound policy,

Bush's new public relations tactic built on the work done by a political scientist from Duke University who had been added to his National Security Council staff. Peter Feaver, a loud Bush supporter with a military and security background, had been part of a small group at Duke that had analyzed polling data from 2002 and 2003 and concluded that the public would rally around the president if he was convincing in framing a worthy purpose for the conflict and persuaded Americans that eventual success (or "victory") was both achievable and likely. In the kind of lurching that always suggests a presidency in distress, this approach barely lasted into 2006 before other White House political advisers persuaded Bush that realism about the situation and outlook was the more productive rhetorical path. What never really changed was the policy and the increasingly troubling nonresults on the ground.

Another major political technique involved a concept often summarized with the word "conflation." The dictionaries define it as the result of things or concepts having been brought together, or melded, or fused. Even before the invasion, White House communications aides discovered that to a still fearful country, the continual juxtaposition of rhetoric about Saddam Hussein with rhetoric about the 9/11 attacks would create an impression (created by the occasional use of unverified or false intelligence tidbits) that the two were related. According to polling data the typical American actually believed that there was a connection between Saddam Hussein and the 9/11 attacks, and a significant minority still does.

After the invasion, the communications strategists then employed the conflation of Iraq with the global struggle against terrorism, a maneuver that worked so well in the short term that it managed to overshadow the indisputable fact that resources had been shifted from the latter to fill the manpower and equipment needs of the former. The two quite dissimilar situations were not only conflated, but Bush himself was able to label the ongoing war in Iraq the international struggle's "central front." It worked, that is, until it didn't work anymore, when the reality on the ground in Iraq inevitably overpowered all attempts at conflation. Indeed, once the truth trumped political manipulation, the public's confidence in both struggles crumbled.

From the trumpeted capture of Saddam Hussein, not unlike the toppling of his statue and the president's appearance in flight gear on the deck of an aircraft carrier beneath a huge sign reading "Mission Accomplished," the coming and going of artificial benchmarks in Iraq in fact punctuated the bungling of the conflict and the sad country's descent into deadly chaos and civil war.

After one year, "sovereignty" was restored to an interim government by quasi-proconsul Bremer, temporarily obscuring the fact that among the institutions over which the Iraqis still lacked sovereignty (and would for another three years) was its military.

There were elections to choose an assembly to haggle over a new constitution, and then a referendum to consider the resulting document; both celebrated events that muted the fact that a constitution was only negotiated and then approved because it avoided the central questions that divide Iraq—the form of its federalism, the distribution of the oil that makes up roughly 90 percent of its economic output, and the nature of fundamental rights in a federation, including the rights of women.

And at the end of the cycle, there were still more elections to choose a government under this new system, and then a long period of negotiations while the composition of a cabinet was hammered out politically. Again, the orchestrated celebration of these events blurred central facts that inevitably emerged more clearly—in the various rounds of voting, a pluralistic democracy was not emerging; the voting showed repeatedly that around 90 percent of the Iraqis were simply dividing themselves into the ever-hardening positions of their religious sects, tribes, and regions. After each round, the basic issues left undecided were to be faced in the next round, and so on until hardly anyone believed the Americans and the Iraqi politicians anymore.

Eventually, more than three years of truculent ineptitude cost Donald Rumsfeld his reputation and then his job—more than two years after the scandalous, systematic mistreatment of Iraqi prisoners should have done so. Eventually, it also cost the Republicans control of Congress. But the cost of this catastrophe to Iraqis and to American soldiers and their families was significantly greater.

The congressional elections, however, did not produce change in administration policy; instead they produced a hardening of the president's determination to persevere, transforming the public's view of him from principled to merely stubborn. In a rare example of independent action by Republicans while they still controlled Congress in 2006, a balanced bipartisan commission was created to study the Iraq situation and recommend change. Eventually, two highly regarded Americans agreed to share the chairman's job—James Baker, Republican secretary of state during the first Gulf War, and Democrat Lee Hamilton, a former chairman of the House Foreign Affairs Committee. Each satisfied himself ahead of time that Bush would both cooperate and listen to what they had to say after the election.

As it turned out, the cooperation was extensive, but the listening was at best grudging. The report issued by the Baker-Hamilton Commission (officially known as the Iraq Study Group) had three principal themes: a grim description of the status quo; a recommendation that military forces gradually move out of urban combat roles by the spring of 2008 and instead concentrate on fighting foreign terrorists and training the Iraqis; and another recommendation that Bush engage Iran and Syria diplomatically to help stabilize the volatile region as well as the security situation inside Iraq.

Bush did not contest the commission's findings; in fact, his choice to succeed Donald Rumsfeld, national security veteran Bob Gates, was both a commission member while still in private life and an endorser of its analysis during his Senate confirmation hearing. Bush did, however, push back hard against the diplomatic advice—at least until he took it belatedly and began talks with the Syrians and Iranians in the spring of 2007.

On the military side, Bush wanted to go in the opposite direction—toward more troops more engaged in the fighting. His model was not the bipartisan Iraq Study Group under Baker and Hamilton. Instead, it came out of a kind of last gasp from the neoconservatives who had been the war's most enthusiastic advocates—above all Fred Kagan at the American Enterprise Institute and a retired top Army general, Jack Keane; they had been supported in their work at least since the fall of 2006 by Congress's best-known hawks, Republican John McCain and Democrat Joe Lieberman. Their main contention was that a larger force—at least thirty thousand more—deployed in and around Baghdad for at least eighteen months and in the province (Anbar) most threatened by international terrorist groups could be decisive.

In a classic illustration of a president making the mistake of taking a halfway measure almost halfheartedly, Bush in January of 2007 ordered the troops to the war zone for up to a year and found a new group of military brass to run it. As violence and casualties continued to escalate, Bush then proceeded to blow a surprisingly uncertain trumpet—pleading for time to give the so-called surge a chance to work, but allowing high-level leaks to the press suggesting that he was already beginning to consider a Plan B that sounded suspiciously like the Baker-Hamilton recommendations for a diminished presence in 2008. Adding to the confusion, other top officials, including Bush himself and Gates, began comparing their latest Iraq "thinking" to the U.S. role in keeping a residual force in post-armistice Korea for more than sixty years.

Beneath the veneer of order and purpose that Bush likes to project, he had in fact compromised his presidency by lurching in different directions at the same time while the situation on the ground continued to worsen. Meanwhile the new Democratic Congress began to use hearings, test votes on funding proposals, and a continuous drumbeat of rhetoric to press its own case for a withdrawal timetable. From the illusion of triumph he had let the situation deteriorate so completely that by mid-2007, 70 percent of the public disapproved of his handling of the war and around 60 percent preferred that U.S. forces be withdrawn from Iraq within a year. It was not the fault of faceless terrorists or Democrats; it was Bush himself who had led the country into a deadly quagmire by committing a cardinal presidential sin—lurching from policy to policy, from PR campaign to PR campaign, without decisively confronting the underlying mess his invasion had created.

Compounding it all was the fact that the United States and its uncertain allies were not fighting one war, they were fighting two. The war in Iraq diverted precious resources from the ongoing conflict in Afghanistan. As time passed, inattention to much more than the daily details of fighting ultimately led Americans to realize that the war in Afghanistan had not only resumed, it was starting to go badly in a country that barely existed as a nation outside its garrisoned capital of Kabul, and that a NATO–plus–United States occupation with roughly forty thousand troops was likely to go on indefinitely. As in Iraq, the rate of death in Afghanistan (well over five hundred so far among the allied occupiers, roughly 60 percent of them American) escalated sharply after 2003, and sharply again after 2004.

Unlike the invasion of Iraq, the overthrow of the extremist Taliban regime in Kabul, which had sheltered Osama bin Laden and al Qaeda for years, was widely supported in the United States and Europe, and even across much of the Arab world. It also even had the support, quite helpful at the time, of the extremist regime in Iran.

But shortly before the Taliban melted away from Kabul there was an odd but ultimately revealing episode that ended up underscoring the astonishingly brief attention span that characterized Bush's handling of the first armed response to the 9/11 attacks.

With bombing having already begun and with intelligence agents, Special Forces, and a very small military force already linked with America's surrogate fighters, the anti-Taliban Northern Alliance, the advance nevertheless seemed to stall far from the Afghan capital.

That was all it took to ignite a firestorm in Washington, all directed from the right at Secretary of State Colin Powell. He was portrayed by spokesmen for the movement's White House and Pentagon hotheads (especially editor William Kristol of *The Weekly Standard*) as almost a fifth columnist in the heated post-9/11 atmosphere. The Powell sin, the critics had charged since shortly after the attacks, was in being lukewarm to the overthrow of the Taliban even as he was gung ho in the hunt for al Qaeda members. There was never any evidentiary weight to the charges, but they illustrated how committed people around Bush were to overthrowing the Taliban and (or so they claimed) making sure that no government would ever be able to sponsor and nurture terrorists to that extent again.

But shortly after the Taliban fled, the movement's top strategists turned on a dime and began agitating for a second front against the enemy they had targeted for years, Saddam Hussein's Iraq, and the Bush administration authorized significant transfers of men and equipment for that purpose. What had been a vital cause in October of 2001 had become an afterthought by the following spring.

In the process, they all but forgot about Afghanistan, even as the nascent government of President Hamid Karzai was attempting to begin a difficult rebuilding after decades of war and turmoil.

In Iraq, the Bush administration, among other appalling actions and inactions, committed the basic sin of failing to recognize and respond to obvious trouble. In Afghanistan, the basic error was the neglect of a situation whose relevance to the worldwide struggle with terrorism was almost universally accepted. In the process it allowed the situation to degenerate and severe dangers to reemerge.

The initial advantages were significant—something like three million hopeful Afghan refugees returning to their homeland from a substantial international diaspora, and a mobilized, developed world community that made more than $15 billion in reconstruction aid pledges at a so-called donors conference in Germany not long after the Taliban fled.

But the advantages were neutralized. Five years into the post-Taliban era, at most half the international pledges had been honored. In the case of the United States, Bush averted his eyes, in a manner that called to mind his father's loss of interest after the Soviet Union's occupying force had departed more than a decade before.

For 2002, the first full year of reconstruction in Afghanistan, Bush requested from Congress the niggardly sum of $250 million, a tiny fraction of the nearly $50 billion being requested that year for anti-terrorism activities and the prewar buildup to the invasion of Iraq. On a per capita basis, the $67 sum for each Afghan is even more paltry when measured against other significant postwar reconstruction programs: it was, for example one-fourth the size of the efforts mounted in the 1990s in Bosnia and East Timor.

Afghanistan is not only a desperately poor country, it is also famous over the years for its reliance on poppy economics, warlord and tribal governance in the remote provinces of this harsh land influenced only slightly by often weak central governments, and rampant corruption. Of 177 nations followed by the United Nations' major economic development agency, only four rank below Afghanistan in terms of persistent poverty and nonexistent infrastructure.

Administrations that neglect obvious needs pay a stiff price eventually. The price for this one, far higher of course for Afghanistan than the United States, was a gradual descent into renewed conflict. An insurgency was up and running within two years, supplemented by a large and growing crime infestation, based on the complete absence of successful efforts to combat Afghanistan's central position in the world opium trade. Largely suppressed under the fundamentalist Taliban, poppy cultivation flourished after the regime change—exploding from virtually nothing to more than 160,000 planted hectares within four years, according to the administration's own reports. In 2006, the alarming situation only got worse, with land under cultivation expanding by more than 60 percent and opium production jumping more than 25 percent to nearly 5,700 metric tons in that one year. Afghanistan maintained its stranglehold on more than 90 percent of the world's supply. The drug organizations maintaining this lucrative racket threaten the country's stability in two ways—they pay large bribes to provincial and national government figures for protection; and they are in league with insurgents as the source of much of the money used to procure arms and pay fighters (double what the Afghan armed forces pays).

At first slowly, and then rapidly, a Taliban-led insurgency gained a toehold and then a foothold. By the end of 2006, the number of attacks on government and Western nation soldiers had exploded six-fold in just twelve months, to more than six hundred a month.

The Bush administration's response to the security threat was to lead an effort to enlist the twenty-six members of NATO to provide troops to supplement the ongoing American presence—a sound option sadly not available in Iraq. However, the arrangement had two defects: it permitted each nation to put conditions on its participation, such as requiring deployment in relatively safe parts of the country; and, as in Iraq, the combined force of barely forty thousand troops was even more inadequate than its cousin in Iraq.

The administration had acted soundly in its diplomacy in the immediate aftermath of the 9/11 attacks in the region, pressuring Pakistan's military ruler, Pervez Musharraf, to understand that the international rules had changed and that he would be either a supporter of the assault on the Taliban or a victim of it. As time passed, however, Bush frittered away this advantage. He essentially looked the other away as Musharraf continually made accommodating deals with tribal forces along Pakistan's anarchic border with Afghanistan, leaving al Qaeda and Taliban remnants alike with a reasonably safe haven.

Bush has shown he could go to war under both legitimate circumstances and phony ones; but for six years he demonstrated how catastrophically things could go wrong when the all-important period following relatively easy conquests was first ignored and then mismanaged. He helped create two quagmires instead of two successes, and the fancy work of his political machine could only keep public disgust at bay for so long. The resulting snafus were epic.

In the words of James Dobbins, the administration's first special envoy to Afghanistan in 2001–2002 and a veteran of sensitive nation-building assignments in the Balkans, Central America, and

Asia: "The White House resisted the whole concept of peacekeeping. They wanted to demonstrate a different approach, one that would be much lower-cost. So the decision to skimp on manpower and deploy one-fiftieth the troops as were deployed in Bosnia was accompanied by a decision to underplay economic assistance."

That piece of wisdom could apply just as easily to Iraq.

16

ISOLATION

Americans can have confidence in the outcome of this struggle because we're not in this struggle alone. We have a diplomatic strategy that is rallying the world to join in the fight against extremism. In Iraq, multinational forces are operating under a mandate from the United Nations. We're working with Jordan and Saudi Arabia and Egypt and the Gulf States to increase support for Iraq's government. The United Nations has imposed sanctions on Iran, and made it clear that the world will not allow the regime in Tehran to acquire nuclear weapons. With the other members of the Quartet—the U.N., the European Union, and Russia—we're pursuing diplomacy to help bring peace to the Holy Land, and pursuing the establishment of a democratic Palestinian state living side-by-side with Israel in peace and security. In Afghanistan, NATO has taken the lead in turning back the Taliban and al Qaeda offensive—the first time the Alliance has deployed forces outside the North Atlantic area. Together with our partners in China, Japan, Russia, and South Korea, we're pursuing intensive diplomacy to achieve a Korean Peninsula free of nuclear weapons. . . . American foreign policy is more than a matter of war and diplomacy. Our work in the world is also based on a timeless truth: To whom much is given, much is required.

—**President George W. Bush, January 23, 2007**

THE ASHES OF Saddam Hussein's regime were still warm in the spring of 2003 when Secretary of State Colin Powell arrived in Damascus, with just the right touch of swagger in his step.

Despite Syria's long-standing hostility to Iraq, its post-9/11 support and its vote in the United Nations just months before to support weapons inspections, Powell had some tough demands of this Baathist regime with a deservedly violent reputation. And those demands played out against a backdrop of much less diplomatic colleagues in Washington actively encouraging "who's next?" talk.

The administration, Powell said, was insistent that the regime of Bashar al-Assad halt the flow of weapons and fighters into Iraq, stop the flow of wanted former regime leaders and their trucks full of cash into Syria, cease its support and harboring of militant organizations like Hamas and Hezbollah fighting the Israelis, and cancel all weapons of mass destruction programs, especially those involving chemical weapons. And in the wake of Iraq's collapse, Bush's stern words to Syria had fresh meaning: "We expect cooperation."

With hints of sanctions first and then more, Powell summarized the new tone and mood of the conquering Americans: "We have been successful in Iraq. There is a new dynamic in that part of the world. And we wanted to point out strongly to the Syrians that this is a time for you to take another look at your policies."

There were even bigger fish on the administration's hook—above all Iran and North Korea, who survived from Bush's original delineation in 2002 of an axis of evil—but the post-invasion attention to Syria symbolized a determination not to stop with Baghdad, that indeed part of the motivation for the invasion of Iraq was the dream of "transforming" the entire region. For people who believed their own expansive rhetoric about preemption of threat (unilaterally if necessary), the quick attention to Syria also symbolized their belief, in the words of the cliché, that the road to Jerusalem begins in Baghdad—that the invasion would begin the creation of a new reality in the Middle East that would force a permanent settlement with Israel.

That was the dream.

Before the summer was over it was illusory; in a year it was absurd; and three years later it was a nightmare—and not by accident.

Instead, the mess Bush made of post-invasion Iraq combined with ineffectual go-it-alone diplomacy to isolate the United States in the region and in the world. Instead of democracy on the march in the Middle East, it was extremism. Instead of a world united in sympathy and solidarity with America after the 9/11 assaults, there was a world united in hostility first to Bush personally and then to important American interests.

The initial self-defensive worry that swept Syria and Iran after U.S. intents were made clear was slowly replaced by a defiant spirit. In the face of inept American and European diplomacy, Iran's secret nuclear program accelerated to the edge of weapons development. Their theocracy moved vigorously to provide support and aid to Shiite supporters inside the violently sectarian Iraq.

Instead of responding to the post-invasion American demands, Syria felt increasingly comfortable as it went unpunished ignoring them. Weapons and fighters continued to move with impunity across its border with Iraq.

Ironically, after Powell's soon forgotten foray on the road to Damascus, the administration retreated petulantly into self-isolation, refusing to have any serious dealings with Syria and Iran at all as post-invasion Iraq deteriorated into chaos. Substantive talks did not begin with either country about the situation in Iraq until four years after the toppling of the Baathist dictatorship, and the initial atmosphere was understandably nearly frigid.

A hopeful development in Lebanon—a popular uprising in 2005 that ended twenty years of Syrian military occupation—turned sour and then dangerous after the United States appeared to back a monthlong, inconclusive Israeli military campaign after a murderous provocation by Hezbollah in the summer of 2006. In its wake, a democratic, pro-Western Lebanese government teetered in the face of pressure from a freshly strengthened Hezbollah movement, which in turn enhanced Syrian and Iranian positions within the unstable Lebanon.

And behind all the turmoil was the continuing, festering wound of the unresolved dispute between Palestine and Israel. For his first three years, Bush could justify American inaction based on the refusal to deal with the Palestinian Authority's Yasser Arafat because of Arafat's refusal to act decisively against a campaign of terrorism inside Israel. After Arafat's death, however, the administration made a grave situation even more perilous by dealing ineffectively with his successor, and thus helping prepare the way for the victory of Hamas in parliamentary elections. The collapse of the peace process during the Bush years was important and alarming by itself, but it also had important ramifications as Iraq unraveled. Again and again, Bush's attempts to enlist moderate Arab regimes in helping stabilize the country were met with the cold reality that collaboration with the Americans was politically impossible in the absence of new initiatives to revive the moribund Israeli-Palestinian diplomacy.

Messing up foreign policy, virtually all of it, is every bit as astonishing a feat as messing up a war. It cannot occur as the result of just one huge mistake or a piece of unbelievably bad luck. It takes work over time, a series of connected blunders each building upon the previous one to transform an empathetic, supportive world into an international community that was largely indifferent to U.S. interests when it wasn't overtly hostile. To accomplish anything of consequence in the modern post–Cold War world, even for the only remaining superpower, requires active allies and vigorous diplomacy. The Bush administration had allies and then lost many of them. Once again, as in the struggle against terrorism and the war in Iraq, ideology, hubris, secrecy, and politics trumped common sense and the basic mechanics of successfully getting from Point A to Point B.

There were significant clues to what was wrong in the months leading up to the 9/11 attacks, two of them flowing directly from Bush's statements during the 2000 presidential campaign, the other something of a surprise.

Like many politicians in both parties, Bush and Vice President Dick Cheney had been contemptuous of the treaty negotiated during

President Clinton's second term in Kyoto, Japan, that was designed to begin an international response to the gathering perils of climate change. Bush, however, went beyond the typical opponent's response of objecting to the specific provisions of the proposed treaty (mandating reductions in the generation of so-called greenhouse gases) to rejecting the entire process of multilateral action. This inflexible position in the face of a growing scientific and political consensus that the greenhouse gases problem was serious, in effect dealt the United States out of a worldwide game in which it had obvious interests. The Kyoto treaty went into effect anyway, and the United States became almost a pariah internationally on environmental matters, and ended up with exactly one ally—the conservative government in Australia. In the process, Bush also lost the center in American politics.

In the 2000 campaign, he had also been quite specific in signaling an intention to revive the stalled conservative dream of building a system that could knock down incoming ballistic missiles. This would require the unilateral withdrawal from a pact limiting antimissile systems that Richard Nixon had negotiated with the former Soviet Union nearly thirty years before. One reason Bush was so inattentive to the increasingly loud alarms of his counterterrorism officials about al Qaeda in 2001 was that so much of his time was devoted to managing the abrogation of this treaty. For his trouble, Bush not only confirmed his growing reputation as a unilateralist, he ended up skewing the U.S. relationship with Russia, whose disturbingly autocratic leader, Vladimir Putin, could have cared less about missile defense. But Putin skillfully used his acquiescence to the Bush initiative to moderate what should have been intense opposition to Putin's use of two powers he cared very much about— his influence over Europe and his neighbors as an energy-supplier, and domestic suppression of democratic opposition.

The only dangerous regime in the world against which an antimissile system might make some sense, assuming it would someday prove reliable after tens of billions of dollars in development costs, was North Korea. Here, in something of a surprise, Bush made a sudden move early in his presidency to jettison the Clinton administration's nearly successful bilateral diplomacy in favor of a more confrontational approach to a country whose nuclear ambitions were a universally acknowledged threat. After six years, however, Bush's policy had no discernible impact on the steady march by North Korea toward membership in the nuclear weapons club (albeit with a program that remained primitive on its best days). Even with the political advantage gained by the discovery of North Korean cheating in one facet of its program, the result of Bush's "tough" approach was a situation that grew far more dangerous deep into his presidency.

Bush's early international efforts were not entirely one way, however. Despite his campaign statements disparaging nation-building in general and NATO's operations in the former Yugoslavia in particular, he did not act on them once in office. The delicate mission, which included U.S. troops, continued throughout his presidency. He also began a hopeful initiative to increase the U.S. role in confronting the AIDS pandemic, especially in Africa.

And in the wake of the 9/11 attacks, the administration was offered the world's sympathy and active assistance. There was far more to this outpouring of emotion and support than the crowds that spontaneously gathered in scores of world capitals or lined up at American embassies to sign condolence books. Iran, Syria, and Pakistan were of material help in the run-up to the toppling of the Taliban in Afghanistan. And for the first time in its history, the leaders of NATO activated the clause in the organization's formative treaty declaring an attack on one member an attack on all—the root of what remains a multilateral effort, despite its severe difficulties, in Afghanistan.

In their indispensable volume on international public opinion, *America Against the World,* pollster Andrew Kohut and *National Journal* columnist Bruce Stokes note that the United States has had to cope with resentment, jealousy, and cultural antagonism due to the belief that World War II left only this country standing undamaged. The environment has been further complicated, they also note, by uniquely American baggage that is continually brought into international activity. There are the strong notions of "exceptionalism" that underlie U.S. behavior and the strong dose of a much more religious character that underlies that attitude. They also document an element of payback and comeuppance even in the overwhelmingly positive reaction that followed the terrorist assault.

And not all of today's harshly negative attitudes are attributable just to feelings about Bush personally or about U.S. policies.

"Today's anti-Americanism runs broader and deeper," they write on the basis of voluminous surveys done for Kohut's Pew Research Center.

> Not only is US foreign policy more strongly opposed, but now the influence of the American lifestyle is also rejected even as American products are still widely accepted. And, for the first time, the American people are also less liked. Judging by trends in international surveys, the negative image of many things American seems unlikely to change anytime soon in much of the world. Whatever global goodwill the United States had in the wake of the September 11 attacks appears to have quickly dissipated as US policymakers broadened the focus of the war against terrorism.

This, of course, has never been how a much less internationalist American public opinion sees itself—"as an exemplar of democracy whose citizens enjoy unparalleled personal freedom and opportunity."

Nevertheless, Kohut and Stokes present the evidence that "the gap between the self-image of America on a white horse and the dim view of America from abroad has never been greater." They also argue that in the context of political and economic globalization, international opinion matters much more than it did a generation or even a decade ago.

To an extent, low opinions of Bush became generalized more toward the United States itself after the president's reelection. The moment of solidarity in the fall of 2001 first dissipated and then became intense antipathy prior to the invasion of Iraq and afterward. This did not happen all at once, but the major contributors to it were the policies and actions of the Bush administration.

The first of his contributions was after the assault on Afghanistan, when Osama bin Laden and many of his followers managed to escape. It is in this period that the U.S. attention to Iraq began to increase exponentially and it is also from this period that the context broadened to include Iran and North Korea. Methodically, Bush managed to make a mess of the United States' dealings with both countries.

For a generation, the spread of nuclear weapons has been correctly seen as among the most serious of the mass annihilation dangers confronting the world, and stopping it has consistently ranked at the top of national and international priorities. Imagine, therefore, the reaction had President Bush begun his administration by announcing that one of his major goals was to pave the way for Iran's theocratic, terrorism-exporting regime to take several important steps on the road to building a bomb; that he wanted to see Iran defy the world as well as the United States, resume experiments in the conversion of uranium into gas, and then go from zero to installing something like three thousand centrifuges all spinning to enrich the uranium into forms suitable for weapons. Absurd, perhaps, but these were the results of the policies he pursued.

Nor was that all. As a direct result of administration blunders, Iran emerged as a stronger-than-ever sponsor of Hezbollah's subversion of Lebanese democracy and threat to Israel, an increasingly popular and populist foe of the United States throughout the Muslim world, and a growing threat to the chances for a nonsectarian, stable Iraq.

The key to Bush's policy—which veteran CIA analyst and National Security Council staff member Flynt Leverett has called "strategically incoherent"—has been an unwillingness to negotiate deep differences with the Iranian regime in order not to legitimize it and undermine pipe dreams of its overthrow, and possibly to enable contingency planning for a not-ruled-out bombing campaign in the future.

This dream—unrealistic at best—blocked reality, repeatedly. It also torpedoed promising post-9/11 contacts with Iran before they had a chance to improve relations. After the terrorist attacks, Iranian and U.S. officials were meeting on the average of once a month before, during, and after the United States–backed uprising in Afghanistan, whose Sunni Muslim leaders were opposed by their Shiite Muslim counterparts in Iran. According to American officials, Iran proved useful both in helping form alliances with the warlords inside Afghanistan who attacked the Taliban and in avoiding problems on the Iranian side of the border as the assault proceeded. Iran also significantly assisted in the formation of an interim government after the Taliban fled, and acted frequently against al Qaeda elements that sought refuge there, often at specific U.S. request.

Not even Bush's silly decision to declare the axis of evil's existence stopped all contact. People forget easily, but in the spring of 2003, the Iranians transmitted a proposal for bilateral discussions through the Swiss diplomats that both countries deal with formally, in the absence of public diplomatic recognition, an agreement that has existed since the hostage crisis of 1979–1980. Significantly, the move to start a comprehensive dialogue came as the influence of the United States was at its apogee in that region; the American bargaining position would never be stronger.

Bush, however, discarded his card, refusing to deal with Tehran comprehensively, which meant that the contacts on specific issues like Afghanistan gradually stopped, and never resumed as post-invasion violence began erupting in Iraq.

Instead, the task of communication was delegated to Britain, France, and Germany under the European Union's auspices for two fruitless years of unproductive talks. The parties made decent attempts at progress (for most of the time, the Iranians suspended their uranium-enrichment-related activities), but the hoped-for participation of the United States never materialized.

With insurgency raging in Iraq and Bush's position in the region and the world weakened, it was the Iranians' turn to be provocative. As the negotiations limped toward failure, the Iranians replaced a relatively pragmatic president (Mohammad Khatami) with a radical specialist in anti-American and anti-Semitic showboating (Mahmoud Ahmadinejad). In the fall of 2005, Iran resumed converting uranium to gaseous form, and followed predictably with the start of uranium enrichment using centrifuges, first a small and then a very large number of them.

Instead of diplomacy designed to resolve the increasingly severe problems, Bush dispatched his second-term secretary of state, Condoleezza Rice, to arrange for economic and political pressure through the United Nations. For most of 2006, she undertook a fool's errand that only succeeded in progressively watering down the sanctions she sought to have imposed. Because of opposition inside the Security Council, notably from Russia and France, the resolution that ultimately passed contained no discernible teeth, vindicating the positions of the hard-liners in Tehran much more than the hard-liners in the Bush White House.

Nothing symbolized the sad state more than the intense maneuvering by Bush's supposedly good friend Vladimir Putin before he agreed to support the weakened sanctions package. He not only extracted a price for his vote that was unrelated—support for Russia's membership in the World Trade Organization—but Putin also managed to exempt a sizable nuclear reactor Russia is building inside Iran from the resolution's ban on exports of nuclear-related materials to the rogue nation. In other words, a yearlong campaign for sanctions produced a resolution whose impact on Iran will be minuscule, but that will permit construction of a reactor from which Iran eventually will be able to extract plutonium for future weapons. And in the meantime, Iran's destabilizing meddling in

Lebanon and Iraq only increased. Negotiations, Rice kept insisting, were out of the question and unnecessary, adding in an illogical coda that talks were beside the point because Iran already knew what the United States expected it to do.

There is no Republican-Democrat, liberal-conservative split over Iran. The threat is widely recognized. The administration's ideological myopia, however, managed to transform a distant threat into something much more ominous, almost as if it had maneuvered itself into a situation where a full-scale aerial assault on the country (with unforeseeable consequences and no guaranteed results) remained possible. The administration was still trying in mid-2007 to muscle another sanctions proposal through the Security Council in New York, while the International Atomic Energy Agency was reporting that Iran's uranium enrichment abilities had improved substantially.

If anything, the situation with Korea was worse. The die was essentially cast months before 9/11 with a ruthless mixture of ideological fervor, hubris, and world-class goofs. As with Iran, the question of how one deals with a dangerous, unstable rogue state that seeks nuclear weapons but often cannot feed its own oppressed people has no partisan overtones whatsoever. The only question of value is what works, and Bush managed to transform an ugly, frustrating situation into a far more dangerous mess that threatened to ignite a nuclear arms race in northern Asia even as North Korea's nuclear capability increased significantly.

When he took office, the intelligence consensus was that from secret activities in the late 1980s North Korea had produced enough weapons-grade plutonium from its Yonbyon nuclear reactor for at most two devices. North Korea had added nothing for at least a decade and was observing a moratorium on its primitive ballistic missile development as well. But six years later, the device total was most likely in double figures, one had actually been tested, and missile work (still primitive by nuclear club standards) was proceeding in the open.

Of all the temptations an incoming president should resist, the instinctive, quick rejection of long-standing foreign policies of his predecessors should be at the top of the list. In the case of North Korea, a difficult but stable situation was tossed aside without the development of a workable alternative, and it all happened in plain view during the first week of March 2001. In the space of two days, Bush managed to humiliate his new secretary of state, infuriate the leader of the ally actually facing North Korea's alleged might, and set relations with North Korea on what turned out to be an unaltered course to confrontation.

The day before the arrival of one of Bush's first head-of-state visitors in Washington, South Korean president and human rights hero Kim Dae-jung, Secretary of State Colin Powell described what he assumed was administration policy, namely continuity. The United States, Powell said, would "engage with North Korea to pick up where President Clinton left off [which was tantalizingly close to an agreement ending North Korea's nuclear ambitions in return for economic assistance and security assurances]. Some promising elements were left on the table and we will be examining these elements."

The next day, March 7, Bush himself took everything off the table, putting negotiations off indefinitely, adding conditions, and clearly signaling hostility and the opposite of continuity.

The result was a rupture with Kim and cancellation by North Korea of the next scheduled midlevel contact with U.S. officials, and an eventual halt to regular deliveries of heavy fuel oil as part of North Korea's plutonium-freezing agreement with the Clinton administration in 1994. More important, there was a halt to substantive discussions.

For those addicted to insider games in the capital, the abrupt turnabout was a victory for "hard-liners" Dick Cheney and Donald Rumsfeld, facilitated by National Security Advisor Rice, over the hapless, pride-swallowing Powell. Much more significantly, it was a victory for the establishment of a new policy promoting what government-overthrowers like to call regime change over negotiations in tandem with the now torpedoed "sunshine policy" of peaceful change and reconciliation then being followed by the South Koreans.

Where a dangerous, unstable nation like North Korea is concerned, no line is necessarily too hard; the question is whether the policy is effective. In this case, know-it-all-ism backfired. In barely eighteen months, North Korea had withdrawn from its obligations under the forty-year-old Nuclear Non-Proliferation Treaty, booted U.S. inspectors out of its Yonbyon facility, and more ominously once again started to reprocess plutonium from the reactor's used fuel rods into weapons-grade material.

But in an ironic twist, Bush's new policy of regime change and confrontation got an unexpected political boost from the North Koreans themselves, who rarely miss an opportunity to make pointless trouble. In mid-2002, intelligence agencies detected a secret effort, dating back into the 1990s, to develop the capacity to enrich uranium for additional bomb-making material, a discovery then inevitably leaked into the public domain.

In the short term, making loud use of this discovery was typically brilliant politics because on the surface all blame for the impasse could be passed back to President Clinton and could help justify a refusal to deal directly with the North Koreans. Bush could solemnly declare his need for "a strong diplomatic hand." And Condoleezza Rice, who is better known for her affinity for clever television sound bites than substantive accomplishment, said sternly, "The United States tried direct dialogue with the North Koreans in the '90s and that resulted in the North Koreans signing onto agreements that they then didn't keep."

That was not as big a whopper as her department's pre-Iraq invasion quip about weapons of mass destruction that didn't exist ("We don't want to discover a smoking gun in the form of a mushroom cloud"). But it was only technically accurate and deceptive in the extreme.

Yes, North Korea cheated by shopping around for an enrichment capacity, though there remains a dispute as to how many years it will be before they have a functioning facility, much less the ability to make a bomb this way. What her statement cleverly obscured was the fact that the capability the world knew the North Koreans had actually used to make weapons—from reprocessing plutonium from spent fuel rods—had been verifiably frozen for a decade and now it was being put to work again to make more bombs.

Effective administrations always understand the difference between relief via short-term politics and the longer-term, more lasting damage that inevitably is done when underlying problems are not addressed. The issue of how to proceed with North Korea still festered, and once again the administration chose to hide dreams of regime change behind the facade of multiparty discussions involving China, South Korea, Russia, and Japan as well as the United States and North Korea.

In nearly three years of activity, nothing of consequence resulted. In fact, the administration spent more time negotiating with China and South Korea than it did at the table with the North Koreans, its lust for "tough" U.N. sanctions colliding with the fears of North Korea's neighbors of the chaos that would follow should the regime collapse. The eventual U.N. resolution was as weak as the one directed at Iran. Eventually, North Korea spent the summer and fall of 2006 firing off missiles (mostly duds) and exploding its first device.

The one exception to this long run of ineffectiveness turned out to be full of helium. In the spring of 2005, massive hype followed what appeared to be a breakthrough in the six-party talks—an apparent agreement by North Korea to return to the basic concept of the 1990s, of nuclear dismantlement in exchange for economic assistance and security guarantees. However, the all-important details were missing, and the alleged breakthrough quickly disintegrated after Bush's Treasury Department acted against a bank in the Chinese territory of Macau. It accused the bank of helping launder proceeds from North Korea's counterfeiting and drug-smuggling activities, effectively freezing some $25 million. The North Koreans predictably went diplomatically berserk, and serious nuclear-related discussions again stalled.

The entire dispiriting mess was hilariously symbolized in September of 2006 during the annual meeting of the United Nations General Assembly in New York. Desperate for a favorable headline, Rice arranged for the formation of a new group of five additional countries with Asian interests (including Canada) that she said would focus on security issues in northern Asia. For the first meeting, North Korea declined its invitation to join, and neither China nor Russia showed up for the gathering.

This led career diplomat Christopher Hill, who has the thankless task of handling the North Korean issue day to day, to remark drily, "It turned out to be the Six minus one plus two plus three minus two."

More to the point, North Korean expert Kongdan Oh of the Institute for Defense Analyses told *The Washington Post* that fall, "We had the three-party talks, the four-party and the six-party. As the number of parties has gone up the speed of the failure has gone faster."

After the nuclear test in October, a somber summing up came from former Defense Secretary William Perry, the most hawkish of the Clinton administration officials, who helped produce the 1994 deal freezing work at the Yonbyon reactor. He was still advocating preemptive air strikes against North Korea's nascent long-range missile complex before the test-firings the previous summer, followed in the fall by the nuclear explosion: "I am very pessimistic," Perry told *The National Journal*. "I think we have blown it. We had many opportunities in the last six years to contain this problem and either by wrong actions or inaction we have let ourselves get into the situation we are in today."

That was probably a bit too strong. Early in February of 2007, there appeared to be another diplomatic breakthrough—an agreement by North Korea to dismantle its reactor in return for substantial energy assistance. This was a potential deal very much like the freeze achieved by the Clinton administration thirteen years before, only now North Korea remained free to continue with its enrichment program. Almost immediately, however, substantial implementation obstacles arose, including no progress on returning the cash frozen in Macau. The agreement also ignited a firestorm among hard-line conservatives and a few midlevel resignations from the White House and State Department. If all this had happened during Bush's first year, one could say that some progress had been made but the road ahead remained uncertain; but this was after more than six years of unsuccessful policies.

Eventually, the cash was unfrozen and the deal Hill had negotiated could at last go forward, but six years had been spent basically returning the situation to its status on the eve of Bush's decision to embarrass his first secretary of state in March of 2001. One reactor was once again shut down, but North Korea had several additional nuclear devices, a less primitive missile program, and at least the potential of enriching uranium. A rare Bush accomplishment in fact consisted of partially repairing the damage he had already done.

President Bush took America to a war that was allowed to morph into a murderous quagmire on the false claim that unconventional weapons lurked somewhere in Iraq, posing a threat. The two countries that actually had such weapons programs, including nuclear ones, were left essentially alone for six years to develop them further.

He also took America to war chasing a dream of transforming the entire Middle East into a region of more democratic governments at peace with Israel. Instead, in addition to the horrors of Iraq, his policies have inflamed the region and enhanced the status of its worst actors.

Behind all the missteps, mistakes, and missed opportunities lay the stark fact of the country's fading reputation in an interconnected world where allies are essential to progress, especially in the struggle that matters—against organized terrorism.

Among the many astonishing findings reported in Andrew Kohut and Bruce Stokes's book are these results from extensive Pew Center surveys around the world conducted in the wake of the invasion of Iraq. Fully 82 percent of the Germans surveyed said the United States had become less credible since the war, as well as 78 percent of the French, 72 percent of the Moroccans, 74 percent of the Turks, 64 percent of the Pakistanis, 63 percent of the Russians, and 58 percent of the British.

Conservative politicians are often tempted to use numbers like these as a badge of honor, but even President Bush knew better as he began his increasingly disastrous second term.

Ironically, his most visible response was to place one of his most loyal and longest-serving aides from Texas, Karen Hughes, into a souped-up public diplomacy position inside Condoleezza Rice's State Department. Hughes internationalized the rapid response and vigorous counterattacking system for which the White House was so justifiably famous in domestic politics. With enhanced communications tools, officials all over the globe were mobilized to monitor local media and plan instant responses to public relations problems in real time.

Bush never missed an opportunity to say his old pal was doing a great job.

LESSONS

I've been in politics long enough to know that polls just go poof at times. I mean, they're a moment; that they are—let me put it to you this way: When it's all said and done, when Laura and I head back home—which at this moment will be Crawford, Texas—I will get there and look in the mirror, and I will say, I came with a set of principles and I didn't try to change my principles to make me popular. You can't make good decisions if you're not making decisions on a consistent set of principles. It's impossible. Oh, you can make decisions, all right, but they're inconsistent. What I think is important is consistency during difficult and troubled times, so that people—they may not agree, but they know where I'm coming from.

—**President George W. Bush, speech at
Tipp City High School, Ohio, April 19, 2007**

PRESIDENT BUSH'S POLLS did more than just go poof.

As his days dwindle down to a precious few, his handling of the presidency has cost him what once were his most appealing qualities—and in a way, the foundations of his standing as president.

In the *Washington Post*/ABC News surveys early in his administration, most people (including most people who disagreed with him on major issues) considered Bush honest and trustworthy—by 63 to 34 percent in the last survey before the 9/11 attacks. In January of 2007, the result was 57 to 40 percent negative.

Another part of his foundation was a once widespread feeling that the outwardly affable Bush understands ordinary Americans and their problems. That was the view by a 61 to 37 percent margin in a survey in early 2002, shortly after the terrorist attacks. By 2007, the result was 67 to 32 percent negative.

Americans also once saw strength in him. Just before the 9/11 attacks sent these ratings to the stratosphere, Bush was seen as a strong national leader by a 55 to 43 percent margin. In early 2007, the result was negative by almost the reverse margin, 54 to 45 percent.

And above all, Americans had long considered Bush the kind of person to be trusted in a crisis. That was the view, by 60 to 37 percent, in the late summer of 2001. Nearly six years later, the verdict was 56 to 42 percent negative. One important reason for the harsh judgment was an overwhelming view of Bush as stubborn and unresponsive. By 63 to 36 percent, the American public declared him unwilling to listen to different points of view.

That's because he wasn't.

The war in Iraq eventually—after mid-2005—became the elephant in the room, but the collapse of the president's political support occurred because of the reaction to virtually everything he touched and chose not to touch—from Social Security and energy to global warming and his tax cuts, from his handling of the economy to his mishandling of Hurricane Katrina, from blundering into Terri Schiavo's tragedy to his squandering of a once gigantic looming budget surplus.

It is helpful to revisit the fiasco of those U.S. attorneys to see—even in a relatively minor mess that should never have become major—how ineffectual he could be in the alleged service of principled consistency.

The political question early in 2007 was not whether he could retain or replace any of the ninety-three high officials. The simple question was why nine of them were canned. Or, put even more

simply, who in the administration had put together the list of endangered names?

It is known that right after Bush's reelection his White House
counsel, Harriet Miers, soon to be embarrassed by her doomed
nomination to the Supreme Court, suggested replacing all of them.
It is also known that political policy guru Karl Rove responded that
this was excessive but left the door open to the mysterious process
that ensued. What more they did, they refused for months to say.

And then, the comedy of errors. The former counsel to Attorney
General Alberto Gonzales, Monica Goodling (also the liaison to the
White House), referred to the list as the intellectual property of the
then chief of staff to Gonzales, Kyle Sampson.

Sampson said he hadn't compiled it, Gonzales had.

Gonzales said he hadn't but pointed to the deputy attorney general
at the time, Paul McNulty. Gonzales then went to Capitol Hill and
testified that one thing he would have done differently is get Mc-
Nulty more involved with the U.S. attorneys issue.

For that, Bush lost the effectiveness of his attorney general and
then lost him literally, squandering the special reputation of the Justice Department in the process. Even before Gonzales's departure
following two failed attempts at presenting a coherent and credible
narrative of the U.S. attorneys mess on Capitol Hill, with delicate
wartime issues coming to a head and with the first major, if failed,
attempt at change in immigration law in twenty years, Gonzales had
been off the field, useless.

Much like Donald Rumsfeld at Defense, Gonzales resisted resignation and Bush resisted firing him, even as the opposition grew
to include important congressional Republicans. Their recalcitrant
stance was supported by Vice President Cheney, who rejected the
idea of doing anything in any area that might be considered "weak"
in the administration's relations with Congress. So, in the end, the
long denial of a widely accepted reality robbed Gonzales's departure of any major potential benefit to the president.

This was not aberrant Bush behavior as president. It was typical, and at least a reminder if not an object lesson in how not to be president.

When the next president is elected in 2008, she or he will have had the advice of at least one person who shaped the strategic thinking and many of the tactical moves that produced the victory.

That person should not be permitted within a mile of the policy-making machinery of the new president's White House. There is already too much politics in the operation of the modern presidency, much of which is unavoidable, even necessary. But Bush's use of Karl Rove was an epic mistake that institutionalized politics at all levels of policymaking and was compounded by a further elevation of the political consultant after Bush's reelection.

Rove brought with him at least three pieces of dangerous baggage—the conviction that polarizing politics more suited to an election campaign could get the president all of what he wanted in a narrowly divided Washington and country, a conviction worsened after 9/11 into an effort to make overt political use of the so-called global war on terror, and the awful habit of elevating politics into a way of life in the management of pre-invasion and post-invasion Iraq. Like many alleged gurus in politics, Rove was hot for a spell, but his departure in the summer of 2007 came at the nadir of the administration's (and Rove's) political reputation. President Bush, from the beginning, failed to understand the limits of partisan politics in governance, and opted for too much of the wrong kind—the partisan as opposed to the art of the deal. Rove was a symbol of Bush's misplaced governing emphasis, however, not the cause.

And Rove was but the tip of a White House iceberg Bush formed to insulate himself from the ordinary give-and-take of successful governance. Loyalty in the service of discipline and the veneer of order produced neither in the end or even in the beginning. John Di-Iulio's appalled description of the "Mayberry Machiavellis" in the summer of 2001 was both accurate and prophetic.

The infamous Bush White House "bubble" was assembled by

Bush himself, who committed a cardinal governance sin in the process. An effective White House is as much a network of presidential alliances as an effective government. The tighter the circle, however, the more closed the system. Blithely, Bush relied almost entirely on a network of cronies, the people least likely to broaden a White House's base and talk back to the boss—Karen Hughes, Dan Bartlett, and Harriet Miers formed Card's inner circle—all Texans with skills honed in Bush campaigns and experience serving Bush. Even the top assistants from the real world—Condoleezza Rice, Josh Bolton, and Larry Lindsey had been with the Bush campaign from its formative moments. The new president showed none of the political judgment and inner strength that led Ronald Reagan to pick the campaign manager of his opponent, James Baker, as his first-term chief of staff. Reagan reached out; Bush, to his eventual harm, closed ranks.

This was all compounded, moreover, by the disaster that flowed from Bush's unprecedented grant of influence and authority to his vice president. According to Walter Mondale, who was the first modern vice president, under Jimmy Carter, to be made in effect a full partner in the operation of a presidency, he and Al Gore shared one abiding conviction—that all the additional influence and clout had to be used in service to the president and his goals and wishes, that any independent agenda was intrinsically wrong and certain to boomerang.

Dick Cheney, selected to provide reassurance about Bush, brought his business CEO background back to Washington instead of his deep political experience. The result was still another large layer of insulation as well as extreme beliefs about executive supremacy and secrecy that complemented Bush's own worst instincts. The result, instead of a helpful ally, was an éminence grise—too much Iago when even a Falstaff would have been preferable.

Cheney's separate identity and personal agendas in domestic and foreign policy are without precedent in American history. There is strong evidence that even as Cheney operated the system that ultimately selected him as Bush's running mate in 2000, it was not the post-2001 Cheney whom then-Governor Bush selected. The strongest evidence is that Bush was seeking to reassure the country with a seasoned Republican politician much as outsider Carter had calmed similar concerns by selecting Mondale in 1976. One of his interviews, for example, was with former Missouri Senator John Danforth, a pillar of the moderately conservative Republican establishment. However, once Cheney became the relentlessly assertive figure that gradually turned off three-quarters of the American people, he was no less the president's responsibility. The vice president may be a constitutional officer, but other than presiding over the Senate, he has no job and no power that the president doesn't give him, no job and no power that the president can't take away without notice. Cheney remains Bush's responsibility.

Cheney's self-elevation was not without other consequences. Donald Rumsfeld was not Bush's first choice for defense secretary. But after former Indiana senator Dan Coats sat for a disappointing interview, the way was open for Cheney's fellow wunderkind from the Nixon-Ford era. Again, the best evidence is that Bush was looking for a modernization and reform true believer with Washington experience—not a man who would rival Cheney in myopia and stubbornness as the invasion of Iraq morphed into a murderous quagmire of an endless occupation before the country's shocked eyes.

And Cheney's own chief of staff, I. Lewis Libby, Jr., a Washington establishment lawyer with rich governmental experience, turned into chief scapegoat for both Cheney and Bush—absorbing the criminal rap for his role in using the disclosure of a veteran CIA official's identity (Valerie Plame) to get back at her husband (Joseph Wilson) for having helped debunk one of the pre-invasion weapons myths, that Saddam Hussein was seeking uranium from the African government of Niger. Lying to the FBI and to the grand jury, as well as obstructing justice in this fiasco, shielded his bosses, not Libby; this was not why he joined the Bush administration.

The temptations of power are always huge, but the Faustian bargains made by the legions of people who served Bush in exchange for the alleged prestige and trappings of public office may not have seemed worth it as more and more of the administration kept unraveling during the second term. Even the first-term-only servants—onetime Secretary of State Colin Powell being the most prominent—paid a heavy price for their enabling conduct.

The presidency is not closed to people with fervent, passionate ideological convictions (Ronald Reagan comes to mind). It is also not closed to people with more eclectic, catholic tastes (Dwight Eisenhower, for example). But more than two hundred years of American history have shown that successful presidents are open, adaptive animals who know or learn how to tack frequently as they try to move forward.

Every president in modern times has special difficulties shifting from the madness of interminable campaigns to the very different requirements of national leadership, but the ones who make the transition are quality politicians in the best sense of that word—always testing notions, thinking ahead, changing as circumstances warrant, holding their most important operatives accountable to the highest standards.

Now think of Dick Cheney, hunkered down in secret with his energy task force and delivering as shortsighted a series of ineffective measures tailored to business interests as has ever happened in this vital policy area—all to Bush's as well as the country's detriment.

Or think of chief of staff Andrew Card, dispatched in secret to stage-manage Bush's reversal on the question of establishing a Department of Homeland Security. In his sealed little world, with terrorism on everyone's mind, think how easy it could be to forget about the importance of maintaining a link between the head of a little agency called FEMA to the president himself in case of natural disasters like hurricanes.

Or think of Bush himself, insulated and greedy for all his tax cuts, lunging for the gimmick of a time limit on his proposals, gambling that ultimately he could extend the cuts permanently. Instead of fitting moderately smaller cuts into a budget and achieving nearly all of a major conservative goal, he ended up endangering the goal itself.

It wasn't just Iraq; it may not have been even mostly Iraq. It was everything. Part of the genius of the American system is that it is geared to reward a competent leader who sticks to the time-honored basics of politics. It is not a stretch to suggest that Woody Allen's famous maxim about success can hold for presidents—80 percent of it is just showing up.

Bush never did when it counted, leaving an even simpler maxim for the next president—Never Again.

INDEX